CUISINES OF
HIDDEN MEXICO

CUISINES OF HIDDEN MEXICO

A Culinary Journey to Guerrero and Michoacán

BRUCE KRAIG
DUDLEY NIETO

ILLUSTRATIONS BY NICOLÁS DE JESÚS

JOHN WILEY & SONS, Inc.

New York • Chichester • Brisbane • Toronto • Singapore

This publication is designed to provide accurate and authoritative
information in regard to the subject matter covered. It is sold
with the understanding that the publisher is not engaged in
rendering professional services. If legal, accounting, medical,
psychological, or any other expert assistance is required, the
services of a competent professional person should be sought.

Library of Congress Cataloging-in-Publication Data:
Kraig, Bruce.
    Cuisines of Hidden Mexico : a culinary journey to Guerrero and
  Michoacán / Bruce Kraig, Dudley Nieto : illustrations by Nicolás de
  Jesús.
        p.   cm.
    Includes index.
    ISBN 0-471-12129-0 (pbk. : alk. paper)
    1. Cookery, Mexican. 2. Guerrero (Mexico : State)—Description
  and travel. 3. Michoacán de Ocampo   (Mexico) :—Description and
  travel. I. Nieto, Dudley. II. Title.
TX716.M4K73 1995
641.5972—dc20   95-32185

Printed in the United States of America

10 9 8 7 6 5 4 3 2 1

CONTENTS

v

PREFACE

This book grew out of a television documentary, a co-production we did with Janice Thompson for public television in Chicago in 1994. The documentary, "Hidden Mexico," is about food, its history, and uses among the people we visited. These subjects are interesting in and of themselves, but we were concerned with other themes in Mexico, all of which touch upon food in some way—environments, ecology, folk customs and art, religion, social organization, and the whole history of the Mexican peoples. Food is an entryway into a whole culture and its history. In few countries is that more apparent than in Mexico, where food takes on unseen depths of meaning. . . apart from being just plain delicious.

The account given here is really our journey through parts of the two states in which the documentary was shot, Guerrero and Michoacán. It is about people we met, places we visited, and, of course, where and what we ate. Because we who made the program are interested in food history, there are good doses of it in these pages. In Mexico, to paraphrase a great American writer, it is hard to escape the past. History lives everywhere in the country, coloring all aspects of life. Fortunately for gourmands such as ourselves, that means preservation of ancient cookery techniques and ingredients. Through even a cursory examination of them, we can reconstruct the layers of peoples and cultures that make up the Mexican nation. It is an endlessly interesting tale that we only touch on in these pages. We hope that reading our adventures and what little of Mexican culture and history we provide will stimulate readers to explore that great country and, of course, to experiment with its foods.

The recipes in this book were tested in an unusual way. Dudley and I convened groups of friends at my house to test them. Ten to fifteen experimenters gathered on Sunday afternoons to try the recipes under the supervision of Chef Dudley. Jan, alias The Boss (the documentary's producer and director), kept everyone in order by starting the proceedings with shots of our favorite tequila, Herradura Gold, and then wine and beer throughout the rest of the day. Each event looked like a medieval battlefield, groups of two or three preparing each dish, rushing from stove to counter, battling over food processors and large pans, grinding by hand, kneading, and grabbing

Dudley for advice . . . . "Semi-organized nihilism" is the phrase. But it worked. The dishes came out (mostly) well, with the participants having done necessary corrections. All agreed that the hard labor was great fun and most of our friends have asked to come back for more. Everyone certainly learned a lot about Mexican cookery from Dudley, and about good tequila and wines from Jan.

Fairness dictates that we mention our victims'—testers', rather—names. First are Bruce's university colleagues Lynn Weiner (history, Roosevelt University) and Tom Moher (computer engineering, University of Illinois, Chicago). They introduced us to Anne Roosevelt (executive director of Museums in the Park, Chicago), her daughter Margaret, and her cooking chum Travers Patterson. Elizabeth Richter (vice president, WTTW/Chicago), Sylvia Avey (program director, WYCC, Chicago) her husband John (NBC, Chicago), and Laureen Ong (assistant general manager, SportsChannel, Chicago) are friends from the television world who are also food fiends, ready to cook and gorge at a moment's notice. From the art world, Richard Francis (chief curator of the Museum of Contemporary Art) and his wife Tamar, an avid foodie and equally adept cook; Bill Goldman (a champion *guacamole* maker), our chief art consultant in Michoacán; and Bob Ward, our man in Guerrero and a melted cheese demon, all worked cheerfully. With football season over, Jan got her friend Gary Barnett (head football coach at Northwestern University) and his wife Mary (a folk art curator and Bill Goldman's colleague) to come on the same day as Nellie Yuret (an executive with United Airlines, world traveler, and diner), my university colleague Ray Sparrowe (professor of hospitality management and splendid cook), with his wife Tish. We picked on friends from other walks of life, some of whom had more experience in cookery: Kim Cella (Dave, our cameraman's serious culinary wife); Ralph Scalise (a teacher, Dave's second and all-around terrific assistant in everything) and his wife and enthusiastic cook Barbara (who learned that making dough does not always mean pirogis); Ann Marie Ryan (whose Italian roots make her a celebrated and written-about cook and caterer); Catherine Chapman, a multi-lingual international lawyer, and Jan's longtime racquetball adversary, who learned how not to make *atole*; our old friends, the great Spanish restaurateur, Emilio Gervilla (of Emilio's Restaurants) and his sensible wife, AnnMarie; Dudley's creative pupil and now a chef himself, Don Hill (who cooked with us in an event in England) and his cheerful, energetic wife Rema (also an executive at United Airlines); and René Sota, Dudley's colleague in culture who runs Spanish-language schools in Chicago and Mexico. Special mention goes to our fellow traveler, Carol Haddix, editor of the Chicago Tribune's *Food Guide*, who is always ready to cook as long as there is enough good food and wine, and without whose field notes we would never have been able to reconstruct our journey. Last, are Mart Guillu, Dudley's rational wife (we say "keeper") and Mike and Ted Kraig, two sons who cooked with scrupulous care not just because they love good food, but out of pity for the person they call "The Little Man." Least we forget, our thanks to senior editor Claire Thompson at John Wiley and Sons, for encouraging us to make this book, who even appeared at one of our cooking fests to check up on us.

The documentary, "Hidden Mexico," on which this book is based, could not have been made without the help of many people. Particularly, we should mention Elizabeth Richter from WTTW/Chicago, who has been a steadfast supporter of our projects, in addition to her duties as test cook and chief food taster. On the Mexican side, we'd like to thank the Mexican Government Tourism Office, and especially the genial Sr. José Luis Sánchez-Navarro, now director for conventions, meetings and incentives, who arranged everything for us. Mexico's Consul General Oliver Farres cut all kinds of red tape for our crew, and his then press attaché (now with the Secretary of Education's office in Mexico City) and still our friend, Hilda Dávila de Chávez, helped enormously. Gonzalo Sánchez Galindo, the cultural attaché and head of the Mexican Cultural and Educational Institute and his assistant Julia Rendón rendered the greatest service to us in more ways than we can name. Nor could we have gone to Mexico without the assistance of Taesa Airlines and the special attention given our project by its Chicago manager, Christopher López, all our kidding of him not withstanding. Not least, our deepest gratitude goes to Arthur Velázquez, president of Azteca Foods in Chicago and one of the city's leading benefactors, for giving the project the necessary grant to shoot the documentary in Mexico.

Our last note is on the illustrations in the book. They were rendered by the Nicolás de Jesús, about whom you will read. He is an internationally renowned artist from the Alto Balsas school of artists in Guerrero. Many of the scenes show his "village life" style. Others are of skeletons in all sorts of activities, many of them humorous. Nicolás, like many other artists in Mexico, draws his inspiration from José Guadalupe Posada, the early twentieth-century artist who invented the style. His work, with long links to the pre-Columbian past, used skeletons to satirize Mexico's elites and its "pretentious" middle classes. It is all black humor that is so very Mexican—the mixture of grim reality and laughter. Nicolás is firmly in that great tradition.

Bruce Kraig
Dudley Nieto

INTRODUCTION

W e had shot a documentary on food, food history, and folk culture in the states of Guerrero and Michoacán and were now doing the really hard work: editing. Our crew had traveled to Mexico with aid from the Mexican Government Tourism Office and its kindly director, José Luis Sánchez-Navarro. The office and the director are long-time friends and knowing that we wanted to do the project, had helped us to set up the shoot in those states, which meant a great deal of work for the office. Many arrangements had to be made via fax and telephone: setting up visits to towns and villages, making sure we had unobstructed views of festivals, and much more. Communications within Mexico are not always the best, especially in rural parts of the country. In addition, local officials are always wary when learning that a television crew is coming to videotape scenes of everyday life—these scenes are not always the vistas beloved of tourist bureau brochure makers. The officials in Chicago went out of their way to help. As the Consul General said when we met at a consulate function before the trip, "I'm the fellow with the machete. . .who's been cutting the jungle of red tape for you!"

So, off we had gone, and we were now putting the program together. After heroic efforts on our behalf, our friends at the Tourism Office were anxious to see some of the results. At the time, all we had was what is called a "rough cut." This is only the first version of a program, edited together for timing and pacing with shots that may not make it into the final version. Such a cut will have no dissolves, special effects, graphics, or music and probably only a "scratch" narration. Usually, producers do not want this version seen by anyone unfamiliar with editing techniques because its imperfections might disappoint. We wanted officials in the Tourism Office to check for accuracy (if for no other reason than to let their chiefs in Mexico know that their judgment in helping us had been sound).

On the appointed day we brought the first half of "Hidden Mexico" to the office. The whole staff gathered around a large conference table in the viewing room, presided over by their cheerfully avuncular director. The light dimmed and the video began with a short on-camera description of the program's theme: Mexico as a kind of cultural layer cake whose levels can be seen through food. After only a moment or two, food scenes appeared on screen. First fruit licuados, drinks, in Acapulco's market. "Oh yes, *zapote*," someone said. "Delicious." Then came a row of goat-meat stands, this served with a *guajillo* sauce on banana leaves. "That's very good," came another voice from the dark. "One of my favorites." A woman stirring a large pot of *mole* with big portions of chicken in it evoked murmurs of approval. "Guajillo and *chile ancho*," several suggested as the probable sauce base. We had traveled down the coast from Acapulco to the Barra Vieja and a well-known beachfront restaurant that specializes in grilled fin and shellfish. The camera showed how *huachinango* (red snapper) is selected by customers, weighed, cleaned, placed on grill racks, and sauced, while the narration described the action. When the sauce, made of four chiles—*costilla, guajillo, ancho,* and *mulatto*—was described, a collective sigh went up from everyone around the table. "Wonderful! M*uy bueno*! I wish I could have that right now!" they declared over the sound of smacking lips.

The rest of the showing went on in similar fashion. When they saw *jumiles* or encina-leaf beetles being crushed into a simple tomato-chile sauce and served in a tortilla, they began discussions about the merits of this and that insect as food, about how wonderful things taste when made in a *molcajete* (stone mortar), and about the subtleties of this or that chile and herb in that particular part of the country. By now the group was hardly listening to the splendidly informative narration (by your informant, of course), but instead swapped food stories about each item they saw on screen. They grew more and more restless, and each described his and her own version of any dish, the way that a mother, grandmother, or aunt makes it. By this point everyone was in something like a feeding frenzy, bits of chiles, herbs, goat, or fish bobbing in the maelstrom. And then the program segment ended. We turned on the lights, blinked, and found an empty room. Like one of those film tricks where a person or object is made to disappear from some place, everyone rushed out the door. Well, almost. The director's beaming face popped around a door jamb: "We're all going out for lunch. Café Oaxaca has an excellent *mole negro*. . . ." We quickly followed. Who could resist?

This is a true story, only a little embellished for art's sake. The people involved were not professional or amateur "foodies," but ordinary, if cultivated, Mexicans. What the story means is this: there are only a few peoples of the world for whom food is so central to their lives. I mean this not on the elemental biological sense of the word, but the cultural. The French and Chinese come to mind as the two paradigms of food-centric peoples. Food, as a French anthropologist once wrote, is for thinking. If so, Mexicans occupy the same plane as these two peoples.

If so much of Mexican culture turns on food, then it cannot be the simple *tacos, burritos*, and hot sauces that most North Americans think it to be. To compare Mexico with China and France, the two countries considered to have the world's greatest and most refined food traditions, is perfectly apt. Mexican cuisine is full of rich flavors and textures. The Mexican palate is subtle, tuned to an almost limitless number of nuances. It is not only *haute cuisine* or plain home cooking that shows these characteristics, but even humble street food. Each seller (usually a woman, a home cook, hence the keeper of the tradition) has her own way of preparing each specialty. No two are ever exactly the same.

How Mexican taste sensibilities developed is a matter of history. Mexican cuisine is a blend of several major food traditions—native American and European. But underneath there is something more, deep flowing cultural ideas that run back into prehistory. I suggest that the native peoples of Mesoamerica had a complex cuisine long before Spaniards, French, and Germans ever arrived on the scene. The indigenous peoples, in their villages and in the new convents, churches, and towns, adapted the new foods of the immigrants and brought them into their own tradition. That is what Mexican cuisine really is.

The mixture of history, tradition, and culture is probably best summed up in a Mexican expression: "People lacking developed taste buds can never understand our culture, our history, us as a people." It is true. So, when you eat authentic Mexican dishes, it really is history and culture you are consuming.

As we learned, there is much more to Mexican culture and food than a collection of historical facts. As we prepared for our journey to Mexico, a Mexican friend said: "We Mexicans wear masks. . . it is hard to know what's behind them." True, much is hidden, in much the same way that seemingly simple foods are far more complex than one might think: the histories behind them, their social meanings (from reifications of family/village life, to prestige systems), their economic production (villages and small farms, much grown locally and processed by hand) and the art with which they are made can be deceptively simple. The people from which the Mexican culture comes have unexpected depths—they are smiling, friendly, and yet reserved. There is something in their eyes that makes one think of the Mexicans' faces as masks shown to the world. Is it history? The blending of the reserve of the Spaniard, the once-despised Indian and the mestizo in between? The product of a historical society that was (and still is) heavily layered? Is it the otherworldliness of their culture—Catholic, yet pre-Columbian? There is something more in the mysteries that make up Mexico, always something more that is hard to reach. We like to think that food is one way, an access point, to those mysteries. That idea lies behind our adventures in Mexico.

1

STARTING IN CHICAGO

Chicago I

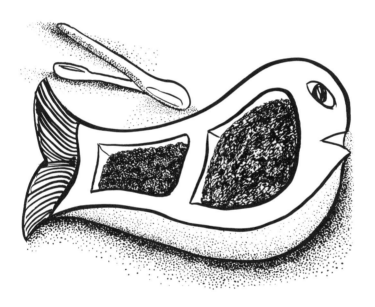

Our journey through Mexico's southwestern states of Guerrero and Michoacán was not simply a visit to the country's interesting tourist attractions and eating places. It was a trip through time, backward into Mexico's history, using as a vehicle the history of foodstuffs and characteristic dishes. Mexico's cuisines are, like the culture and the peoples themselves, products of a long history that began on both sides of the Atlantic Ocean and would one day involve the history of the whole planet. For example, one of the region's classic dishes, *carnitas michoacanas*, is composed of big hunks of pork that are literally boiled in oil for several hours, shredded, covered in a sauce made of

5

various chiles mixed with a little fresh orange juice, and served with corn *tortillas* made by hand on the spot—accompanied by a spicy-hot table sauce. It is a very Mexican dish and even more delicious when eaten in the region's small open-air restaurants.

Even the most superficial analysis of *carnitas michoacanas's* origins shows its antiquity. Pigs were probably domesticated in southwest Asia and brought along by farmers who migrated along the Mediterranean coast into Iberia as early as 6000 B.C. Pork become so intrinsically Spanish over the succeeding centuries that pigs were among the first European exports to Spanish America. The sauce is typically New World—the chile pepper having been domesticated in Mexico by at least 4500–5000 B.C., from whence it spread around the world. The orange, even those called Valencias, came from further afield. It was first cultivated in southeast Asia or southern China deep in prehistory and only came to Spain with Moors in the eighth century A.D. As for the *tortilla*, it is the symbol of Mexican fare, made from corn, the staple crop of indigenous peoples of the Americas. Like so much that is Mexican, even the simplest street food comes from complex historical processes.

On the other hand, some histories are short and there are more immediate causes of what we see in a culture and its cuisine. Mexico is no exception. The famed Mexican beer tradition dates to the nineteenth century and German immigration, while some of Mexico's most famous cheeses came from German Mennonites who settled in the northern and central areas of the country where a dairy industry took root. The cheese style is still called *Menonita*, while herds of black and white Holstein cows make parts of Michoacán today look like a kind of south-of-the-border Wisconsin. And then there is fast food. As recently as 1993 one fast-delivery pizza chain is reported to have opened three hundred stores in Mexico. These pizza and hamburger chains are explicable in a country that shares much with North American cultural forms, especially advertising. But what does one make of U.S.-born, antiseptically decorated Tex-Mex chain restaurants becoming evermore popular in Mexico and partly replacing one of the world's great street food traditions? One explanation Mexicans give is that the new imports are attractive by virtue of cleanliness. Such is the power of North American cultural ideas.

In a way, our journey into Mexico mirrors the history of food described here. Simple notions of historical causality are that every event has long- and short-range causes, and we are, after all, historians of food. For one thing, we were going to see ways of life and ideas that were both old and new. We knew that visiting rural villages would be like stepping back into past worlds, but worlds with plenty of modern influences in them. Further, our interest in exploring parts of Mexico and doing a documentary on what we found goes back some years. It has to do with tradition, the immediate needs of television, and both personal and professional aspirations.

My interest in Mexico began with one of my family's oldest friends, Dr. José Pérez Alamá, "Uncle Pepe" to us. Now retired, he was one of Mexico's leading heart surgeons whose practice was located in the north central city of Aguascalientes. Valencian by birth, he and his family had fled Spain as a result of the dictator Francisco Franco's victory in the Spanish Civil War. Although my parents had been friends with Pepe for some years and he had visited us in the United States many times, it was not until the late 1970s when I first visited him and his family. I was working on a writing project concerning Mexican prehistory and the only thing I knew about Mexican food was the archaeological record for the origins of agriculture. My interest in corn, beans, chiles, and the other New World domesticates had more to do with their crucial role in the rise of civilizations in Mexico than with matters gustatorial. That would change as a result of the visit.

Pepe was interested in Mexican prehistory, so, after his early morning rounds at the hospital, we would hop into his vintage Ford Mustang (he still drives it) or onto his Harley and head off to tour ancient sites that were as yet untouched by archaeologists. The country is dry, semi-desert, but we stopped along the way to examine the local flora, especially cacti. We sampled this and that herb—I can still taste the wild oregano from the nearby hills—while Pepe discussed the virtues of traditional folk medicines. The *tuna* or cactus fruit is especially good for certain gastrointestinal disorders that afflict both visitors to and natives of the country. The cure actually seems to work. As we climbed over the remains of walls and buildings, mostly earthen mounds by now, Pepe talked about the nature of "our," meaning Mexican, history and prehistory. One trip took us to nearby Zacatecas, a city almost literally paved with silver from the nearby mines. That night we sat out on an open terrace at a hotel set atop one of the city's hills. We looked out in the darkness at the wide valley surrounded by more hills, and above us was a vast net of stars. My old friend began to tell a story of the ancient god-king Quetzalcóatl, who sprinkled the earth with star beams and thus created the *maguey* plants so important to Mexicans from ancient times to now. He told it as if it were part of everyday Mexican history.

Pre-Christian (indian) myths of the indigenous peoples, archaeological sites, and folklore were all part of my "uncle's" conception of his Mexican culture. But in most ways he was hardly Mexican at all, except by accident of residence. In his personal habits and in many of his attitudes, he was Spanish—like much of Mexico's (and Latin America's) elite society. Why this identification with a Mexico whose roots lie in its Indian population, people who are often seen as the bottom of the social heap? It did not occur to me until much later that whatever the social and economic distinctions within the country, and they are very wide, Mexico is a great *mestizo* nation. As a part of the nationalist movements of the early nineteenth century that created the Mexican nation, a new mythology was created that drew on the distant past to justify the new political entity. In this way, ongoing social processes were recognized as something uniquely Mexican. The country is a society that is both layered and mixed in its traditions, population and, of course, in its foods. That is its fascination.

At home in Aguascalientes, Pepe's housekeeper and cook Lupe cooked in the required Spanish style. An early light breakfast, lunch, late afternoon snack, and then a late-night light dinner. The food was often simply grilled vegetables, alone or with meats or fish. Olive oil was the cooking medium, never the all-purpose lard that Mexicans traditionally used (less so nowadays). Spanish wine accompanied many meals, hardly ever beer. However, Lupe knew much more about food than that: she was my guide through the markets. Twenty-five years ago Aguascalientes was a small city, not the large corporate center it has become today. We could walk everywhere, which was preferable to the eccentric urban bus service of the time. We walked to the central market to do the daily shopping, stopping along the way at this or that street food vendor as I learned about the glories of Mexican street food. Those impressions were reinforced by tours of the market with its small *fondas* or cookstands and, of course, the vendors who sold everything, including fresh fish, meats, all kinds of vegetables and fruits, herbs, and chiles. How very different from the food stores of North America where hardly anything was fresh! Clean, yes; fresh, not often.

That first introduction to Mexico and its foods led to a cookbook and much more writing about food. Later that summer I traveled to Mexico City to work in the *Museo Nacional de Antropología é historia* located in Chapultepec Park. While looking for inexpensive dining places, I discovered a small restaurant not far from the central Avenida Juárez. It was run by a North American woman, Alice de Aguirre, who had married a Mexican and settled in her husband's country. It was an idiosyncratic place serving a mixture of North American (butterscotch pie, for instance) and Mexican fare. It was eclectic, very good, and struck me as another model for Mexican culture. Alice and I became friendly, and, upon learning that she was in her seventies and not well, on an impulse I asked whether she would give me some of her recipes for a cookbook. She agreed and it became the core of a cookbook on Mexican cooking. Many of the recipes also came from my Uncle Pepe's household and the recipes that his late wife had collected from the region around Aguascalientes. Mexican cooking is regional, so a good portion of the book was north-central Mexican in character.

While I was composing the cookbook and testing the recipes, a former student of mine became the editor of a local newspaper in the Chicago suburb of Oak Park. We met at the small bookshop he ran, and when we swapped information about what we were doing at the moment, he suggested that the paper could use a weekly food column. Needed or not, the column has been running for fifteen years. The subjects are hugely varied, including everything from food history to restaurant reviews, literally anything related to food that comes to my mind. It was through a review in this column that I came to know Dudley Nieto. How we became friends has to do with love of good food and art.

In 1988 Dudley had opened a small Mexican restaurant in Oak Park called El Rebozo. Although there were many Mexican restaurants in the Chicago area, none did really fine cooking and most only approximated the kind of home-cooked regional dishes found in Mexico. Mostly the food was the usual North-American Mexican, derived from the northern Mexico-U.S. border areas and featuring gobs of melted cheese on everything. That style of fare is not necessarily "bad," since it can be well made. Nor is it "bad" for reasons of inauthenticity, since it is a new cuisine created from a mixture of cultures. However, most restaurants serving Mexican fare of this sort simply do not prepare it well. Besides, with four other Mexican restaurants in the

The enchilada *eater*

town, what could yet another one be? So for some time I avoided the place (wrongly, as it proved) on general principles.

All my visits to restaurants are accompanied by my resident critic, Jan Thompson, who in real life is a television producer and director and professional Mexican food fan. One night she could not resist the urge for her favorite cuisine, and, after much debate, we decided to give El Rebozo a try. The restaurant turned out to be decorated with some works of art, a few prints done in native style, some carved masks and decorated boxes, paper cutouts, and obviously hand-woven shawls or *rebozos*. "Very nice," we said to ourselves, "but let us try the food." There is an acid test for Mexican restaurant cooking of this sort: whether the beans are made with lard (hence authentic home-cooking and better tasting) and the *mole poblano*, the most famous of all Mexican sauces. We ordered dishes that included both. The beans were perfect. And then we tasted the *mole*. It was an epiphany, the best *mole* I thought that I had ever tasted. Even Jan the Critic agreed. When the smiling, cherubic-faced Dudley came around to ask how we liked the dish, I nearly drooled in delight. He, in turn, said that the *mole* should be good since he was from Puebla and this was his mother's recipe. This was the most Mexican response any cook could give, and we became friends at once.

Dudley's home city, Puebla, is accounted to be the home of Mexico's finest cooking traditions. Perhaps that reputation comes from the very Spanish character of the city, something it retained long after other cities had become more "Mexican." That flavor later attracted Spanish immigrants, including Dudley's father, yet another refugee from Franco's Spain. After peregrinations in the United States and Cuba, he married a *poblana*, Dudley's mother, and settled in her native city. It is an old family tradition dating, they claim, to the English defense of Spain in the Napoleonic Wars, that one son be given the English name Dudley (pronounced Dude-lee in Mexican Spanish). Dudley grew up in a family that was international and liberal in outlook and very interested in matters cultural.

At home Dudley learned Spanish cookery from his father, who cooked large family meals on Sunday, and Mexican traditions from his mother. It is the time-honored way that Mexican cookery has been handed down through time. Many recipes are secrets held closely by the women of the family. As such, they are the symbols of the centrality of women in Mexican life, with women the keepers of not only the household and kitchen, but of society itself. This may be one reason why food is so important in Mexican culture. It is certainly one reason why Dudley himself became deeply interested in cooking, food history, and other expressions of Mexican culture.

Contingency made Dudley a chef. His youthful intention was to become a physician. After receiving an initial degree from the *Universidad Autónoma de*

Puebla, he came to Chicago and enrolled at Northwestern University Medical School, but eventually family exigencies required him to take a degree in occupational therapy instead. While in school, he took a part-time job at a well-known Mexican restaurant to support his children. It often occurs that someone who thought that their life work would be in another profession falls into the world of restaurants. So it happened with Dudley. Eventually he became hooked on cookery, more as an art and an expression of culture, than as a business. When he opened El Rebozo as a first venture in restaurateuring, his intention was to make it a place where patrons could not only take in many parts of Mexican culture besides the cuisine, but also encounter a gallery where Mexican artists could show their work and sell it. That is how we became enthusiasts of Mexican folk art, among other styles, and it is one reason we all eventually traveled to Mexico.

Jan and I often dined with Dudley and talked about history, food, and art. Dudley would bring out new dishes for us to try. As we munched, a project came to us. There is nothing like a *margarita* (incidentally, an invention of the 1940s) or two to stimulate the creative spirit, particularly when accompanied by good food. Our friend was full of enthusiasm about the Mexican heritage and suggested that we all go on a field trip. Perhaps, he said, we might do a book on the subject. He knew just the region, his home state of Puebla and neighboring Oaxaca. We should go for the *Día de los Muertos* (Day of the Dead) festival held in the first days of November. The *molotes* Dudley often served us were argument enough. He explained that the little fried *empanadas* filled with *tinga* (*chipotle*-spiced shredded pork) were typical street food in Puebla. Well, Jan suggested, if we went why not a television documentary? Excellent idea, said our friend Dudley. That was in 1990. We did not get to Mexico for another four years, and then it was to travel through Guerrero and Michoacán, stopping to see not the celebrations of departed ancestors, but of those of renewal: Easter.

In the intervening time, Dudley sold his restaurant and his career as a chef took off. He has gained an international reputation for fine "authentic" dishes from several regions of Mexico. Recipes for some of them are reproduced in these pages. We, meanwhile, continued to explore things Mexican, becoming friends with many people in the Mexican art community in Chicago. William Goldman, perhaps Chicago's main authority and collector of Mexican folk art, became a friend, so we learned much more about this kind of art and were eager to visit the places where it was created. In particular we collected the works of Nicolás de Jesús (who has illustrated this book). He comes from a small village in the center of the state of Guerrero called Ameyaltepec. In this dry mountain village, a school of artists working mainly on bark paper has grown up in the last thirty years. Nicolás asked us to visit many times, and Dudley said that he always wanted to visit that particular region of the country. Ameyaltepec would prove to be one stop on our journey.

Then, in 1992, almost by accident, Jan and I traveled to China to make a documentary on food history and folk cultures in China. The program was co-produced with WTTW/Channel 11, the major public television station in Chicago. It was a considerable success winning a local Emmy award. Encouraged by that, our little team renewed its long-standing dream of making a documentary in Mexico. We intended to show as much of the rich life of the Mexican people at all levels, through the country's food and history, something we had tried to do in China. Because of the timing we decided to go not to Puebla and Oaxaca, but to Guerrero and Michoacán. Eventually, all our planning came together with the help of officials of the Mexican government in Chicago and Mexico. With a small grant from Azteca Food Company in Chicago and the encouragement of WTTW/Channel 11, our co-producer, we collected a crew and equipment. Our journey was years in the making, but what was that compared to the centuries of history we were going to explore?

The team turned out to be quite a diverse assortment of people who managed to get on well together despite trying conditions. Television productions, in general, tend to be nerve-wracking, never more so than when in a foreign country and in the field or, literally, fields. Fortunately, since we were doing a documentary about food, all of us got to eat and drink interesting things, and thereby tended to become fairly merry at the end of the long days—at least when arrangements were not too disorganized.

David Cella was our senior cameraman. A strapping fellow, well able to hold a twenty-five-pound camera steady for hours on end, David's normal beat is sports—the Chicago Bulls and the White Sox—in the first instance as a roving cameraman on the stadium floor. Jan, whose career has also been in sports, had known Dave for years and always liked his work. He also told us many tales about our favorite basketball team and the world's favorite player. Dave came along because ever since his days in the Air Force he has always been interested in the cultures of other peoples and, like our other friends, wanted to acquire some tangible remembrances of them.

We needed a second camera operator and sound person, and when a friend who was going to do it suddenly could not, I thought of someone who had been a student—one of the best—in one of my graduate courses at the university. Ralph Scalise is a distinguished teacher at Elk Grove Village High School, focusing on social studies, Italian, and just about anything else having to do with anthropology, archaeology, and exotic and foreign lands. Incredibly energetic, he and his wife have traveled to many interesting corners of the world, all the way from Amazonia, Peru, and the Australian outback to the Arctic, all the while collecting materials, slides, and videotapes for his classes. He had shown these to me and done a marvelous presentation in our class, so he seemed a natural choice. Ralph ended up doing some shooting, but much of the time he was Dave's invaluable assistant, earning the name, "Tripod Boy." Always cheerful, he took on the job with great enthusiasm; we would hardly think of doing another documentary without him.

The third, and most important member of the technical crew was Jan Thompson, to whom I happen to be married. She is an experienced documentary maker, composer, university lecturer, world traveler and, especially important, food aficionado. Petite in appearance, she is a regular Erich von Stroheim of a director when at work. (I threatened to get her a set of jodhpurs and boots to go with her riding crop.) She was the producer, director, general editor, and composer of the final documentary. Fortunately, she has a good appreciation of the absurd and of good food and drink. Without her single-minded devotion to it, the project would not have happened.

The eating side of our cast, apart from Dudley and me, was Carol Haddix, food guide editor of the *Chicago Tribune* and an eminent food writer. She is an old friend and fellow trencherperson who went with us to China. Having eaten Mexican-style food many times in the United States, she was interested in seeing what the cuisine was like in the native country, since she had never been. It was a good thing for us that she did go because the journal she kept has been invaluable in reconstructing our journey. In return, we introduced her to the joys of first-rate tequila, Herradura Gold, Añejo, and *Reposado* mainly, plus iguana, *jumiles* (pine beetles), and a few other treats found only in Mexico. She has been dubiously grateful ever since.

Two other crew members crossed categories, acting both as diners and as cultural consultants. Bill Goldman is, as mentioned, Chicago's foremost collector of Mexican folk art. A retired school teacher, he knows almost every artist in Michoacán and those he does not know personally, he knows of through mutual acquaintances. He has been a major consultant to museums and exhibitors for years. Before we met, Dudley would say that we absolutely had to see his apartment because of his extensive art collection. When we finally did, we could hardly believe our eyes: every inch of space on the walls, windowsills, and tables was packed with objects. Some were pre-Columbian, most were first-rate examples of regional folk art. The place is a museum unto itself, and we say to one another when Bill is not listening that it should be preserved intact in a special wing of the Art Institute of Chicago. The collection truly is that good. Besides being an art expert, Bill is as nice a human being as anyone could hope to find. His colleague and fellow collector, Bob Ward, is an expert on the arts and crafts of Guerrero and has one of the best mask collections anywhere. He can tell you not only where a mask comes from, but what artist made it, or what son or daughter of what artist made it. So taken with Mexican art did he become that he left his own business to become one of the heads of a large framing company. There, he creates mounts that are as handsome as the art within them. All of our consultants are wonderful people, but when it comes to art, it is as if a full moon rose over Bill, Bob, and Dudley at the same time—they become wer-shoppers. Using the excuse of commissions to purchase things for shops and restaurants, they tore into every artisan shop and studio they encountered, buying so much that we could hardly load the stuff onto our vehicles. Eventually, we had to arrange to have it packed into huge crates for shipment back to Chicago. In truth, it is hard not to buy examples of the work we saw—it was splendid and the prices very reasonable. Nevertheless, the phrase "mad shopper" was invented for our friends.

Lastly, two more consultants came along for portions of the trip. Marta Guillu, Dudley's wife, works for the Mexican Government Tourism Office. She was a chief troubleshooter for us in Guerrero, and most importantly she kept Dudley from eating and buying everything in sight. Later, in Michoacán, Dave's wife Kim decided that she should come down to keep an eye on her husband. A professional psychologist with a recent doctorate, she was doubtless interested in our group dynamic, pathology perhaps. She is also keenly interested in food, is an avid cook, and takes classes from the best teachers in Chicago. Based on what she saw and ate (she once ordered three entrées at a meal to see how they should be presented—Dave had to eat them all), she has given valuable assistance in both testing the recipes in these pages and making sure we all remained sane, something like the counselor on a starship.

Finally, everything in hand, we were ready for our adventure. First, though, a little snack. The dish that endeared Dudley to us is one of the best street foods in Puebla. *Molotes* are little *empanadas* filled with a kind of stew done in the Puebla style.

Tinga Poblana

1½	lbs.	boneless pork shoulder, cut into 2-inch cubes, water to cover
1		small onion
2		cloves garlic, peeled
1		bay leaf
¼	lb.	Mexican *chorizo*

2		onions, cut into rings
3		cloves garlic, crushed and chopped
3		tomatoes, peeled, seeded, and chopped
1–2		canned or bottled pickled *chipotle* chiles, chopped
1	T.	dried oregano

Cut pork, place in a deep pan and cover with water. Add 1 whole onion, 2 cloves garlic, and 1 bay leaf. Bring to boil, reduce heat to simmer and cook until pork is soft, about 45 minutes. Remove from water and set cubes on a cutting board. With two forks, gently shred the pork. When done, set aside. Place *chorizo* in a deep skillet and sauté over medium heat until just browned and much of the fat has flowed from the *chorizo*. Remove *chorizo* and set aside. Add onion rings and 3 cloves chopped garlic to hot fat and saute until browned. Drain fat from pan. Add tomatoes, *chipotle* chiles, and oregano to pan and bring to boil. Reduce heat and allow to cook down until a thick sauce forms, about 5-7 minutes. Return *chorizo* to pan and stir in the shredded pork. Cook until meats are warm. Serve with warm tortillas.   *Serves 4*

Note: If using *tinga* for the *molotes* recipe that follows, refrigerate the stew until it is thoroughly cooled, otherwise the hot mixture will "break" the masa coat.

Molotes

1-½	lbs.	corn *masa*
½	t.	salt
1	C.	hot water
		tinga poblana
		cooking oil, at least ½-inch deep in frying pan,
		heated to 350°

Mix *masa*, baking powder, salt, and water together in a large bowl and form a dough. Divide the dough into 10–12 pieces. Roll out 10–12 thin circles. If you have a *tortilla* press, place plastic wrap or waxed paper on both sides of the dough and press out. Or, place a sheet of waxed paper on a flat surface and cover with another sheet. Roll out with a rolling pin. Or, if you feel skillful enough, pat out the dough into tortillas. Once *tortillas* are rolled, place a portion of *chorizo poblano* in the center of each *tortilla* and fold over. Slip each *molote* (the filled *tortilla*) in hot oil and fry for 1–2 minutes or until browned. Remove from oil and drain on paper towels and keep warm. When all are done, assemble by placing around the edges of a serving plate with a spoonful of sour cream on top of each and *guacamole* in the center.

Serves 4–5 as appetizers

Note: You can substitute *masa harina*, plain unbleached white flour for the corn *masa*, but the finished product will not be exactly the same as the original.

Note: There is an easier way to make *molotes* or any *empanada*. It is a device called the "Tartmaster," made and sold by Kitchen Connection. It is a spring-loaded press requiring only that the dough be rolled out, filled, and covered with a top layer. Then the *empanada* is sealed and cut all at once by the "Tartmaster." It works just as well on corn flour dough (*masa*) as it does on regular wheat flour.

Chicago II

Some time ago, English friends who work in culinary history came to Chicago for a visit. They knew that the city was famed for its ethnic communities and foods, so we went on a tour of various neighborhoods, ending in my favorite part of town—the Mexican section. The streets there look as if

"Ah, gorditas, *so tasty!*"

Eating tamales

they had been lifted from some neighborhood in a Mexican city—the shops with signs in Spanish and the decor typically in homemade Mexican motifs. My guests had never eaten real Mexican food. England has a few restaurants that masquerade as Mexican but are really devolved fast-food versions of the cuisine.

We stopped at La Guadalupana on 26th Street, a grocery store that makes wonderful *tamales* with green sauce. Our friends took one bite and expressions of delight crossed those smiling English faces. We then proceeded to a sit-down lunch down the street at Mercado Aguascalientes. The place is a small supermarket with one section given over to a small restaurant. The kitchen is open, just a tiled service counter, staffed by cooks who specialize in *gorditas*. The word has several meanings, since it technically means "little fat things," but is usually used to indicate thick, hand-made *tortillas* toasted on a flat griddle and then covered with whatever sauce and ingredient one chooses. The result is an open-faced sandwich eaten from the hand. The place looks just like the small *fondas* in any Mexican market, only here in a supermarket setting. My English friends and I gorged on a variety of these treats: beef, chicken, *al pastor* (pork), and even the special Mexican dishes, tripe and *sesos*, or brains. Foodies must be experimental, after all.

What we ate was essentially street food, although these dishes are also served in small restaurants all over Mexico. Here the sauces were from the north central region. The visitors were amazed at how good the fare was and how extraordinary the ambience is to European eyes. Very Mexican, I told them, something like Chicago's immigrant neighborhoods of years past before they became more or less assimilated into the mainstream culture of the city. Better see it now, I suggested, because assimilation is already happening to the new citizens from south of the border. Second generation Mexican-Americans are rapidly loosing major elements of their parents' cultures. Not only do they not wear traditional dress—for instance, girls wear *rebozos* only in festivals—but many have forgotten the ways of villages and towns "back home." In two ways, though, traditions remain: use of Spanish (not indigenous languages, though), and food. No matter how assimilated and no matter whether raised on American fast food and supermarket foods, most Mexican-Americans retain a deep appreciation for the cuisines of the "homeland." Many a young woman has secret family recipes passed down through generations of mothers and daughters. Food is, and one hopes always will be, at the heart of what it means to be Mexican, no matter what the degree of incorporation into other societies. That is why a trip to Chicago's "Little Mexico" is so deliciously rewarding.

Mexico and its citizens not only share the North American continent with the United States and Canada, but have played an increasingly greater role in shaping the cultures of their northern neighbors. Two major trends are at work here: migration and assimilation. Food is an obvious sign of the magnitude of these trends. In 1994, for example, bottled *salsas* surpassed ketchup sales in the U.S.; by 1994, one of our major national fast-food chains is dedicated to selling the famed Mexican street food, *tacos*. Nowhere are all the elements of Mexican life in North America better seen than in cities with large Mexican populations. Chicago is one of them. Although the hispanization of large areas of the city has been quite recent, Chicago serves as a model of how Mexican and Anglo cultures interact as they go on to form some new syntheses. The result is something like a nice green *salsa* on Chicago's greatest culinary creation, the hot dog.

Historically, Chicago has been one of the country's most diversely ethnic cities. Waves of immigrants from both abroad and within the United States settled in Chicago from the time of its foundation to its rise as a center for commerce and industry in the nineteenth century. Neighborhoods and larger sections of the city are remembered by locals as belonging to this or that ethnic group. To old-time Chicagoans the area called Andersonville on the city's North Side, for example, has always been Swedish. Taylor Street still means Italian, and Maxwell Street once meant Jewish. Chicago is in a continuous process of change as various populations move in and out of the city. Continuity and ethnic changes in neighborhoods are marked virtually block by block. An as-yet unpublished study by Evelyn Thompson on Chicago's ethnic food stores graphs this interesting phenomenon. An example is Clark Street, one of the city's old main thoroughfares that runs from Andersonville in the 5000 block northward. In these blocks stores change from general Middle Eastern/Lebanese/Assyrian to Swedish, Japanese/Korean, then to Filipino, to more Middle Eastern, followed by Cuban/Puerto Rican stores, several Mexican stores, one or two Greek/East European stores, then a string of Mexican stores spreading along more than ten blocks, and ending, almost, with the ancient Romanian Kosher Sausage Company. Streets become kaleidoscopes of world cultures. Yet, in almost all of these stores, some food products from the neighboring traditions will be found. Adaptation to and absorption of other cultural forms is simply human. It is also the nature of Mexico's history and the basis of its cuisine, both at home and in other parts of the world.

A little more than thirty years ago, Chicago's Mexican population numbered only about 7,000. Most had come to Chicago in the 1920s to work on the railroads, a small part of the great emigration to El Norte that began early in the century. Roughly one-tenth of Mexico's population emigrated northward during this period. Later immigrants to the United States and Chicago arrived after 1942 as part of the *bracero* program. That was an agreement between the governments of Mexico and the United States to bring needed workers to the north to lessen the labor shortages brought on by World War II. Most of the immigrants were country people with little formal education but with a willingness to work, usually at manual labor. Contrary to the image portrayed in popular North American culture in the past, Mexicans are typically hard-working people both at home and everywhere they settle. In the north, with few exceptions, Mexicans filled lower levels of the economic pyramid. In the west they became the muscles of the agriculture industry. At the same time, Mexicans were drawn into other industries such as construction and factory work. In Chicago they formed about one-third of the labor force in the steel mills of the far south side of the city. Factory and railroad workers earned higher wages, enabling the new North Americans to establish themselves in solid communities. These would expand dramatically in the decades between 1960–1990.

Census figures in that year put the Mexican population of Chicago at more than 350,000, but unofficial estimates range from 500,000 to upward of one million in the northern Illinois region. While there are still a considerable number of temporary workers, hence the large estimated numbers, many Mexicans came to stay. And they changed the characters of the towns and neighborhoods in which they settled. The stores along Chicago's Clark Street are graphic testimony to an ongoing cultural phenomenon—the recreation of familiar places, or in Latin-American terms, *barrios*.

The *barrio*, or neighborhood, replicated the village community that the Mexicans left behind, but with some differences. Because the immigrants came from many parts of Mexico, from varieties of localities, each with its own cultural style, the new communities merged into something pan-Mexican. Perhaps a new identity formed, one often called *chicano* in the west and southwest. Public celebration of Mexican national holidays, *Cinco de Mayo* and the 16th of September especially, became focuses of Mexican sentiment that crystallized into parades and feasting. The Mexican-style churches, with their mixtures of pre-Columbian and European practices, have always been important community centers. Special attention is paid to the dark-visaged *Virgen de Guadalupe*, who protects *los indios* and, by extension, the poor folk of Mexico. It is evident that many who came to the new *barrios* were poor in material wealth, but rich in culture and in the traditions of simple country food.

As Chicago's original Mexican community began to grow during the 1960s, other sections of the city became hispanicized. Most of the early settlers came from a variety of northern states, with even larger numbers from Jalisco, whose capital is Guadalajara. By the later 1980s on, the largest numbers had immigrated from the southwestern state of Michoacán, the state that currently provides the largest number of immigrants to the United States, and to a lesser extent, from the state of Guerrero. Eventually the Pilsen and Little Village areas in Chicago bore the heaviest concentrations, becoming nothing less than "Little Mexicos" in their own way. Pilsen is a classic story of urban life. As the name suggests, it was once home to a large Czech, or Bohemian as it is known in the city, population. These groups moved westward, eventually to suburbs such as Cicero and Berwyn (where there is still a fall festival devoted to the *houby*, or mushroom, complete with a parade). Their places were taken by yet newer Americans who created colorful new urban environments.

Now instead of bakeries making rye bread and *houska*, *panaderías* load their shelves with *bolillos* and *pan dulce*. Butchers now make *chorizo*, and their cold cases are graced with whole hog heads instead of *kiska* and *prasky*. No longer are the names above the shops central European. Instead they are in Spanish, and the windows are rococo with colorful signs and decoration. Best of all, there are the foods of Mexico, mainly plain home cooking of a northern or central-Mexican style, with some dishes from Michoacán. Not far away, in the old Maxwell Street area, there is an open-air Sunday market where produce sellers and street-food vendors sell raw and prepared Mexican foods.

Maxwell Street is a storied name in Chicago lore, a microcosm of the city's immigrant history. It is west of the Loop, running south from Roosevelt Road. More than a street, it is a district that was once home to the city's immigrant Jewish community. The name itself is used to identify a kind of hot dog, in its true form an all-beef Polish sausage, that has its origins in Jewish street food. Later, the area was home to Poles, Czechs, and Lithuanians, then some African Americans, and now mainly Hispanics. On Sunday, the great market day, the street would be congested with pushcarts and shoppers. Some sold food, but otherwise it was a giant flea market. The common wisdom was that if you had had something stolen, chances are it could be found the next Sunday on Maxwell Street. In recent years, the adjacent streets became Mexican open-air food markets. The stands resembled mini-versions of their Mexican prototypes, where fresh *cilantro, epazote*, and even more exotic fruits and vegetables could be found. Unfortunately, after a huge battle with vendors and preservationists, the city closed down the Maxwell Street location. Happily, the Mexican market has been reborn just a couple of blocks to the east. It is a wonderful resource, because more and more foods from Mexico make their appearance there every week. Dudley goes every Sunday to shop for basic ingredients. We needed fresh amaranth to make a special dish called *huazontle* and found it at Mexican prices. Corn fungus, *zapotes, tomatillos*, even the occasional insect for really special dishes, can all be found there. As Chicago receives more immigrants, the market becomes increasingly "authentic."

No group of people are without art, music, or food. The Mexican community has become home to a fine art tradition that centers on the Mexican Fine Arts Museum (on 19th and Wood) and on artists' workshops, especially the *Taller de Grabado* (on Halsted Street and Cermak Road). It was at these places where Jan and I learned much about the art of Mexico and the artists who create it. Some, like our friend Nicolás de Jesús, move back and forth between the two countries, drawing inspiration from both. There is, however, an increasingly large group of artists who live and work in Chicago and who now can be called Mexican-American. Apart from its intrinsic value, what makes much of their work so interesting is the cultural mixture that it often depicts. It is a small version of that major element in the creation of Mexican civilization: mixing, amalgamation, and layering all jumbled together into a cultural stew or *cocido*. It does not take long to become hooked on all this. Chicago itself is a cultural pastiche, and the Mexicans have added much more color and spice to the grand tradition.

Here is a version of the dish my English friends ate and loved. Potatoes are not to be found in every version, but they give an interesting flavor and consistency to the final product.

Gorditas

The name tells us that these are fat little cakes. To be really authentic, they should be made by cutting lard into the *masa* or cornflour dough. The resulting cakelet remains soft for a longer time than plain tortillas. Each *gordita* can be eaten plain, but is usually covered with one or more ingredients and sauce. This one, made with avocados and pork, is in the style of Aguascalientes or Jalisco and parts of Michoacán, and very much in the Chicago-Mexican tradition.

¹/₂	lb.	potatoes, boiled
1	C.	prepared *masa*
1		egg, lightly beaten
1	T.	lard, vegetable shortening, or corn oil
2	T.	or more plain white flour
2		ripe avocados
2		tomatoes, peeled and seeded
2		*serrano* chiles, seeded
1		medium onion, chopped
¹/₂	C.	cooked shredded pork
		salt and freshly ground pepper, to taste
		lard or oil for cooking

Mash cooked potatoes, place in a large bowl and mix with *masa*, egg, lard (or vegetable shortening or oil), and flour until a firm dough has formed. Adjust amount of flour as needed. Form into thick cakes about ³/₄-inch in thickness and 3 inches in diameter. Set aside. Heat a heavy skillet or griddle over medium heat and place enough lard or oil in it to cover the surface with a light layer. Place *gorditas* in the skillet and toast until lightly browned, but not too hard. Remove from the skillet and keep warm.

Peel and pit the avocados. Mash them until they are quite smooth. Have ready a small saucepan filled with boiling water. Plunge the tomatoes, chiles, and onion in the water until tomato skins are easily removed. Remove from pan and drain. Place tomatoes, chiles, and onion in the bowl of a food processor (or better, in a *molcajete*) and puree. Place in bowl and mix with mashed avocado and pork. Mix well and season with salt and pepper. Cover each *gordita* with the mixture and serve while warm.   *Makes* 8–10

2

GUERRERO

Mexico City

Our crew and equipment assembled, we took off for Mexico, thanks to the kindness of Taesa Airlines. Taesa is a budget air transport that flies "redeyes:" travelers leave the northern cities in the United States at 2:00 AM and reach their Mexican destinations by late the next morning. Airline officials cheerfully proclaim the virtues of sleep deprivation by pointing out that vacationers can be "on the beach" by early afternoon and have the whole day to recover. Doubtful at first, since we were not planning to lounge on a beach, we discovered merit in taking this flight. The other passengers were one of the benefits. Because the flight was broken in Durango, many of our fellow fliers were cowboys who were clearly from that state. The state is beef cattle country, and the men dress accordingly. Their weather-darkened faces, many with drooping black moustaches, looked out from beneath classic western hats. Their clothing was pure trans-Rio Grande—fringed leather jackets, cowboy boots, and silver-inlaid belts. They could not have been more authentic than if they had come straight from a movie set. Seeing these marvelous-looking *vaqueros* brought us immediately into another culture, not exactly the one we had come to see, but an introduction to Mexico nonetheless.

Flying over Mexico at the hour of dawn, we looked out on an extraordinary landscape. Beneath us lay a horizon-to-horizon scene of rugged gray-black country, broken by the narrow valleys of the Sierra Madre Occidental and finally flattening into a huge central plateau that gave way to the broad Valley of Mexico. There sprawls Mexico city, a megalopolis whose population is now estimated to be approximately 14 million, although some say 20 million. We landed, spent the night, and were almost happy to take off again for our first shooting locations, Guerrero and Acapulco. Visiting the capital, all of us were struck anew by the size of the place and its immense problems. We stayed at a hotel conveniently near the airport. In the morning, streets leading from the district into the center city were jammed with cars and buses, like any city, only the air was also packed with particulate matter. Hungry after a long flight, the whole crew jumped into two taxis, still inexpensive, and cruised down one of the main boulevards looking for a likely restaurant. Outside the center, the city has a grimy quality, no doubt partly from the air quality, but also from economic causes. The population explosion has clearly overwhelmed some of the city's services, and additionally, as in all such situations, country people who migrate to the city tend to follow ways of life better suited to rural villages than urban life. Although this kind of problem is particular to North American cities, Mexico City has similar disadvantages.

As we drove along, Bob Ward suddenly spied a branch of one of the city's chain restaurants, El Portón. Clean, he said, and the food is pretty good. This place looked like many of the other new restaurants: lots of windows, natural wood tables, plants strategically placed. . . in short, the international style of corporate feeding. However, this restaurant was in Mexico, where food means more than simply central commissary fare. While the menu itself was in the familiar, laminated style and the dishes looked more or less familiar, what actually appeared on our tables surprised us. Everything was fresh. The juices we ordered were made from fresh fruits right on the spot and the coffee, likely from Oaxaca, was delicious. It was mid-morning, time for the Mexican *almuerzo*, and many of us wanted something hearty. We ordered *guacamole* all around. It arrived chunky and finely seasoned and we wolfed it down with plenty of *totopos* or fried chips. *Chilaquiles*, basically fried *tortilla* strips in sauce, is a standard dish that is done in different styles according to the region. These came with excellent charred beans that, we were told, is Mexico-City style. All of us ate *tacos* with grilled (skirt) steak, also in the regional style. Accompanied by good green sauce, a roasted tomato sauce, and piles of fresh *tortillas*, this was a reasonable reacquaintance with the joys of simple Mexican food.

Well stoked, everyone headed into the gritty heart of the city for different activities, some to shop in the regional craft shops near the *Palacio de Bellas Artes* (Fine Arts Museum), others to visit Chapultepec Park and the *Museo Nacional de Antropología é historia*, which is, without question, one of the world's greatest museums. I know the museum well and, time being short, opted to walk through the downtown area, along Avenida Juárez to the Zócalo. Since Carol Haddix had never been to Mexico City, she put on her running shoes and came along. The Alameda, Mexico City's central park, is ordinarily very attractive. Thinking about the place brings up an image of a Diego Rivera mural now in the park's Alameda Museum. It is his "Sunday Afternoon Dream at the Alameda"—the one showing him as a child along with important political figures, his painter-wife Frida Kahlo, the great artist José Guadalupe Posada, and "La Catrina," a female skeleton dressed in Sunday finery. Powerful art such as this conditions one's views of the world. But this time no such pictures were to be seen. Instead, different symbols confronted us. Much of the east end of the Alameda was surrounded by a wooden fence because of construction work on the *metro* (subway) system. This temporary structure, annoying though it was for tourists, was something of a monument to the government's determination to rebuild the old historic district and to remake Mexico into something more modern by revitalizing the past. Mexicans have done this before; indeed, historic renovation is one of the cornerstones of their nationalism.

That was made evident when we got to the Zócalo (or *Plaza de la Constitución*), the original Spanish city's central plaza. Here stands the Metropolitan Cathedral, begun in 1573 and not finished for another century. At ten acres in extent, the Zócalo is enormous, and on this day it was filled with people. Many were visiting the church, some as tourists, others as worshippers. As usual, it was virtually impossible to view the ornate exterior because of all the scaffolding. The cathedral is under constant repair because it is sinking into the marshy subsoil that lies under much of the central city. Stalls had been set up around the building. Some were distributing political literature related to the upcoming presidential elections; others sold souvenirs, T-shirts, cheap jewelry, and the like; and still others served the street food for which Mexico is justly famous. Carol and I walked by them, eyeing the assorted *tacos*, *churros*, *buñuelos*, and other treats. The smells of frying foods are almost irresistible, but we managed to do so because we had an appointment for dinner at a fine restaurant later that evening. Simply observing the scene was enough, for the place was packed with people. Here in the heart of the old city, we got an immediate sense of its pulse, its vibrancy, and something more.

The whole Zócalo area, with its impressive buildings, is monumental and also acts as a monument to several themes in Mexican history. The National Palace on the eastside represents the glory of the old Spanish Empire, while the cathedral indicates the power of the church in traditional Mexican life. The word *zócalo* itself, meaning "plinth" or "base," refers to a large platform that was built to be the base of a projected monument to Mexican independence. Although the platform was long since removed because the statuary was never put up, the idea of nationhood or nationalism remains, as does the name. Nearby there is an even older symbol of power: the ruins of a tremendous pre-Columbian temple. As Mircea Eliade, the historian of religion, has pointed out, all peoples have "sacred places," special sites that are seen as centers of the world or locations where the sacred and the mundane worlds come together.[1] This, the Zócalo, is one of those places, an ancient one.

Just to the northeast of the cathedral stands the *Templo Mayor*, or chief temple. . . of the Mexica, that is. By Mexica we mean Aztecs, the former likely the proper name of the group which settled along the lakes in the Basin of Mexico. There, beginning in the mid-fourteenth century by historical reckoning, the Mexica created a state and then an empire. At the empire's peak, the capital city, Tenochtitlán, was a huge complex of public buildings, markets, and private houses. Near the center was a roughly 120-foot-high double temple pyramid complex dedicated to the gods Huizilopóchtli, the god of war, and Tláloc, the god of rain. That a major building had once existed near the cathedral was well known. Spanish sources tell us that the conquerors of Tenochtitlán pulled down the temple and used the stone to build their own temple—the original cathedral. But the Mexica building's exact location was not clear until February of 1978, when some workers digging trenches for electric lines came across an extraordinary find: a colossal oval stone carved with the figure of a goddess named Coyolxauhqui ("she who has bells painted on her face"). Carved in 1469, it lay at the foot of the last temple, clearly meant as a recollection of a compelling myth, a story that has passed down to the Mexica descendants.

I well recall seeing the first excavations of the temple site not long after its discovery. Only part of the base had been exposed, but on it was the terrifying head of a snake. Anxious to see what had been done with the excavation, Carol and I walked over to have a look. A long section of the pyramid's base now lay exposed. Signs have been added to tell visitors about the construction (seven phases), the decoration (brilliant polychrome), and what gods are represented. However, it is inside the museum that the awe and mystery of the temple and the Mixtec religion come to life. On the second level, museum curators have placed the eight-ton stone depiction of Coyolxauhqui. It is an exquisite and horrifying piece. The goddess has been decapitated and dismembered. She is surrounded by snakes, even wearing a snake belt with a human skull attached to it. With her bare breasts prominent, she is clearly a deity associated with reproduction. It is a splendid piece of art, but hard for modern civilizations to understand. All is explained in a room devoted to Aztec religion. Logical as the explanation is, many beliefs, and certainly some of their ritualized expressions (human sacrifice, for example), remain alien. That some of these old ideas live on in folklore and modern religion cannot be doubted. Perhaps here is one reason for the otherworldly quality of life in Mexico.

So, what was the story of Coyolxauhqui? It is part of a cycle about Huitzilopóchtli, the "hummingbird god," a triumphant warrior and sun deity who demanded human blood as his due. Coatlicue, the great mother goddess, was sweeping a temple on Serpent Mountain when she was suddenly impregnated by a ball of beautiful feathers. Her daughter, Coyolxauhqui, considered this a dishonor of the highest order. In rage, she incited her 400 brothers to attack their mother and decapitate her. Coatlicue's image is often that of a headless corpse with serpents representing blood flowing from her neck. Just at the moment of Coatlicue's death, Huitzilopóchtli emerged from his mother's womb with weapons at the ready. Invincible, he slew his sister, removed her head, and threw her down the side of the mountain. Falling, and tumbling, her body broke into pieces. At the same time, the 400 brothers were scattered into the heavens and became the stars. The story corresponds exactly with the finds at the chief temple. Virgin birth, matricide, and sibling murder may all sound like the elements of a modern pulp novel or movie, but there are spiritual and ritual meanings in the story.

The tale is cosmic. Coatlicue was the Mother Earth, from whom all springs, including the heavenly bodies. Coyolxauhqui represented the moon—which represents the female side of the cosmos and life in virtually all ancient myth systems—with her head acting as the literal orb. She was slain by her brother, the sun, whose morning rays banish the moon and stars. From the mother came all life—depictions always feature human breasts that nurture—and death. The ancient peoples of Mexico believed that from death came life and from bones came vital seeds. In the same way that corn was harvested and decapitated, so seeds would come the next nurturing crop. From human life came renewed human life. Rituals carried out these beliefs verbatim. The Coyolxauhqui stone was placed at the base of the temple, while serpents representing Serpent Mountain line the main staircase. Can we doubt that human sacrificial victims were tumbled down these same steps in remembrance of this powerful myth? The hearts and blood of these victims were necessary to ensure that Huitzilopóchtli arose every morning to bring the sun's life-giving rays.[2] Explicable though the myth and its ritual enaction might have been to the Aztecs, it is nonetheless irrational to modern-day civilizations. Standing on the very site where such slaughter took place and such ideas were celebrated made both of us shudder.

After that, Carol suggested some refreshment, so we stopped in at one of the city's favorite places, the *Casa de Azulejos*, or "House of Tiles." The building is unmistakable, covered as it is in handsome blue tiles, and is a treasure of the colonial period. Inside is a Sanborn's restaurant, along with a newsstand and gift shop. What is so nice about Sanborn's are the curving counters, the revolving stools, and the cheerful waitresses who hustle about serving sandwiches, coffee, cakes, and ice cream creations. The atmosphere is something like a cross between old-fashioned counter-service restaurants and the tea rooms of fancy department stores in North America. One expects to find ladies and gentlemen of a certain age taking their afternoon break from shopping in such a place. Naturally, we had to have caffeinated drinks and one of the sweets displayed in the dessert case. It was an area of calm in the chaotic sea of urban life and very reassuring after having contemplated ancient horrors.

At the end of the long day, our crew separated for dinner. Several were off to an old standby, Bellinghausen, in the Zona Rosa. Dudley and Martha visited friends to discuss food stuffs, art, artists, and places on our itinerary that they might know. Jan, Carol, and I got to dine at one of Mexico City's new upscale restaurants. It happens that Jan has distant relatives in Mexico. A cousin to Jan by marriage, Catherine Austin is Mexican by nationality but half North American. She was completely bilingual, an official with the office of Secretary of Commerce. We had corresponded for some months before arriving in Mexico and received an invitation to dine with Catherine and her brother Steve. Knowing that Jan, Carol, and I were interested in new trends in food, they took us to Circunstancia in the Plaza Garibaldi. This part of the city, not far from the center, has become one of the hot places for an evening out. Most tourists will know it for the large numbers on *mariachi* bands that congregate there every night. On a warm evening it is a cacophony of guitars and blaring trumpets played by silver-bedecked musicians. We later learned that the now ubiquitous trumpets only entered this popular musical form in the 1940s. Before that, the more euphonious guitar, voice, and occasional harp were the instruments of choice. This night the streets were filled with so many players that we could hardly make our way to the restaurant. A colorful sight, but how many versions of "Guadalajara" can one person stand? Once inside the restaurant, we discovered what might be called "Nouvelle Mexican" cuisine.

Circunstancia's decor is dark, similar to something one might find in a trendy place in California's Santa Monica. We sampled many dishes, beginning with soups—a *poblano* cream with a touch of spice and an ultra-rich cilantro camembert were interesting. *Huitlacoche*, a corn fungus very much like mushrooms and one of Mexico's greatest delicacies, was featured in several dishes. One was an appetizer: *huitlacoche* in puff pastry with a delicate tarragon cream sauce. Among other appetizers we sampled were a dip, roquefort mousse with *tortilla* chips, and a kind of *chile en nogada, chile poblano* with fruits and nuts in a beet sauce. All were very interesting, mildly seasoned, and good. For entrées, we tried a beef tenderloin with a red chile sauce with cream, garnished with slices of roasted red peppers. Cream-finished chile sauces can be excellent; this was no exception. Then came a *huachinango* (red snapper) baked in foil with pistachio nuts and orange slices, an unusual and fine combination. Finally, we tried a shrimp with *huitlacoche*. Its sauce was made almost entirely of the fungus, sharp and very much of its origin. That is, it tasted like *huitlacoche*. None of these dishes could be described as Mexican either in the sense of traditional fine dining or, of course, ordinary restaurant food. Bearing some affinities to "California cooking," this kind of food preparation will become better known north of the border in the course of time. It worked well, we all thought, especially after several bottles of a nice Mexican red wine and plenty of interesting conversation with our charming hosts.

On that high culinary note, we left for the western states we had planned to visit. Experiencing Mexico City again left us all with mixed thoughts. It is a vibrant city, a cultural center, and a real world-class capital that is trying to upgrade itself physically. There is, however, still something of the Third World about it, a trace of Mexico's old problems. The city's infamous air pollution, evident problems of the infrastructure (though the transport systems work well and the *metro* is still one of the best run and best looking in the world), and marked social divisions between rich and poor show how far the country still has to go to reach the long-ago revolutionary-era promises of prosperity and justice for all. Perhaps, though, Mexico City represents a vision not of the past, but of the human future.

Physical Setting

Flying out of Mexico City toward the south and west, our view was once again a snapshot of the country's deeply folded terrain and one of the reasons for it—volcanic activity. (The other reason is uplift caused by the movement of continental plates.) As we headed southwest, huge twin volcanic cones glided into view on the left, still hazy from the morning mist rising from their snow-covered peaks. What stories the ancient peoples of the region must have told about *Iztaccíhuatl* (Nahuatl for "White Lady") and the more infamous *Popocatépetl* ("Smoking Mountain"). They seemed like twin gateposts, marking the entrance into the hidden Mexico we had come to explore.

Geography has everything to do with life in Mexico. Immensely varied landscapes and climates exist within a relatively small space. Hills and mountains dominate the country, most of them standing some 3,000 feet in elevation. Interspersed among these are valleys and depressions, some, but by no means most, with water sources in them. Water is life in the uplands' essentially dry climate, and, today as in centuries past, these are the places where villages are located. The Sierra Volcánica and the Sierra Madre del Sur run along the western side of Mexico. These, too, are cut by rivers and natural hollows. One of Mexico's main rivers, the Río Balsas, runs some 450 miles through the highlands, beginning in Jalisco in the north, then onto Guerrero and the interior of Oaxaca. We would follow this river as we traveled to the dry upland villages of Guerrero. Basins form the core agricultural areas of Michoacán, our second destination. Pátzcuaro is one such basin. But in this state, the river Cupatitzio flows through a low-lying zone and makes it a sub-tropical garden spot. The mountains rise as an escarpment along the Pacific coast; below them is a strip of tropical low-lying land. Once home only to fishing peoples, some of this area is now resort country, notably Acapulco.

Microenvironments change with an unexpected suddenness. Climbing the hills beyond Acapulco, especially during the dry season, one enters an almost Martian landscape of arid land and scrubby vegetation. The higher the elevation the worse the land, a situation painfully evident to us on our journey to Ameyaltepec, artist Nicolás de Jesús's village, located high up in the mountains of central Guerrero. Mexico's climate is mainly biseasonal. Rains fall during the year's warm months, usually May until the late autumn. Moist ocean air flows over adjacent lands and up over the bordering mountain country. The coastlines of Guerrero and Michoacán receive heavy rains in this season, with precipitation ranging from ten to twenty inches a month. Places in the nearby mountains—Acapulco, for instance—are, in comparison a tropical Edens where palm trees and fauna such as giant *cucarachas* flourish. The interior gets its rain as well, but like much of Mexico, there is not really enough water to support an ever-growing population. Here, in the cooler months when the damp weather belts move to the south, the skies are clear with little or no precipitation. (Although this is not so often true any longer in the massively polluted capital city.) Like Mexico City, the lands along the Río Balsas or Alto Balsas, may only receive about twenty inches a year. Ground water and rivers are the fluid of life, and yet they are overburdened. Going through the hot lands where people in the dusty villages live a hardscrabble life, always short of water, one can well imagine why North America seems to be promised land. We can also understand why the pre-Columbian peoples venerated water and the gods who brought it. Yet within these lands, in every small village and hamlet, there is another kind of wealth. It lies in the complex imagination of the people.

Perhaps that imagination, manifested in the arts, springs from the environment as much as from the ethnic mix that comprises the Mexican people. The land is a kaleidoscope of local ecological zones juxtaposed upon one another. The big divisions are the *tierra caliente* (the "hot lands": the coastal regions, the southern jungles, and northern deserts), the *tierra templada* (the "temperate lands" of the center, including much of Guerrero and Michoacán, running in a broad strip northward through Guadalajara to the U.S. border), and the *tierra fría* (the "cold lands" of the highest elevations). Although these divisions would make major cultural regions understandable, each of these three zones can be found in various states or small regions. Guerrero, as we noted, is one of them, while Michoacán is even more varied. In the latter state, dry hills, lush lowland lake country, and forests can be found within the radius of a forty-five-minute drive from the capital, Morelia. Then there are the forests scattered across the highcountry. Where there is enough moisture, coniferous and oak forests grow. Forests create even smaller microenvironments that give rise to different faunas and flora—and different foodstuffs. The famed *jumiles* (insects) of Taxco appear only on the wooded flanks of the hills upon which the city is built. Their preparation is exactly the same today as it was in prehistoric times. Down on the coast, one can dine upon iguana, also a pre-Columbian delicacy. The plants, animals, and foods of all the local environments are all important parts of the complex life of Mexico as it is borne out in various cultural forms.

For all the country's diversity and resources, traveling through it gives rise to questions about how long the environment can support an ever-increasing population (expected to rise to upward of 100 million by the turn of the millennium). It comes as no surprise that only thirteen percent of the land is arable and that only ten percent of the land gets enough rain to farm without irrigation. Those miles upon miles of barren hills seen from the air tell much about the thin margin upon which Mexican agriculture is based. Yet the country produces abundant food supplies. Markets in every town are filled with foodstuffs and street food is a national passion. Mexico yields enough arable land to make fruits, vegetables, nuts, and other farm produce among the country's major exports. The *ejido* system of collective farms seems to have succeeded to this extent. All production comes at some cost, however. The country's water supplies are under siege, and many environmentalists doubt that current production levels, much less future expansion, can be maintained. Further, questionable techniques such as heavy fertilizing and massive pest control can be seen in many Mexican fields. The runoff from such fields has virtually killed some rivers and reservoirs. Together with the heavy timber harvesting (about twenty-five percent of the country is woodland) that depletes water tables, it is no wonder that many Mexicans say that their nation's main problem is not frequent currency crises, but water.

Fortunately, an environmental movement has risen in response to these and many other problems. Some steps have been taken to reverse situations that could have become completely catastrophic, such as the destruction of the monarch butterfly's forest wintering grounds in Michoacán. Just how much of Mexico's rich natural heritage the environmentalists can save is open to question. It is very much akin to the same problem with Mexico's cultural heritage: how much can and will be preserved? That is one of the things we came to Mexico to discover. Again, history's twins, tradition and change, are both Mexico's parents and children.

On to food. These are three versions of a dish we all ate upon arriving in Mexico City, *chilaquiles*. Nothing is wasted in the Mexican kitchen, not even old, stale *tortillas*. These are cut into strips and used in much the same way as noodles are in European cooking; that is, mixed with sauces and/or cooked with other foods. They may be used in many different ways, and the following recipes are but a few of them.

Chilaquiles

(from Jiquilpan, Michoacán)

4	medium tomatoes, roasted and peeled
7	*arbol* chiles, toasted and seeded
$\frac{1}{4}$	medium onion, sliced
2	cloves garlic, peeled
$\frac{1}{4}$ C.	lard or vegetable oil

6		dried *tortillas*, cut into strips
2		eggs, beaten
		salt and freshly ground pepper, to taste
¼	C.	*queso fresco*, grated
¼	C.	sour cream

Roast tomatoes on a griddle or under a broiler and peel. Toast chiles and seed then. Place in the bowl of a blender or food processor together with the onion and garlic and purée. Reserve. While doing this, heat lard or oil in a deep, heavy skillet. Add *tortilla* strips and brown until crisp. Add beaten eggs and saute gently until cooked. Add chile mixture. Season with salt and freshly ground pepper, to taste. To serve, sprinkle grated cheese on top and a teaspoon of sour cream for each portion. *Serves 4*

Super Chilaquiles

This recipe is simpler, calling for bottled *chipotles*, which are available in many Latin markets.

2		large tomatoes (about ½ lb.), peeled and seeded
1		small onion, chopped fine
1		clove garlic, chopped fine
1	t.	*epazote*, chopped
1	t.	chopped fresh coriander
		Salt to taste
12		*tortillas*, cut into ½" strips
		bottled *chipotle* chiles, cut in strips
½	lb.	bacon, sliced thinly and fried crisp
½	C.	cooked pinto beans
1		avocado, cut in medium slices
¼	C.	grated hard cheese
		lard or oil for frying

Make a sauce from the tomatoes, onion, garlic, herbs, and salt: fry garlic and onions in a small amount of oil until soft, add tomatoes, coriander, and *epazote*; cook for 2–3 minutes, then place mixture in a blender or processor and purée. Add salt, return to the pan, and heat gently. In a separate pan, fry *tortilla* strips until golden brown and drain. Add strips to sauce and cook until soft. Place mixture in a serving dish and cover with strips of chiles, bacon, beans, avocado, and grated cheese. Keep dish warm or serve at once. *Serves 4–6*

Chicken Chilaquiles

This is a particularly delectable dish. *Preheat oven to 350°.*

½	lb.	*tomatillos*, peeled
2		*serrano* chiles, seeded
1		small onion
1	t.	*epazote*
1	t.	fresh coriander
		salt to taste
		lard or oil
12		stale *tortillas*
1	lb.	chicken breasts, cooked and shredded
1	C.	sour cream
1	C.	shredded white or asadero cheese

Prepare a green sauce: boil *tomatillos* in enough water to cover until soft, then grind in a blender together with chiles, onion, *epazote*, coriander, and salt. Heat 1 tablespoon of lard or oil, add *tomatillo* purée, and cook for several minutes. Cut *tortillas* into strips and fry until just browned. Drain and add to green sauce. Cook slowly, stirring constantly until *chilaquiles* are soft. Place in a heated serving dish or casserole and cover with the chicken, sour cream, and shredded cheese. Place in an oven preheated to 350° for a few minutes until the cheese melts. Serve covered with shredded lettuce. *Serves 4–6*

The Journey to Acapulco

Early the next morning, we all collected our equipment and set off for the airport, on our way to Acapulco, where we planned to begin the program. From the air we looked down upon the tan-colored terrain of central Guerrero, its mountains in the north giving way to a weathered, deeply creased landscape. We could see, here and there, small villages and towns set in the arid country. We knew that later our journey would take us into this country. As so often happens when flying in Mexico, the hills dropped away beneath us and suddenly we were over the ocean and a wide flat beach. As the plane circled ever lower, we could easily see gentle breakers on the shore and, not far inland, broad stretches of palm trees. It was the very image of a tropical island landscape, so different from where we had been only a few minutes earlier. Mexico is a land of sharp contrasts, indeed.

Emerging from the aircraft in Acapulco was an immediate introduction to a tropical climate—it was sunny, hot, and humid and felt like a sauna. After a winter in Chicago, it was a delightful change. Moving all of our equipment was not delightful, but what was a little perspiration when the prospect of the famous resort's pleasures were before us? At least, that is what we told ourselves—but in fact, we were here to put in twelve- and fourteen-hour work days. We were greeted by local representatives of the tourism office, who loaded us on to the bus we would be using while in Acapulco, and set off for the city. The airport is located some twenty kilometers down the coast, but getting back and forth is not a short trip. Mexico's roads, as we discovered, are usually not like U.S. Interstate highways. Terrain is usually the problem since it is often so hilly that winding roads are common. Two-lane, rough-pavemented highways run through the towns, and endless work projects make the going slow, if interesting. The road to Acapulco is like that, rising onto high ridges that run along the coast. The view from on high was spectacular, especially as we passed by the bay of Puerto Marquéz. Described in the tourist literature as a lair for pirate ships in the seventeenth century, this small, circumscribed bay is rapidly developing into a junior, if newer, Acapulco. Finally, we dropped down onto the narrow strip of beach that fronts Acapulco. Whatever one might think of resorts, this one has a splendid geography and climate going for it.

Our hotel turned out to be a very large building just off the beach and close to the main road running along the bay front, La Costera Miguel Alemán, or simply La Costera. Clearly, the place had once been an upscale hotel. The views of the bay and its islands were superb. Now slightly down-at-the-heels, the hotel was packed with teenagers and college-aged tourists there on spring-semester break. It was not an ideal situation. Not that any of us dislike young people, but there were so many that it took literally fifteen or twenty minutes to get on an elevator—none of which were very efficient in the first place—in order to reach the rooms on the upper floors. Never having participated in any such trips, most of us regarded the scene as one would a painting by Hieronymous Bosch. A kind of culture shock grew upon us, all the more so when we all sat down to discuss what we were going to do and why. Everyone had seen the countryside we had flown over and knew something about the villages. Since this was a journey not only in space but in time, all of us had to be aware of the historical dimensions of what we saw, wrote, and put on camera. If that sounds somewhat professorial, it is. . . the prelude to a series of lectures on food history. Sitting near the hotel pool with margaritas (Acapulco's greatest invention!) in hand, we ignored the roiling mass of wet pubescent humanity and cast our minds back into the distant past. For even this highly artificial place is the product of its environment and human history.

Historical Overview

The Villages

Climate, land, and water are elements crucial to Mexico's farming villages. Although the country is highly urbanized, villages are still significant features of Mexico. They always have been, or at least since they first formed several thousand years ago. Many people living in towns and cities still have something of the village mentality embedded in them, because the village is the ancient base of the nation's life. Habits of thought are hard to break, even supposing it is desirable to do so. Like most human settlements in ages past, these villages fit into their local environments and are adapted to natural conditions, as hard as those may be. Again, this is one reason for the great variety of life in Mexico. Anyone traveling through the countryside, upland and down, sees these places nestled into the landscape. With their buildings forever in seeming states of decay, once whitewashed adobe walls cracked and stained, they appear to have been there forever, artifacts of long-ago times. At least most of us *norteamericanos* think so. It is an image of Mexico given to us by the popular media, once by books and photographs, now by movies and television. Mexican villages? Scenes from "The Treasure of the Sierra Madre," "Viva Zapata," or "The Magnificent Seven," come to mind. You know them: windswept dirt streets, sun-baked adobe, white-garbed *campesinos* with broad *sombreros*. The fact is, parts of Mexico do look like this, but mostly in the dry northern lands or in the backland villages of Guerrero where we had yet to travel. Environments with greater biodiversity produce very different-looking dwellings.

Nonetheless, villages do have some aspects in common. They are as much signs of social, economic, and cultural forces as products of history. Certainly Mexico is socially stratified, and nowhere is this more evident than in rural areas where, in Mexico's rapidly changing economy, subsistence farmers are seen as relics of ages past. Nor are villages stuck in some kind of time trap. Most are near market towns or cities, so that there have always been interactions between those venues of more rapid change and the primary producers of agricultural products. No village that we saw had remained untouched by modernity. Even Ameyaltepec, high up in the desolate hills of Guerrero, has electricity and a telephone. In Michoacán and Guerrero, as in other states, some villages are devoted to subsistence, while others engage in cottage industries, including arts and crafts. But the fact remains that many villagers are economically poor in the states in question, particularly indigenous peoples, which gives rural Mexico the aspect of a Third World nation. That is why so many country people have migrated to

Mexico City. How to bring these people into the mainstream of a modern economy is the problem.

Modernity is also a dilemma. Villages have always been the mainstream of Mexico's history. Achieving economic solvency in these places and at the same time preserving the best of the past is the difficulty. Why? Because there is a wealth in these villages that goes beyond mere money. It lies in the traditional ways they have preserved. These customs are the stuff of Mexico's authentic history. Real history is not so much the words and deeds of rulers and warriors, but the works of the ordinary people of villages and towns. The expressions of that history and of historical processes, in these contexts, lies in art and ritual and in foods. It was here, among the common folk, that the great mixture of peoples that is Mexico was born. This is where, in the words of, if not the full meaning of, turn-of-the-century writer and politician José Vasconcelos, the "cosmic race" was forged. And, as Dudley constantly reminds us, a cosmic cuisine: it is *the* metaphor for Mexican culture and history, and the native foodstuffs of Mexico have had the most profound effects on human history.

Origins of Mexico

If we suppose that Mexicans are the sum of their past (and who is not?), then we ought to look at their origins. Any visitor to Mexico who has the slightest interest in history—and that means archaeology, too—knows that virtually every guidebook and museum starts the story with the earliest peoples in Mesoamerica. Could it be that the great stream of modern Mexican society is still fed by these small, ancient springs? Most scholars of Mexico tend to conclude that there is something in that idea. Researchers who take environmental backgrounds into account agree. Food historians know it because Mexican comestibles are based on what the first peoples of the region gathered and, especially, what they grew. A quick glimpse, then, of Mexico's prehispanic past and how it lives on in the people of today.

The "New World" has always been new for human beings. Until perhaps 20,000–25,000 years ago, the American continents were populated by other animals, but not by humans. The first Americans traveled from Asia, across a sixty-mile-wide band of land that is now the Bering Strait. The time must have been before the end of the last Ice Age, some 13,000 years ago, because when the great ice sheets melted, the land bridge was inundated. The small bands of immigrants spread out across the two continents and established home territories. Thus, the first Mexicans may have appeared in their new homeland as long ago as 25,000 years, although stronger evidence suggests about 12,000–10,000 B.C.E.

Perhaps the early rapid dispersal of these small groups led to the stunning variety of languages spoken throughout the Americas. It has been said that Mexico once held more than 500 distinct languages before the Spanish conquest. Even though scholars have placed these languages into families, Mexico still has fourteen large linguistic families spread over such a relatively small space that it is difficult for us to comprehend. One is reminded of Dagestan in the Caucasus Mountains, a country of less than 2 million people that is divided into forty-three different language groups. Today indigenous peoples often identify themselves by their language group. In the region we were visiting, Nahuatl, one of the Uto-Aztecan languages, is mainly spoken. It is our friend, Nicolás de Jesús's native language. However, once the Nahua group had many rivals, among them the Purépecha of Michoacán, as we would discover.

The country to which these peoples came must have seemed like a paradise. The climate was not like it is today, but warmer and wetter, and there were considerable numbers of large grazing animals and many smaller ones in the newly grown forests. The original settlers were hunters and gatherers, peoples not unlike aboriginal groups in Australia, but they had the benefit of a better climate. We usually think of people who live this lifestyle as hunters of big game who, after a successful field trip, squat by their campfires chewing on large roasted haunches of their prey. In reality, archaeologists studying early sites all over the Americas have shown that life differed from this picture. Most discarded bones belong to small animals, such as rabbits, rodents, lizards, snakes, and various invertebrates. We know, too, that these hunters also gathered plants of all sorts and that this, without question, was done by women. Based on comparisons with more recent hunter-gatherers, it is clear that women supplied most of each band's foodstuffs. It was they who invented agriculture. . . and not only in Mexico, but in places all over the world.

Paradise, if that is what it was, did not last. Climates changed and as they did, the early hunter-gatherers gradually adapted to those changes. About 7000 B.C.E. Mexico's climate grew warmer and drier. By now the bands were long accustomed to collecting their food seasonally, that is, going from place to place within their home range during each area's optimal season. More and more their diet shifted toward plant food, especially annual grasses. One of these was the small podded ancestor of corn. By this period people were using grinding stones, mortars, and pestles (later to become the classic *metate* used all over Mexico) to prepare grain. Because annuals are self seeding, their potential harvest season is short. Gatherers knew just when to collect them, but with the climate causing harvests to be unpredictable, deliberate planting became necessary to survival. This step, likely taken in central Mexico around 5000 B.C.E., would lead to farming villages and, eventually, to the great indigenous civilizations of Central America.

Not that full farming villages came about immediately, or that all the plants eaten in pre-Columbian times were actually domesticated. For several thousand years, most peoples continued to be seasonal migrants, only now they genetically manipulated plants to their advantage. Maize, what we call corn, which became the eventual base upon which all Mexican civilizations rested, composed only about five percent of the total foodstuffs in their diet. It did not look like modern corn; instead, it had small pods on stalks that more closely resembled large grasses than the familiar large stalk of today's varieties. Interestingly, one of the first domestication areas may have been Balsas region. There avocados, chiles, certain kinds of squash, at least one kind of bean, and perhaps amaranth also seem to have begun the long road to full domestication. What that means is that farmers, or gardeners, to use a better term, selected plants whose characteristics they wanted, saved the seeds, and planted them in their small plots of land. By gradually altering the plants' characteristics, early experimenters changed their habitats, yields, size, and colors, among other elements. The many varieties of corn and beans, for instance, stem from these early days.

Some food plants remained wild and still are. Mexicans eat a wide variety of *quelites*, or "greens," that are gathered in season. Usually these are the young shoots of annual plants, such as purslane (something we consider a garden weed, but widely used in the Americas for food), *epazote* (in the *chenopod* family that includes beets and spinach), and various forms of amaranth.[3] We can well imagine a prehistoric meal featuring boiled *quelites*, *epazote*-flavored beans, and chile sauce, accompanied by *tortillas* made from corn and all cooked in clay pots over an open fire. We discovered that it is not hard to find the same meal today in villages all over Mexico or in market foodstands.

By around 2500–2000 B.C.E, the small groups were established enough to have formed permanent villages all over Mexico. Archaeologists call the whole period the Formative Period. This period of village life is usually divided into three phases, starting about 2000 B.C.E. and lasting until roughly 300–150 B.C.E. This process of settlement into distinct regions coincides with a wetter climatic phase. It could well be that with better conditions, populations rose rapidly, making it necessary to produce more food. This is when corn really developed into something like its modern forms with large cobs, big kernels, and multi-layered husks. The growth of stationary villages meant that food sources had to be close by and that surpluses could be stored. What did the early villagers live on? Their domesticated plants included at least three major kinds of squash (including pumpkins), many kinds of beans, avocados (although not the "alligator" and smooth green ones common in our stores, but types of *criollo* avocados with edible skins), varieties of chiles (from hot to mild), certain amaranths, gourds, and *chayote*.[4] Notice that the tomato, another New World plant, is not included in this inventory. It seems to have been developed as a domesticate much later, as was the green, husked *tomatillo*. Corn, the eventual staple crop, was likely already categorized into three main types. These are popcorn, close to the original wild types; flint corn, with a high starch content that was used for hominy; and flour corns, which have soft starch that makes them easily ground into flour.[5] It may be that Mexicans had already discovered that corn should be prepared with lime. In its natural state, corn lacks certain amino acids and niacin. Human diets heavy in corn can produce a serious vitamin-deficiency disease called pellagra. Treating corn with lime, such as boiling it in lime water or mixing corndough with wood ash or shell, solves the problem. That is exactly what the ancient Mexicans did and still do. It is not likely that the food preparers understood scientific nutrition, only that hard corn kernels could be ground more easily when boiled, and there is limestone aplenty in Mexico.[6] Besides that, it tastes good. In several villages we ate *tamales de ceniza* that were absolutely delicious, and they tasted even better when we realized that they represented at least a 3000-year-old preparation.

By the time stationary villages were created, several animals appeared in farmyards. Compared to the Old World, there were very few domestic animals in the New World. Horses had disappeared and there were no cattle or

Washing nixtamal *(ground corn) in a vessel* (tlalchikiuhtli *in* Nahuatl)

Trapping grasshoppers

pigs. The first domesticate was the dog, which served not for hunting, but was served for dinner. Representations of small, fat, hairless dogs abound in pre-Columbian art; the pottery figurines of Colima are famous. As scavengers, dogs eat almost anything: cheap grain, garbage, excrement. Dogs were the first recycling systems—they ate things people could not and people ate them. Because dogs passed from the menu with the Spanish conquest, the historical breed had disappeared, or at least until they were recreated through back breeding by dog fanciers. The variety has been given the old Nahuatl name, *xoloitzcuintli*, or "young dog." We saw some in Taxco: small, lean creatures, hairless, black in color, with heavily boned eyesockets. The other domesticated animals were turkeys, perhaps Muscovy ducks, bees, parrots (in the jungle areas), and cochineal beetles. The latter feed on prickly pear cactus and were used both for flavoring and dye (red, of course). Insects have always played an important role in the cuisine of the indigenous, and now Mexican, peoples.

No one supposes that these few animals provided large amounts of protein to the human diet. Throughout all of pre-Columbian Mexican history, local peoples hunted game. Before modern times, there were many more forests that served as home to game animals. We know from comments by

Toasting grasshoppers

early Spanish chroniclers of Mexico that the Aztecs ate deer, peccary, rabbits, mice, armadillos, snakes, gophers, opossums, iguanas, frogs, salamanders, and many more wild beasts. Today, several of these can still be found on regional menus. In Guerrero and Michoacán we saw iguana, salamander, and armadillo available in markets and some restaurants. There is one other wild creature that served as a major protein source: fish. Lakes, and there were many more in the past, provided a dense biomass and plenty of fish. On the coasts, including the Acapulco area, early fishing villages have been found. Evidence of fishnets indicate that the kind of fishing still done along the coast is quite old. The final result, grilled fish with chile sauces, splendid preparations that our crew gorged upon, is yet another delicious relic of the past.

Early Civilizations

Out of the Early Formative Period villages came cities, states, and civilization. It did not happen all at once or in all places. Once begun, though, the process we call civilization spread to many parts of Mesoamerica and in a remarkably uniform way. Elements of the earliest civilization so far recorded appear time and again in the others. That happened either through the diffusion of ideas through trade and other contacts or, in some cases, conquest. Two things are certain about how civilizations came about. One is the rise of religious-political elites who controlled the military force. Another is that trade routes wound through and into every part of ancient Mesoamerica so that hardly any group was untouched by some outside culture. The story is familiar because it was repeated time and again.

The earliest civilization was that of the Olmecs, whose heartland lay in the east along the Gulf of Mexico in the Veracruz region (although some scholars think the culture originated further south). This is lowland, hot, humid jungle country, not the sort of place where archaeologists look for primary civilizations. Nonetheless, it was here that trends also existing in other parts of Mexico coalesced into the formal political organizations we call cities and states. When the Olmec civilization was first discovered, researchers were amazed at the extraordinary art and monumental buildings that the Olmecs built. Colossal stone heads weighing up to twenty tons, frowning baby-faced, helmeted things, had been found lying in an apparently haphazard way in the jungles. Discoveries of figurines, made of pottery and carved stone, showed much the same style, often strange mixtures of a human baby face and a snarling jaguar. How mysterious they seemed! Indeed, their language and their apparent sudden appearance puzzled the first students of this culture. The name Olmec was not their own, but Mayan, meaning "people from the land of rubber."

In the past thirty years, much has come to light. Linguists now reckon that the Olmecs probably spoke some form of the Mixe-Zoquean, possibly Xipe-Totonac languages, whose speakers are said to be the descendants of ancient Olmecs. In the three best explored sites, San Lorenzo, Tres Zapotes, and La Venta, carved hieroglyphs have begun to be translated by researchers and scholars working backward from the modern indigenous languages. We now know that Olmecs used a calendar that was remarkably like the famous Mayan one, which was the model for all others in Mesoamerica. San Lorenzo is, so far, the oldest site, dating back to at least 1500 B.C.E. At first the place was a largish village with about 1,000 inhabitants. About a century or so later, large buildings and works projects appeared. The foundation for a major temple was laid, a large platform about six feet in height that likely carried a structure built with poles, woven branches, and thatch. We now know that this was not the first such platform, since some have been discovered from an earlier date further south in Belize. Eventually large-scale pyramids would be built, one at La Venta standing about 110 feet high on a base measuring 240 by 420 feet. These public buildings, usually the temples, that were the focus of public religion, would have taken hundreds of thousands of man-hours to build. That means organization of lots of labor for the job, and that, in turn, means central control: priests and kings, always a hallmark of states. Maybe the huge stone heads are portraits of the warrior-kings of these Olmec states.

By about 1100 B.C.E, the mature Olmec artistic style had developed. Most striking is the image of the were-jaguar mentioned previously. Many faces on figurines have thick lips with the upper lip curled upward and the lower lip turned down at the corners, often with jaguar fangs. Clearly, the jaguar was sacred to the Olmecs. Michael Coe, the excavator of San Lorenzo, suggests that the Olmec myth about this animal was that once upon a time a jaguar mated with a human woman to produce the creature depicted by the figurines.[7] Perhaps he was the earliest version of the Aztec war god Tez-catlipoca, who also had something to do with fertility. Whatever the exact meaning, and if later religions are any model, it was very complicated, the jaguar became a widespread symbol in all pre-Columbian religions. The rituals live on. In Guerrero, far from the animal's jungle home, villages such as Totoltepec perform jaguar dances in full costume. This reminds us that this fantastic religious art represented rituals in which the participants wore masks and costumes. The Olmec dancers thus acted out sets of myths about the jaguar god. The idea is compelling, so much so that Dudley bought a complete costume in one Guerrero village we visited. It hangs on display, and, despite our many entreaties, he refuses to perform the dance.

The prestige, wealth, and symbolic power of these states came from the collection of exotic materials via long-distance trade. Black magnetite and black obsidian were major imports from the volcanic lands of the interior. Virtually all minerals had to be imported, including the huge stones used in carving the stone heads and in building the monumental structures. Some came from as far away as the Tuxtla Mountains, more than one hundred miles away. The state itself depended upon getting prestige goods. Wide-spread trade relations sent Olmecs into other regions and put them in contact with other peoples. That is why archaeologists have found many Olmec influences in the Valley of Mexico to the northwest, in Oaxaca and Mayaland in the south, and the inhospitable lands of Guerrero. There are arguments among scholars about the degree of Olmec influence on other peoples. Were they responsible, through their demands for raw materials, for the development of the ancient Maya, as was once thought, or did they stimulate al-ready ongoing developments? The answer seems to be the latter.

So, why did the earliest states arise in the jungle lowlands? Apart from the military and political skills of individual leaders, one reason is that the region held rich agricultural potential. Tropical jungle lands are never good for farming, but the Olmecs devised systems for using the rich land around rivers. These areas did not require the kind of labor needed in the dry lands of the interior to produce a great deal of food. The families that got control of the rich lands by whatever means also came to control the flow of goods and then to lead the state. Religion was a powerful cement that held the allegiance of the people. That is likely why the jaguar deity was so important, since he was the symbol of secular, warrior, and divine power. The potency of those religious ideas is still carried out in folk rituals in traditional villages.

The height of Olmecan power lasted for several centuries. By 400 B.C.E., La Venta had been destroyed and the Olmec peoples returned to village life. States in the highlands where raw materials were to be found had eclipsed them. In places such as Oaxaca, intensive agricultural systems grew up so that their populations grew ever larger. Eventually leaders there took control of trade and religious sentiments and became great kings. Their cultural forms may have differed in art style and in their choice of deities, but the similarities with Olmecan forms remained. And this fundamental bit of reality remains: no matter how complex the societies, how powerful the state, everything rested upon the platform of agriculture. When states fell, as happened from time to time, what remained were the villages carrying on their traditional ways of life. There they are still, ages old.

Some of the traditions maintained by the villages are, of course, religious. Not only are jaguars an Olmec legacy, but other deities as well. In the bleakest mountains of central Guerrero, not far from the capital of Chilpancingo, a painted cave was discovered. Deep inside there is a brilliant polychrome Olmec mural depicting a god who has with him a feathered serpent. Whatever the Olmecs called him, this was surely the predecessor of a deity worshipped for the next 2,000 years, called Quetzalcoatl by the Aztecs. In another nearby cave, at Oxtotitlán, another painted cave shows an Olmec king wearing a mask that represents the gods of the underworld. This and several other figures demonstrate the ongoing theme that was so important to agricultural societies, that life and death are associated with the fertility of the land. Guerrero, with its unforgiving uplands, is a place where one can imagine farmers fervently believing in powers beyond this world who can help them with their harvests. Celebrations invoking such powerful emotions is something we were later to witness in that state.

Wild game always played an important role in the pre-Columbian diet. Deer feature in all archaeological sites as well as in the early Spanish records about what the ancient elites ate. The following recipe is Dudley's interpretation of one such dish; the cheese and cinnamon come from the Old World. The oil might have come from *chian*, a major source of oil in the ancient kitchen.

Picaditas de Venado

½	lb.	venison, cut in thin slices across the grain and sautéed
2–4	T.	olive or canola oil
1½	C.	corn *masa* or corn flour
¼	C.	warm water
½	T.	kosher salt
5		*tomatillos* (green tomatoes), peeled and toasted
2		cloves garlic, peeled and toasted
¼		onion, toasted
1		*serrano* chile, toasted
5		springs cilantro, chopped
		a pinch of powdered cinnamon
		salt and freshly ground pepper, to taste
½	C.	*fresco* cheese, grated

Prepare venison. Beat oil in a heavy skillet and sauté the venison until rare. Set aside but keep warm. Prepare *masa* by mixing in a bowl with warm water. Knead until it has a soft consistency, adding more water if necessary. It should not be sticky. Let rest for 5 minutes in a bowl covered with plastic wrap. Make 6–8 small balls 1-inch in diameter of the *masa* dough and place them in the bottom of a *tortilla* press ("Preparing tortillas" p. 243). Do not press to usual *tortilla* thickness, but instead made them about ½-inch thick. Heat an *ungreased* griddle or frying pan over medium heat until hot. Place each *picadita* on the griddle and bake until lightly browned on both sides. Remove from the pan and pinch up the edges of each *picadita* so that it has a small lip or rim. Set aside to be reheated later. Meanwhile, toast the *tomatillos* on an *ungreased* griddle over medium heat until most of the skin is light browned. Remove from pan and do exactly the same with the garlic, onion, and *serrano* chile. When done, place *tomatillos*, garlic, onion, chile, and cilantro in the bowl of a food processor or blender and purée. Season to taste. Then reheat the griddle and place the pinched-edge *tortillas* on it. Toast until nicely browned but not burnt. To assemble: place 1–2 tablespoons of the purée on each *picadita*, cover with strips of venison and sprinkle with grated *fresco* cheese. Serve warm or cool.

Serves 6–8

There is no question that the ancient elites—the kings, chiefs, and priests—ate more meat than the common people. Nonetheless, their diet was also based on the staples of corn and beans. The following dish is something one of those stocky Olmec warriors might have eaten, with the substitution of deer or peccary for pork.

Frijol de Arriero

(from Guerrero)

1	lb.	red beans
8–12	C.	water
2	T	canola oil
½	lb.	pork spareribs
1		whole head garlic, peeled
1		sprig *epazote*
6		*guajillo chiles*, soaked, seeded, and deveined
		kosher salt and freshly ground pepper, to taste

Cook the beans as directed in the "Preparing Beans" section (p. 244). While they are cooking, heat 2 tablespoons canola oil in a deep, heavy skillet. Add the pork spareribs and brown on all sides. When the beans are about halfway done (about 30–40 minutes) add the browned spareribs, garlic, and *epazote*. Return to a boil, reduce heat to simmer, and continue to cook the beans. Meanwhile, toast *guajillo* chiles lightly on a *comal*, then soak them in a small amount of warm water, enough to cover. When soft, remove seeds and veins. Place the chiles in the bowl of a food processor or blender and grind with a little of the water in which they have soaked until a paste has been formed. Remove the paste from processor bowl. When the beans–spareribs mixture is ready, make certain that there is not too much water left in the pan. (This is not a soup dish.) Stir in the *guajillo* paste and allow to cook for another 10 minutes. Season with kosher salt and freshly ground pepper, to taste. *Serves 4*

Note: Serve this dish with plenty of fresh tortillas. Also, although this is not authentically pre-Columbian, sprinkle *queso fresco* on top.

The workers on all the building projects ate mostly vegetable foods, some cultivated and some wild. It would be nice to think that they had a dish like this from time to time. Mushrooms play an interesting role in the cuisine and medicinal and interesting ritual history of Mexico. The ancient Mexicans had an affinity for fungi in many forms, from field mushrooms to smuts and molds. Some were, and still are, used in religious rituals—the hallucinogenic kinds. This dish is a recreation of what might have been eaten after a mushroom hunt in the woods. Although it calls for shiitake, any large flavorful mushroom, such as portobello, will do. The presence of tomatoes in the dish may not be authentic, since they may not have been introduced into Mexico by then.

Hongos con Salsa

(from Morelia, Michoacán)

1-½	lbs.	large mushrooms or shiitakes, finely sliced
5		whole *chiles de arbol*, lightly toasted, soaked in warm water, and seeded
3		whole tomatoes, roasted or toasted
1		clove garlic, peeled and chopped
1		whole clove
2		black peppercorns
2	t.	lard or vegetable oil
		kosher salt to taste

Slice mushrooms and set aside. Toast chiles and soak in enough warm water to cover, then seed. Set aside the water. Place chiles, tomatoes, garlic, clove, and peppercorns in the bowl of a food processor. Purée with about ½ cup of the chile water. Heat oil in a heavy skillet. Add mushrooms and sauté until softened, about 2–4 minutes. Stir in the chile mixture, bring to simmer, and allow to cook for 10 minutes. Season with kosher salt, to taste.   *Serves* 4

Note: Serve with chopped cilantro as a garnish.

Mature States

Our hotel, just off the main beach-front street, La Costera, was very near a small cultural center and archaeological museum. Despite the usual hectic shooting schedule, several of us trotted off to see what treasures could be found there. Unfortunately it was closed, so even more unluckily, Ralph, the archaeology enthusiast, and company had to listen to yet another disquisition on Mexican prehistory. Acapulco was as appropriate a place as any, since several of the ancient states had either trade relations or dominion over this part of the Pacific coast. The story goes like this.

Once the basis for them had been set, Mesoamerica's great civilizations rose. There were many, with many regional variations. What they all had in common were, first and foremost, farming villages with large numbers of peo-ple to supply food to the new urban centers. After all, you cannot have chiefs and priests without the produce of common folk to support them. Long-dis-tance trade in valuable goods and some basic commodities were under the control of the bosses, because this gave them the prestige they needed to maintain their positions in the world. Among these goods were cacao beans. The modern Latin name for cacao, *Theobroma cacao* tells us something about its value. The first word is Latin for "food of the gods" and the last a Mayan word, perhaps Olmec in origin but known to us from the Nahuatl, *cacahuatl*. Grown in the tropics, in Mayaland, the beans actually served as a kind of money. Naturally, the hot chocolate drink made from them was imbibed only by the elites, the god- or priest-kings, hence the name. Fancy feathers, espe-cially from the quetzal bird of the southern forests, fine cloaks of native cot-ton, precious stones (jade and obsidian in particular), captives, and more made up the trade in all the states of Mesoamerica.

There was also a common set of religious ideas. Deities that appear in the Olmecs's iconography became a standard part of the ancient pantheon in the same way that in the classical period of Europe, Greek and Roman gods merged. Only the names were changed. They include the Rain God (Tláloc, Chac, Cocijo, and others), the Sun God (Tonatiuh and Curicaveri among the Purépecha), a Goddess of the Earth (Coatlicue, as in the Aztec myth), a Goddess of the Waters (Chalchiuhtlicue), and the hero-king-god Quetzalcóatl, the benevolent feathered serpent who brought the blessings of the earth, wisdom, and art. Despite these common attributes, pre-Columbian theologies are beyond comprehension for most of us. There were many, many other deities, their profusion stemming from the large numbers of ethnic groups within Mesoamerica.

Religion means rituals, hence the need for priests, temples, and much else that we associate with these civilizations. Some similar rites were car-ried out among all Mesoamerican peoples. The two best known were the ball game and human bloodletting, including sacrifice. Later in our journey, near the Michoacán town of Uruapán, we visited an archaeological site called Tingambato. It is a small version of the enormous city in the Valley of Mex-ico, Teotihuacán. Like its model, Tingambato also has a ball court. We were shooting various scenes there when Dave and Ralph, sports fans both, sug-gested that we should do something in the court. After much discussion about how we could fit it into the script, Jan came up with a brilliant solu-tion: why not do a program promotion that the station could run as a teaser for the program? Great idea, we all said. Dave stood at one end of the court, half a football field away, and I prepared to walk down a set of steps at the other end into the court and utter deathless words. The rest of our group sat on the grassy banks surrounding the court, munching various fruit and sweets they had brought, commenting on the action, very much as spectators would have done when the field was in real use. Climbing down the very narrow set of steps leading into the court, I managed to say something like this: "We Chicagoans are great sports fans. We love our teams' players and sometimes scream, 'Kill the umpire!' Not here. In this ball court, in the heart of ancient Mexico, it was the umpires who killed the players!" Then we did the public television station promo. The piece never did get on air. Too gruesome, everyone said. Maybe, but that is what the old ball game was about.

Walking into that arena and saying a few lines was a strange feeling. Somehow, speaking before an audience in that place brought a sense, some shadow, of what it must have been like to have been there during pre-Columbian times. What were these places all about? More than forty ball courts have been found among the ruins of the old urban centers. There, amid pyramids, temple complexes, and housing for the elites, were structures built for viewing ritual-athletic events. Varied in size and shape, evidently according to how the game was played, they are usually composed of straight or sloping walls built around an open area that can be up to several hundred feet in length and about half that in width. Some have closed ends so that the shape was two T's set end to end. Many stone carvings, some paintings, and a few eyewitness accounts by the first Spanish intruders into Mexico tell us something about the game, though not all.

The game was played by teams with a solid rubber ball, some small, some large. Like our modern soccer, hands could not be used—only elbows, knees, and heads. Since the ball was very heavy, players wore heavy padding around all the body parts used in the game, including the waist and head. Many carvings of helmeted men may be not of warriors, but of athletes. How the game was scored we do not know, though rings set high on the walls of some courts imply that the ball had to be put through them. This much is known: in a number of places, death awaited some of the players. A frieze on the court in the Post Classic Yucatecan site of Chichén Itzá shows a decapitated player. Blood, in the form of seven snakes ending in flowers, pours from his neck. Beneath the figure is the skull of the Death God, who waits for his due. The interpretation of the scene is that the game was part of the old Mexican theme—from death comes life, in an endless cycle. Only here it was literally carried out in ritual.

When many of us see the name "Aztec," thoughts of awful, bloody, rites spring to mind. Archaeology tells us that human sacrifice may go back to the Archaic Period. It was certainly present in the Formative, likely among the Olmecs, certainly among the Maya and the Zapotecans in Oaxaca. As for the Aztecs, the earliest Spanish sources tell appalling and likely exaggerated stories of massive human sacrifice. Where did the idea come from? Some scholars say that the idea stems from one basic idea: as we have suggested before, the everlasting cycle of death and life and life from death.[8] Rituals are ways of carrying out religious ideas as a kind of drama. More than that, rituals are also transforming processes. Back in the days of predominantly village cultures, the holy men (and women) we call shamans must have done something like this. Through trances, some brought on by alcohol or hallucinogens, shamans entered a spirit world. Maybe they became part of that other world, bringing powers that affected everyone to life. The other world was that of the dead. The dead—dry and thirsty, hunger for precious water and blood. In return, they give life. Bones, the ancients thought, were like the seeds that when watered deliver new creation. Skeletons do not mean a frightening, grim, final end to life, but the hope of its recreation. The antiquity of this idea is substantiated by the fact that some of the oldest graves from Archaic Period villages have human skeletal material with red pigment scattered over the bones.

In high civilizations, kings and priests took over the function of the shamans. We know from Mayan sources that these elites routinely practiced autosacrifice by mutilating themselves in grisly rituals. The blood of kings ensured that life for their peoples would be sustained.[9] In all rituals of human sacrifice, the victim actually became one with the gods. To be sacrificed was an honor, a prelude to deification. Among the Aztecs, a late-arriving people in Mexico, the idea of renewal through death took on larger proportions. They, or at least their official religion, held that the sun god, Huitzilopóchtli, required vital fluid, including the pump that drove it, to rise in the morning. Night swallowed up the unconquerable warrior as he went underground to the land of the dead. Human beings had to help him return. Blood was required, so sacrifice was in order. One must be prepared to make the ultimate sacrifice for the good of all creation, or so it was said. The same idea holds for corn, rain, and other elements of the cosmos that made life possible. Do some of these notions linger in Mexican culture? Perhaps it is somewhat of an incomprehensible past that gives Mexico the dreamlike quality that has been remarked upon so often by writers.

From the list of commonalties among the Mexican civilizations, we cannot omit foodstuffs and preparation techniques. Here is one area where the past is alive today. As we have said, farming villages were the base for all the civilizations of old Mexico. Actually, farming still has that function. Villages means domestication, so a list of plants that the farmers of old developed as staple crops looks something like this: corn (maize), beans, squash, pumpkin, avocado, amaranth, annato (for flavoring and color), *sapota* (or *zapote*, a fruit, in several varieties), sweet potato, *nopal* (cactus, leaves, and fruit), *agave* (for everything, especially alcoholic *pulque*), peanut, papaya, manioc, chile peppers, *chayote, chía* (seeds for a drink and oil. . . and "Chía Pets"); *pitaya* (fruit from a cactus), guava, goosefoot (as in *epazote*), cacao (chocolate), vanilla, *tomatillo* or husk tomato (not at all a tomato), tomato, and others, such as rubber and tobacco. Not all of these plants grew everywhere in Mexico; some are native to hot lowlands, others adapted to dry climates. However, all were known in many parts of the country by the time of the Aztec Empire. These and more are still the basis for Mexican cuisine, as a trip to any decent Mexican market will demonstrate. They did not know it, but the earliest villagers were to give an incalculably precious gift to the world.

Historians call the great periods of Mesoamerican civilizations Classic and Post Classic, with dates running from about 150–1520 A.D. The roster is well known—Maya to the south, Teotihuacán in the Valley of Mexico, followed by Toltecs and then Aztecs. These were not the only high civilizations in Mexico. Once again, there were many groups in Mexico, speaking different languages, each with their own ethnic identity—peoples like the Zapotecs in Oaxaca, the Mixtecas in western Oaxaca, the Purépechas in Michoacán, and many others. Guerrero alone had twenty-four different ethnic-linguistic groups. All, however, shared many of the same cultural characteristics. One reason is trade. The more archaeologists learn about all of these cultures—and there are many sites which remain untouched—the more they know about widespread trade networks. Perhaps the best example comes from Teotihuacán. At its height, this was the largest urban center in the New World, and it would seem that it rose, at least in part, on the wings of insects.

The ruins of this place, not far from Mexico City, are one of Mexico's largest tourist attractions for good reason. At least 500 buildings have been found in the central core, along with two massive pyramids. The largest, the Temple of the Sun, has a base as large as the great pyramid of Khufu in Egypt, though it is not as high. It contains roughly 1 million cubic meters of brick. This was a massive undertaking possible only with a large population. Large it was, with perhaps a quarter of a million people in and around the place in 500 A.D. By estimate, twenty-five percent of the people worked as artisans—potters, stone carvers, jewelers, basket makers, and more. One of the major trade items was cochineal beetles. The region around Teotihuacán was rich in *maguey* and *nopal* cacti, the only types on which this beetle lives. Ground cochineal was highly prized as both a dye and a foodstuff. It still is. Teotihuacán merchants traded it and other products all over Mesoamerica. We know that citizens of Teotihuacán had diplomatic-trade contacts far down in Mayaland, even to the point of one noble marrying into the other city's royal family. Eventually, trade relations became so important that quarters for foreigners were established in the city. At the same time, residents of Teotihuacán either established trade outposts in other regions or strongly influenced locals. Either reason explains why Tingambato in Michoacán looks like a small version of the original. It is not unique.

Food remains on the site show that the people ate the usual varieties of beans, corn, squash, and lots of cactus. Irrigation canals indicate widespread agricultural systems. The fields were not worked with ploughs—these came with the Europeans—but the tools were not dissimilar to the hand tools used today by Mexican farmers in back country villages: hoes, digging implements, and harvesting knives. And for food preparations, what else but the flat *metate* (grinding stone) or *molcajete* (mortar)? What is so interesting about the diet of the residents of Teotihuacán is that eighty percent of the animals eaten were wild, mostly deer. That is highly unusual for an urban center and reminds us that venison has always been a part of the Mexican diet. Incidentally, their diets were not very nutritious. Studies of human remains indicate that the average life expectancy was little more than thirty years of age.

Teotihuacán declined and was abandoned after 600 A.D. The reasons seem to be complex: combinations of ecological problems, politics, and perhaps warfare. The vacant city, burnt over, became a ghost-haunted place, given the name "the place of the gods" by later Nahuatl speakers. Three hun-

Removing sesame seeds

dred years later the preeminent position would be taken by military states, first the Toltecs and then the Aztecs. Much of what literary sources tell us about pre-Columbian Mexico and food preparations describes these peoples. The Aztecs, or the "Mexica" branch of the Nahuatl-speaking peoples, arrived in the Valley of Mexico in the early fourteenth century A.D. They were migrants from the deserts of Northern Mexico who settled on a large lake that covered the lower part of the valley in those days. Highly militaristic, their leader set about conquering local peoples early in the next century. By the sixteenth century, that of their demise, the empire covered much of central Mexico, including much of Guerrero, but not Michoacán. There, the Purépecha kingdom fought off all Aztec attempts at subjugation. The Aztec empire is one reason why there are still some 800,000 Nahuatl speakers spread over central and western Mexico.

The nature of the empire was tributary. This means that the Aztecs demanded tribute of many forms from its dependents; indeed, they depended on these goods to keep their state intact. As wealth poured into their capital, Tenochtitlán, it grew ever larger until the population reached upward of a third of a million in the city, perhaps 2 million in the vicinity. In 1519 when the Spanish conquistadors arrived, it was more than double the size of any existing European city, quadruple the size of London or Paris. This huge population depended on intensive farming. The lake margins were rich in biomass, and to produce even more, Aztec farmer-engineers created *chinampas*. These were literally floating gardens. Stakes were planted into the lake bottom, then platforms of woven branches were tied into them. Layer upon layer of rich lake bottom mud were scooped up and placed on top to build long, narrow "fields." Further fertilization came from garbage, weeds, more mud, and feces, in short, anything organic. The *chinampa* was one of those closed ecological systems where everything is recycled. It worked brilliantly. Up to seven crops a year could be produced on these plots, a significant source of food for an urban population. Until recently, there were floating gardens at Xochimilco in Mexico City, but they fell victim to pollution and urban expansion. Luckily, we were able to visit and shoot *chinampas* at Lake Pátzcuaro in Michoacán, as we will see later.

Much has been written about Aztec food, some based on archaeology, some on Spanish accounts. It is only in recent years, however, that scholars have really begun to sort out the fact from myth. The late Sophie Coe[10] was one of the major scholars in this field, and it is her research on which the following comments on Aztec cuisine are based. Obviously, we want to understand as much about the matter as possible, because the tradition stands as one of the twin foundations of modern Mexican cuisine. Additionally, Mexicans trace their own national history to the Aztec state.

Late Prehispanic Food

One place we were anxious to visit was Acapulco's central market. Here, we thought, could be found many foodstuffs from the tropical coastal region and from the interior of Guerrero. Since many were pre-Colombian in origin, Dudley and I had to know precisely what the diets of that period must have been. We pored over our texts, especially Coe's work and old Spanish sources. One of the few fairly reliable Spanish texts from the early colonial period is *Historia general de las cosas de Nueva España* by a Franciscan monk, Fray Bernardino de Sahagún. Since he spoke Nahuatl, he was able to compose his work using Aztec informants who also illustrated his work with extraordinary pictures of life in the old empire. Sahagún was interested in everything, including foods. Reading his work, among others, while on location gives one a different frame of reference about the subject. What Fray Bernardino mentions can be seen today in markets that, although housed differently, are not too dissimilar to those of 500 years ago. And when the people in the markets are *indigenas*, there is an immediacy to the texts. The examples upon which Sahagún based his observations were taken from among the Nahuatl speakers of the Valley of' Mexico, but they also represent pre-Spanish Mesoamerica as a whole.

The Aztecs, like all other peoples, ate corn, or more properly, maize (*Zea mays*). Incidentally, like the word "potato," the name "maize" comes from a Caribbean language, since that is where Spaniards first encountered it. Among all the indigenous peoples of Mesoamerica, the Aztecs identified themselves most completely with the plant on which their lives were based. Many religious rituals were centered on getting the corn to grow, among them, as mentioned, human sacrifice. At home, prayers were more pacific, hedged with many superstitions. For instance, women breathed on corn before putting it into the cooking pot so that it would not be afraid of the heat. It sounds like a mother caring for her child, and here, indeed, were children of the corn, or at least of the gods of rain, sun, and the grain (the god, Cinteotl, and goddess, Chicomecóatl).

Sahagún describes the eight types of corn that he knew (there were at least 300 varieties cultivated in the New World, probably many more) including a small, hard white one grown in the fields and *chinampas*, yellow, reddish, tawny, flower (white grain striped with color), and colored. This one, he says, has a dark blue husk and was highly prized. Two more follow: black and then a black pinto or speckled breed, the latter with soft large kernels dotted with black. These are still to be found in any market in Mexico. The diversity of colors are one of the striking things about ancient Mexican foodstuffs. Early farmers probably developed these varieties as much for their appearance as for other qualities. The same holds for beans, which also appear in many hues. Design and rich colors in food are as much a part of Mexico's artistic traditions as anything else.

Corn was the foundation of life, but other grains were also important. One source for understanding Mexican foodstuffs are the Aztec tribute lists, compilations of goods sent up to Tenochtitlán by subject peoples. A few of these have survived and give a good idea of what was eaten. Each place sent what it produced most and best. That could include manpower in the form of military service or field labor as well as goods. Textiles were one major item and so were animal skins. Deer hides and live deer are on the list, showing that this animal remained a part of the diet. Since a large number of feathers are on the list, we can be sure that most of the birds had been eaten. Since many were colored, it is safe to say that parrot was on the menu. It still is in South America.

Grain, though, was the backbone of the tribute: corn, beans, *chía*, and *huauhtli*. Beans were surpassed in importance only by corn. Sahagún mentions twelve kinds of beans. The two main ones were large black and yellow beans which could be either boiled or baked. Though they taste good, says the good brother, they "cause. . . flatulence in one. . . and distend one's stomach." Other beans may not have produced quite the same unfortunate effects: white, purple, reddish, whitish, quail-colored (white dotted with black), speckled, small, mouse, small black, and climbing beans are all on the list. Beans are high in protein and, when mixed with corn, can replace meat in a diet. This is important when you consider the lack of large animal protein sources for most of the Aztec peasantry. It holds even today when many of Mexico's impoverished peoples live on such a diet.[11]

Chía (*Salvia hispanica*), the third grain, has an interesting history. The plant has small black seeds with a mucilaginous coating, something like the consistency of overcooked okra, but with crunchy interiors. *Chía* was made into porridge dishes, for which there were many recipes among the common folk. However, the Spaniards did not like the dish, and it eventually passed out of use as a food. *Chía* is, however, a good source of oil. Coe thought that there was little evidence for use of expressed oils in Aztec cookery, though there are words for "greasy" and "frying in a pan." In her opinion, vegetable oils appeared only after the Spanish arrived on the culinary scene. If that were so, then the Aztecs did not fry foods, unlike today's foods, because with no large domesticated beasts, there could have been no animal fats. It would mean that the Aztecs roasted, boiled, toasted, steamed their food, or ate it raw. On the other side of the debate, Professor E.N. Anderson of the University of California, Riverside, one of the country's leading food historians, claims that *chía* oil was used, mainly in the southern parts of Mexico. The question of frying remains open. One thing about *chía* is certain: you can buy it in stores or by mail order in the United States—growing on pottery animals! It is the same stuff.

Huauhtli, the other grain mentioned, is used ambiguously. Aztecs meant amaranth and chenopodium (goosefoot) by the term, used both as greens and seeds. The Spanish used *huauhtli* to indicate *quelite*, from the Nahuatl *quelite* or "greens." There is some confusion today about amaranth and how it was and is to be eaten, partly because of the Spanish word usage. Dudley went to a new Mexican restaurant in Chicago not long after our video had aired. The restaurant owner, a Mexican whom Dudley knows, stopped at his table to remark on the program. She said that it was good, except for the section where we ate *huazontle*, amaranth. "That's not amaranth," she declared. Dudley, understanding what this was about, smiled and asked if she knew how many kinds of amaranth there are. When his hostess looked puzzled, he replied, "At least seven." We had eaten the green parts of the seed amaranth; she had meant greens, or *quelites*. Without question, the Aztecs ate amaranth and chenopodium in all their forms and knew what the differences were. The Spanish did not.

The only way the restaurateur could conceive of seed amaranth was in a famous candy called *alegría*. It is made by mixing together amaranth popped on a griddle with a thick sugar syrup. It is a familiar Mediterranean sweet, only there sesame seed is used. Evidently many Mexicans also believe the religious taboo story of amaranth. This one tells how the Spanish prohibited natives from growing and eating it because of its use in rituals. The fact is, cultivation of grain amaranth and its use in regular meals was not prohibited, only its use in pagan rituals. As we were to discover, it is one of the traditional dishes in the main Christian festival, Easter. And no wonder, since it is the first crop harvested in the spring.

The peoples of Mexico lived on many more foods than were enumerated in the tribute lists. Squashes were one. There were and still are many varieties, from pumpkin to warty, crookneck, and others. Squashes and pumpkins were used for their seeds, just as they are in sauces today called *pipián*. The flowers of these plants flowers are edible, and are now used in some excellent dishes, although once they were only considered food for the poor. Sahagún describes one squash as sweet and tasting of ashes, edible uncooked but better cooked in a pot. We suggest moderation because too much can swell one's stomach. Another, our very own pumpkin, he describes as wonderful because of its seeds that can be eaten toasted or in sauces.

Chiles: if there is one signifier of Mexican food, it is the chile, or rather, the enormous variety that makes up the family *Capsicum annum* and *Capsicum frutescens* (*chilli* in Nahuatl). Every Spanish source mentions them, often in awe of their flavor and spicy heat. The earliest written references are to seven types: the *quauhchilli* or tree chile, the smallest and hottest: the *chiltecpin*, hot at first but loses its heat quickly; the *tonalchilli*, a summer chile; the *chilcoztli*, which gives any food prepared with it a yellow tint; *tzinguauhyo*; and the *texochilli*, large, sweeter, and eaten with *tortillas*. This last chile was smoked and dried, obviously the modern *poblano* and its dried counterpart, the *chile ancho*. There are more, many more. Sahagún mentions many other varieties, each delineated by their heat, flavor, color, and place of origin. These are the very same designations used today, when Mexican claim that there are more than ninety-nine kinds of chiles. They are too numerous to delineate here and often so subtle in differences as to be impossible to describe. Even the old friar, for all his learning, could not do that.

Aztec legends say that while they were poor migrants in the northern deserts, they carried with them the seeds of the plants by which they lived. Two of these turned out to be avatars of Mexican cuisine, and one eventually migrated to the Mediterranean where it took firm culinary root. What else but the *xitomatl* and *miltomate*? The first is our own tomato in all its glory[12]. The second is another plant entirely (*Physalis ixocarpa*), small, green, and sour with a husk on it. Mexicans call it a *tomate verde* or *tomatillo*. The problem of the origins of the tomato has never been solved, but most likely they were first domesticated in tropical regions of the south (Peru or Ecuador, most likely) and not until quite recently. The earliest possible finds (not well authenticated) in central Mexico date only to about 600 B.C.E., and they were not widely known until the Aztec era. The *tomatillo* comes from the central highlands and was surely brought southward by migrant peoples. No doubt because the two plants resemble one another—round, softish-bodied with seeds in them—Nahuatl-speakers gave the newer fruit a familiar name. (It means "something plump.")

No matter the late date for tomatoes, Sahagún mentions a wide variety for sale in markets. He notes the likes of large and small tomatoes, as well as leaf, thin, sweet, serpent (possibly green?), nipple-shaped, coyote, sand, yellow, very yellow, quite yellow, red, very red, quite ruddy, ruddy, bright red, reddish, and rosy dawn-colored. Tomatoes are infinitely amenable to genetic manipulation. The National Seed Storage Laboratory in Geneva, New York, has 5,500 varieties, and we know that many other kinds have disappeared just since the nineteenth century.[13] Tomatoes mutate so rapidly that we really do not know the exact types Sahagún describes. But it is nice to think, while strolling through the markets of Mexico, that some of those on sale are very much like the originals.

One major Aztec plant that is widely used today in the homeland and abroad is the *chayote* (Nahuatl, *chayotli*). It is a spiny green fruit with one large seed surrounded by a fairly pulpy flesh. Minus its husk, the *chayote* is widely available in North American and Asian markets. While doing a documentary a few years ago in China's very rural Guizhou province, we came across the very same *chayote* being sold on the street. What a surprise to see this visitor from Mexico. . . or at least until I realized that all the chiles found in that relatively inaccessible land had come from the same place.

Among other crops, Mexicans then and now grew *jícama*, sweet and delectable and usually eaten raw. Several forms of sweet potato were common. In Mexico it was eaten boiled, roasted, and candied. Sahagún mentions several kinds, saying that they might be cooked or eaten raw. Mushrooms appeared on Aztec tables, but not always for eating. Some were used as hallucinogens in religious ceremonies, much as they are today in remote parts of the country. Sahagún names six kinds, warning that they must be cooked very well (uncooked they cause—guess what?—diarrhea) in pots or on a griddle. Whether he meant sautéed in oil as we do now is another matter. There is another kind of mushroom that must be mentioned, the "Mexican truffle" or *huitlacoche*. It is the smut fungus that appears on corn. Not very appetizing in appearance, it is a soft lump, gray or black when ripe, that tastes delicious. The flavor is not at all like a truffle or any other mushroom, but has a unique earthy quality and a somewhat sticky-mucilagenous consistency. As the inappropriate analogy with a truffle implies, *huitlacoche* is highly prized by Mexican chefs. It is not always available in the United States, but is well worth seeking out.

Avocados (*ahuacatl*) were an important part of a diet that was probably short of edible oils. The Spanish name *aguacate*, comes from the word for "advocate," not the original meaning at all. It is a mispronunciation of the Nahuatl word meaning "fruit of the avocado tree" or "testicle." Churchmen obviously did not like such earthy humor. As with so many other domesticates, there are a number of types of avocados, with four or five predominating. Sahagún thought that when growing on trees they resembled figs, only with different flavors. In his day, they were pressed for cooking and fuel oils. They still are, as we learned when visiting an agricultural station in Uruapán, Michoacán. Avocados varied in their size, the size of their pits, and their place of origin. The largest ones, Fray Bernardino said, came from very warm regions. Smaller ones the size of olives (probably *criollo* types) were also eaten. Avocados are the core ingredient of what is probably the best known Aztec dish, *guacamole*. The real name is *ahuacamolli*, or literally, "sauce made of avocados." Today's versions are pretty much the same as their predecessors: mashed ripe avocados, chopped tomatoes or *tomatillos*, chopped chiles, chopped onions, and some salt, wrapped in a *tortilla* or scooped up with torn pieces of *tortilla*. A splendid creation.

The Aztecs ate great varieties of fruit. Fruits were divided into sour and sweet. There are too many to list, but among the best are *mamey*, several kinds of *zapotes* (literally, "soft fruit"), *guayava* or guava, *guajilote*, *tejocote*, and two kinds of *pitahayas*. All are quite delectable and now increasingly imported into the United States. One other fruit is noteworthy, that of the *nopal* cactus. Cactuses have always played a large role in Mexican cuisine. The young pads of certain cacti can be eaten raw or cooked as greens. Today they are featured in many varieties of salad. The fruit (*tuna* in Spanish, prickly pear in the U.S.), is to be found in every Mexican market. Sahagún tells of thirteen different kinds of *tunas* that are sweet or sour and can be eaten raw or cooked. *Tuna* juice could be used to make wine or boiled down to make sugar. In Zacatecas, the juice is made into a jelly candy called *queso de tuna*.

Usually thought of as a cactus, the *maguey* (*agave*) is really a succulent, related to the amaryllis. This is one of Mexico's most useful plants and was a source of joy to the old Mexicans. Juice from the plant can be drunk as it is, boiled into syrup, or fermented into a wine called *pulque*. Wine, which is naturally fermented juices, can be made from any fruit, but that of the *maguey* was special. The drink of the gods, it was said, because drinking enough of it causes the drinker to enter another state of consciousness. . . or unconsciousness, as the case may be. Traditional *pulque* is made by first poking a long tube into the plant and retrieving the juice by sucking it out. In season, the juices flow prodigiously. Along with the harvesters' saliva, the juice is put into a pottery vessel and allowed to stand until it reaches the proper degree of alcoholic content. Portions of already fermented *pulque* can be added to speed the process. Carol and I drank healthy drafts of this in Michoacán and it wasn't bad. She did not have to eat the worm that lives in the *maguey*, although it is still considered a tasty treat in parts of Mexico. North Americans can have them, too, from the bottom of a bottle of *mezcal*.

We know that the pre-Columbian diet was mainly vegetarian. Historically, most peasant diets have been. Some meat was eaten, of course, especially by the upper classes. Domesticated animals have already been mentioned: turkeys, Muscovy ducks, dogs, bees (the Aztecs ate their larvae as well as their honey), and cochineal beetles. Game was a staple of the elites' tables: deer, peccary, rabbits, jackrabbits, mice, armadillos, snakes, gophers, tapirs, opossums, iguanas, and perhaps forty-five species of edible birds. Eggs from domesticated and wild birds were also a source of protein.

And then there were fish from the ocean, lakes, and rivers. The species eaten are still on menus today, although some rate low on the food preference scale. Frogs and tadpoles that had been gathered from lakes could be bought in any market. Frogs are perfectly understandable to modern diners, but there were other marine protein sources that are not. *Axolotls*, a large salamander, were eaten. They still are in Michoacán, where Dudley had them not long ago. Spanish commentators opined that they tasted like eels. Dudley says it's more like a cross between eels and Scandinavian *lute fisk*. Nor is that all. *Axayacatl*, water bugs, and *ahuautli*, meaning "water amaranth," or the eggs of water bugs, were other sources of protein. The bugs were collected in nets, ground up in *molcajetes*, made into balls, and then wrapped in corn husks and steamed or poached. One Spanish source considered this a good dish. So were the beetle eggs, which were said to taste like fish or caviar. *Izeahuitli* were small worms taken from lakes. When the worms were cooked with salt and chile, diners said they tasted like blackened crushed bread crumbs. They could also be made into fresh *tortillas*. And yes, *maguey* worms are quite good even when not pickled. Roasted and salted, they are tasty enough to be served regularly in the cafeteria of the huge food processor Herdez. The general manager says that the workers cannot get enough of them. To test out our devotion to culinary history, our crew all ate fresh insects when we got to Taxco. Interestingly, we all agreed that we would not have been averse to trying one of these Aztec insect-based dishes.

Here is one of Fray Bernardino's favorite dishes, not insect-based, although who can tell what little creatures may be found in the raw ingredients. This version comes from Uruapán in Michoacán, and calls for the avocados taken directly from the trees that are so abundant in the area. It is not strictly pre-Columbian because lime and all other citruses were brought to Mexico by the Spanish who got them, ultimately, from India in classical Roman times. Incidentally, Mexican food lore holds that placing the avocado pit atop *guacamole* preserves the bright green color. Once exposed to air, avocado flesh turns brown-black, not very appetizing. Whether the pit technique works is open to debate, but who is to argue with tradition?

Guacamole

5		ripe Hass avocados, cleaned
2		*serrano* chiles, chopped
1/2	C.	red onion, chopped
1/2		bunch cilantro, chopped
1-1/2		tomatoes, seeded and chopped
1/4	C.	lime juice
		salt and freshly ground pepper, to taste

Halve the avocado lengthwise by cutting from stem to flower ends around the pit. Twist the halves apart, then scoop out the pit, but do not discard. Scoop out the flesh with a spoon into a bowl and mash roughly with a fork. The result should be somewhat lumpy, not a smooth paste. Mix the rest of ingredients into the mashed avocado and season to taste. Refrigerate, placing the pit on top of the guacamole to preserve the nice green color.   *Serves 8*

The great Mexican "mushroom" *huitlacoche* is used in the following version of *quesadillas* (the Spanish name implies cheese in the dish). It may be hard to find, but is well worth seeking out. Ask at your local Mexican market. Occasionally it is available fresh. There is an excellent canned product made by Herdez (they call it *cuitlacoche*), and it is this one that we always use. It is best to use the fresh *huitlacoche*, not preserved in brine or with other seasonings. This *quesadilla* dish is very much like its pre-Columbian ancestor, at least in its ingredients; using *epazote* would make it more so. The question remains whether native cooks fried foods in oil. Maybe they did, but if not, it works well toasted on a griddle.

Quesadillas de Huitlacoche

(from La Piedad, Michoacán)

1	C.	*huitlacoche*
1		large tomato, diced small
½		medium onion, finely chopped
1		clove garlic, finely chopped
1		*serrano* chile, chopped
1–2		*epazote* leaves (optional)
4	C.	corn *masa*
1	t.	baking powder
2	T.	lard or vegetable oil
1	t.	salt
1	C.	warm water
1	C.	vegetable oil
		salt and freshly ground pepper, to taste

Have ready a *tortilla* press ("Preparing *tortillas*," p. 243). Heat a deep, heavy skillet until hot. Melt lard or heat olive oil in the skillet. Add tomato, onion, garlic, *serrano* chile and sauté for 3 minutes. Add *huitlacoche* and season to taste. Bring to a simmer and allow to cook for 5 minutes. Set aside to cool. Meanwhile, dissolve 1 teaspoon salt in warm water. In a bowl, mix corn *masa* and baking powder together well.

Stir in the salted water and mix well. Using your hands, knead dough until it is smooth and comes away from the sides of the bowl. Add additional water as needed. Have ready the *tortilla* press with waxed paper or plastic wrap. Form dough into 16 small balls, about the size of small limes. Press each ball in the *tortilla* press until the *masa* forms a thin cake. This should be thicker than a normal thin *tortilla*. Place a tablespoon of the *huitlacoche* mixture, more or less, in the center of the dough circle. Fold over until all edges meet evenly. Place a "Tartmaster" cutter over the folded circle so that outer rim covers the open edge of *quesadilla*. Press down to seal edge. Continue until all quesadillas have been made. Meanwhile, heat 1 cup of vegetable oil in the deep, heavy skillet until hot. Oil should be about ½-inch deep. Place *quesadillas* in oil and fry until golden brown, 2–3 minutes. Remove from oil and drain on paper towels. Serve at once.   *Serves* 8–10

Note: Quesadillas come out quite well, if not quite so savory, when toasted on a lightly greased griddle. Simply heat the griddle, spread a thin layer of oil over it, place the quesadillas on it and toast for 3–4 minutes, turning them over until lightly browned. In either case, the following sauce is a good accompaniment.

Salsa Chile Chipotle

2   whole *Chipotle* chiles, roasted or toasted
2   large tomatoes, roasted or toasted and skinned
6   whole *tomatillos*, peeled and roasted or toasted
2   cloves garlic
2   pinches powdered cumin
    salt, to taste
    raw green onions, shredded
    sprigs of fresh cilantro

Heat a *comal*, griddle, or heavy skillet over medium-high heat until quite hot. Place tomatoes on the hot surface and toast until skin begins to blacken. Peel tomatoes and set aside. Do the same with the *tomatillos*. Then place the chiles on it and toast until blackened, but not burnt. (You will have to be careful here, because you want the flavor brought out by the high heat, but not the burnt quality.) When done, place all the ingredients except the green onion shreds and cilantro springs in the bowl of a food processor—or better, in a *molcajete*—and grind until the sauce has a chunky consistency. Adjust seasoning to taste. Place the sauce in serving bowl alongside the *quesadillas de huitla-coche*. Garnish the sauce with shredded green onion and cilantro sprigs. *Serves* 4

One dish all common folk ate and still eat is cactus salad. See the directions on p. 233 for tips on how to prepare the raw cactus paddles. Prepared cactus is widely available now either bottled or in cans, so it is just as easy to use those instead.

Nopales Rancheros

(from Morelia, Michoacán)

4	whole cactus leaves (nopales), peeled and diced
1 t.	salt
	boiling water to cover
3	tomatoes, seeded and sliced
1	small onion, finely chopped
2	*serrano* chiles, finely chopped
8	sprigs cilantro, chopped
	juice of 1-1½ limes
¼ C.	olive oil

To prepare *nopales*, bring water and salt to a boil in a large pan. Add diced *nopales*, return to a simmer, and cook for 5 minutes. Pour *nopales* into a strainer and run cold water over them to cool completely. Drain and place in a bowl. Add tomatoes, onion, chiles, and cilantro. Mix well. Place olive oil in a small, deep bowl. Whisk lime juice into the olive oil until opaque and emulsified. Pour over *nopales* mixture and toss. Adjust salt to taste.   *Serves* 4

Acapulco

The Fort of San Diego

"Most people think Acapulco is a resort city. The fort of San Diego tells a different tale. This was one of the great ports in a world-wide Spanish empire. Beginning in the 1500s, great Spanish galleons sailed east bound for China via the Philippines. They carried huge cargoes of silver. But they carried an-

other treasure which was even more important: foodstuffs. Foodstuffs such as corn and chiles which revolutionized life for the populations of Asia and the world. In return, ships came from the Philippines bearing, equally, foodstuffs . . . and they have great importance in Mexican cuisine."
—from the television documentary "Hidden Mexico"

By now, restless from all the discourse on old matters, the whole crew was ready to get to work. . . and then eat. Or the other way around. Before setting off, we met with officials from the local government tourism office to discuss our plans. Most arrangements for locations had already been made via many fax messages. Now the details had to be worked out. The second chief, a very pleasant English woman and naturalized Mexican, briefed us on what her office considered to be the most scenic locations in which to shoot. Naturally, these were places they would like to have American television viewers see. We wanted to do the fort of San Diego and fishing on the beach. The divers of La Quebrada—the ones who jump from high cliffs—and the water park and aquarium, *Mágico Mundo Marino*, and bullfights are all interesting, but not for a piece on food history and food folkways. Our hosts blanched when we told them what we really wanted to see: the central market in all its grubby glory. How could anyone come to this beautiful resort and want to shoot something that could be seen in any Mexican city? Besides, that is not what Acapulco is, they protested.

Fortunately, just at that moment our friend Gonzalo Sánchez Galindo turned up to intervene on our behalf. He is the Mexican cultural attaché in Chicago who happened to be in Acapulco with his wife for a short Eastertime break. We have always suspected that he had come to keep an eye on and out for us. A cheerful young man, he explained what our program was to be about. We wanted to see how *real* people lived everywhere in Mexico and where their glorious foods came from. Did not Acapulco have one of the best food traditions in the country and a historical importance in the creation of Mexican cuisine? Besides, Gonzalo said, these people have made documentaries like this before (well, one anyway), loved Mexico (we do), and would never show it in a bad light (at least not by design!). With that irrefutable argument, all defenses came down, and our interviewer said, smilingly, that since we were serious about food, she knew someone we just had to meet, Susana Palazuelos, as well as some great places to eat. And that is what we did. . . starting with a nice, leisurely lunch on the Continental Hotel's terrace overlooking the beach. It was a very North American meal, composed of a salad bar, red snapper, fresh sauces, plenty of fresh *tortillas* (some crisply fried in lard), and coconut ice cream. It was very nice and reflected the hotel's clientele, just what our friends in the tourist office had in mind for would-be vacationers. In all events, we certainly could not have had a better ambience.

The fort of San Diego has an interesting history as well as a role in the story of food. In 1512 Acapulco had been a small fishing-farming village for some two millennia. The name in Nahuatl means something like "the place of the standing reeds." Spanish naval explorers discovered the excellent harbor early in the sixteenth century and built a harbor facility there by the 1530s. It was, at first, a port for the local coastal trade that eventually extended down to Peru. Acapulco soon became the Pacific port for a cross-Mexico trade when the great *conquistador* Hernan Cortés and some business partners set up a regular route. As always, the Spaniards were interested in precious metals, gold and silver, for themselves, the Crown, and for a growing international trade. Commerce created colonial Acapulco, particularly after 1565 when it became the terminus for the greatest trade route of all (at least in terms of distance): the trans-Pacific trade to Asia. The fortress is the tangible symbol of an early global linkage between very different worlds.

The main reason Christopher Columbus set out across the Atlantic Ocean in 1492 was to find riches in what Europeans thought of as the East. Asia's wealth was in bullion, and in something almost as valuable: spices. European *haute cuisine* was loaded with them: pepper, cinnamon, cloves, nutmeg, often all of them in one dish. All came from Southeast Asia and all came by sea and land westward across Central Asia, the Indian Ocean, and Turkish-held lands. From there they came into the hands of Italian merchants (Venice, especially) and finally to Europe's upper-class end users. Incidentally, the idea that Europeans needed them to cover the taste of spoiled foods or as preservatives is a canard. Elite diners liked the flavors and, even more, liked the idea that the ingredients were more costly than most people lower in the social and economic scale could afford. Therefore, merchants or monarchs who could get their hands on these culinary delights could become immensely wealthy. Silks, gems, and manufactured goods such as porcelain and lacquerware added to the benefits of direct control of the Asia trade. Columbus, himself deeply religious, set out to make everyone rich.

In the early sixteenth century, Portugal got the jump on everyone by establishing trading colonies in the Spice Islands (the Moluccas) which lie between Celebes and New Guinea (the Moluccas were eventually taken by the Dutch). Spain had to grab what it could: some islands it named for King Philip II. In 1564–65 a round-trip route from Mexico to Cebu in the central Philippines had been found. Not long after that, the Spanish moved their base of operations to Manila's fine harbor, itself the mirror image of Acapulco's. The Philippines proved not to be as rich in spices as the Spanish colonists had hoped. But, as they say in the restaurant business, it was location that counted. The islands were in a good position to organize round-trip trade with China and from there with the New World. In 1572–73 Spanish merchantmen sailed from Manila with a cargo of rich Chinese goods and reached Acapulco four or five months later. Spain's 9,000-mile cross-Pacific trade was born, and by royal decree Acapulco became Mexico's only port of entry and exit.

Each year for two-and-a-half centuries, until the early nineteenth century, one great galleon made the voyage across the vast ocean. The ship's arrival was occasion for an annual festival, still held in Acapulco. Called the *Nao de China*, it is held in mid-November, as it always was, but the current version is nothing like the trade fair from which it sprang. That one saw merchants and adventurers from all over the continent converging on Acapulco to buy, sell, barter, or steal the goods of the Orient. What they gave in return was mainly silver. From the silver mines of Mexico, especially those of Taxco, came silver (processed with mercury largely obtained from China). The Chinese literally regarded silver as the coin of the realm and took as much of it as they could. Trade routes, ran across the Pacific to Acapulco, then overland on rough dirt tracks to Taxco, then on to Mexico City, and from these depots spread to towns in other parts of New Spain.

What was it they traded for silver? From the east, the ship carried Filipino gold, cotton, and coconuts; spices from the Spice Islands; gems from India; fine metal and woodwork from Japan; and in particular, treasures from China: many kinds of silk, fine porcelain, lacquered woodwork, copper and ironwork, ivory carvings, and many more valuable items. The Chinese products influenced Mexican artisans. One of the lacquerwork traditions in Puebla is, by tradition, a direct copy of Chinese techniques. Also, like their European counterparts, Mexican potters made colorful works in imitation of the handsome Chinese ware. Clothing took on Eastern hues and designs, and even religious statuary made by Chinese craft workers were imitated by the locals. One wonders how much of the colorful designs found in Guerrero and Michoacán artwork is indigenous and how much might have been influenced by imported Chinese patterns.

Silver poured from the mines of Mexico, hauled from the ground by Indian laborers at first, then more and more frequently by *mestizos*. Silver, however, was not Mexico's greatest export. No one knew it at the time, but their most influential export was botanical. Native Americans gave several great gifts to the Old World. Corn is one. It appears to have reached China by the middle of the sixteenth century and struck deep roots in the countryside.[14] It is grown everywhere, mainly for animal feed, although also for human consumption. Corn is the grain of poor folks, eaten in the poorest provinces and by those who cannot afford the "better" grains, such as rice and wheat. Being Chinese, they prepare it well. The best corn bread Jan and I have ever eaten was in a small market town in a remote province in southwestern China. However it is viewed, corn has been one of the staunch pillars upon which the boom in the Chinese population has been built.

Corn is only one New World plant that had powerful influences on Asia. There are others: chiles, sweet potatoes, peanuts (these, too, grow in poor soils and are foods of the impoverished), squash, and more. The *capsicum* (or chile) in all its varieties—and they are the same genus whether hot or mild— has other nutritional values in addition to serving as a flavoring agent. They are good sources of carotene and vitamin C when fresh and are high in B vitamins, iron, and calcium when dried. According to E.N. Anderson,[15] their introduction broke the vitamin "bottleneck" in the areas where they took culinary root—warm climates—because they are available in seasons when other such sources are not. All *capsicums* came from the New World. How they got to the Orient is something of a mystery. Most theories suggest two possible routes. One is through India,[16] where peppers may have been introduced by Portuguese traders, and the other is directly into southern China by the Spanish galleons involved in trade with Acapulco. Either way, Acapulco played a major role in dispersing these invaluable food sources.

Humans being what they are, no one nation's pursuit of wealth in the New World would go unchallenged. Spanish treasure ships were prey to pirates of all nations. It is the stuff of swashbuckler romances in novels and movies: Erroll Flynn as the "Sea Hawk" and many others of the same ilk. Reality does not follow fiction. Piracy often meant murder and to the Spanish authorities, even worse, the loss of treasure. In fact, the whole economy of Acapulco and Manila depended upon the arrival of the annual galleon. So in 1616 a fort was built overlooking the old city, its *zócalo*, and cathedral. Pirates apparently still lurked in the neighboring Puerto Márquez, but evidently in all the years of voyaging only forty ships were lost. Standing on the ramparts of the current fort, rebuilt after 1776, one can almost see the billowing sails of a *nao* sailing into the bay, just ahead of a pursuing ship with the Jolly Roger at full sail. And then another thought: the Spaniards stole all that silver and forced enslaved or enserfed native peoples to spend their wretched lives digging it out of the ground. Maybe it was only condign punishment that the exploiters were themselves exploited.

We put such thoughts behind us when that evening the whole crew was invited to Susana Palazuelos's house. Our tourist office liaisons had spoken with her and instantly received an invitation for us. She is one of the *grandes dames* of Mexican cookery and her books have international sales. Carol, as a food editor, knew exactly who she was and was familiar with her most famous book, *Mexico: The Beautiful Cookbook*. Dudley knew her book even better, and when we met actually quoted her recipes to her! Arriving at her home,

Las tres fuentes ("The Three Fountains"), we were overwhelmed. It looked like a movie set, no doubt once a featured house in a "beautiful homes" magazine. A high wall surrounded a large paved courtyard with a fountain in full spout in the center. Three spouts. A semi-circular staircase led up to the living area and to a largely open living room with furniture to match. We sank into the sofas, enjoyed the drinks brought by the serving staff, and chatted with our hostess about food and foodstuffs in and around Acapulco. She obviously knew a great deal and offered to be our guide the next day in the market. We happily took her up on the offer, agreeing to meet her in the market later in the morning.

We descended the same staircase to find that an array of tables had been set up: some buffet tables loaded with food, others for dining. Among the dishes arrayed before us were an excellent red snapper with a watercress sauce; poached new potatoes (Carol, whose Irish heritage shows whenever this tuber appears on a table, filled her plate); chicken *enchiladas* with a delightful spicy touch, made with a cream-finished sauce; and a good rendition of chicken *adobo*. While we marveled at how she had managed to prepare such a meal for a mob of us at short notice, Susana reminded us, after all, she was also a caterer with a staff. While we all munched, Susana expressed her hope that Mexican food would become better known throughout the world. It is not all chiles, she said, but is much finer. Because so many other culinary traditions have affected Mexico, her native fare has taken on qualities from the outside. (She did not mean fast-food hamburgers.) Her cream-finished sauce was cited as an example. Yet there is so much, she said, that is good within the Mexican tradition. Guerrero, for instance, has many regional dishes that are outstanding, for instance, the great seafood, *pozole*, or suckling pig cooked in a special clay oven. That discussion, about Mexico as a kind of culinary melting pot that still retains with its own basic structure, is a gloss of Mexico itself and has many layers of meaning. Little did our traveling companions know that later would come another lecture on this subject. . . within the context of post-Columbian history.

The Market

"Long before floods of tourists arrived, and even when it was Mexico's main port in the trans-Pacific trade, Acapulco was a fishing town. It still is. At dawn local fishermen set and pull in their nets, plying their age-old craft. . . on beaches that later in the day will be covered with sun-worshipping bathers."
—from the television documentary "Hidden Mexico".
Our day began at 5:00 A.M., early even for us, because that is the hour for fishing, as even we duffers know. The scene was glorious: the sun just rising

over the mountains behind us tinted the bay a warm rose color and made the fishers more copper-skinned than usual. We saw hardly a soul besides the gatherers on the beach. They used two kinds of techniques. Some larger boats with nets like insect wings on each side set out for the deeper parts of the bay; others headed out into the ocean. We were interested in those close to shore. Crews of five or six rowed small boats out several hundred yards from shore and set nets into the water. Stretching their nets out, the fishermen stood in a row, then very slowly walked toward the shore, making sure that the nets were straight. Meanwhile, teams of men stood on shore and hauled on ropes attached to the nets. It was a scene from any picture of fishermen from ages past, as the men strained against the weight of the water and the nets to haul in their catch.

Dave ran onto the beach with the video camera; Ralph followed close behind with the tripod, batteries, and other bits of equipment. "Down low" Jan yelled. "Lower, lower!" The idea was to get low-angle closeups of the men's faces and straining bodies, framed against the sky. These are the kinds of shots we had discussed while planning the documentary, based on our admiration for the documentaries of the 1920s to 1940s that depicted people at work as heroic. Dave squatted and we got the shots beautifully. Even to us bystanders it seemed an heroic effort, so much so that several of the now-frequent passersby hopped onto the beach to help. Our driver, Eduardo, was one, smiling and laughing with the fishermen as they hauled on the coarse ropes. Most Mexicans rarely let an opportunity for a party to pass by unheeded, or at least to make work into a communal activity.

Finally, the nets came to shore. The Acapulco Bay fishermen were looking for fin fish, *huachinango* (red snapper), and perhaps even a skate or two. All the jollity came to an abrupt end when the nets turned out to be mostly empty. One skate, a couple of little snappers, and some crab were the prizes for several hours of labor. The fishermen said that meager catches happened from time to time. Maybe they were jinxed by the presence of cameras expecting success, as if the camera were something of an "evil eye." Fishermen are among the world's most superstitious people. Fortunately, they quickly amended, on most days the haul was better, and besides, they had other jobs in the tourist business along the beach. We still felt a little guilty and certainly empathetic toward the fishermen, if not the fish.

We saw fish aplenty when we got to the market. The whole thing is a vast, ramshackle affair, composed of partly concrete structures, partly tin-covered structures, and less permanent stalls with canvas or plastic over them. The place was crowded with Sunday shoppers of all genders and ages and swarms of taxis and private cars dropping shoppers off and picking them up; in short, it is a real local market, only bigger. In front, alongside the main

street, several sets of steps lead down into a wide cement culvert. This was
the open-air fish market. Tables lined both sides of the drainage ditch, and
all were laden with fish of every regional variety. It was good that we arrived
before 9:00 A.M. The sun was up, and, considering Acapulco's heat and hu-
midity, there was some question about just how long the fish would last in
the open. Some were iced down and others were not, but all had just come
off the local boats. Red snapper, grouper, sea bass, kingfish, fish that looked
like mackerel, ocean perch, shark, skate, plenty of shrimp, and an octopus or
two made up the majority of the sea creatures. Shoppers chose their fish,
which could be expertly cut up or presented whole. In one case that we captured on camera, a whole fish was simply slipped head first into a purchaser's shopping bag. No problems with overpackaging and waste wrappers
here. But by then a certain effluvia had begun to rise from the area. . . and
besides, we were ready for breakfast.

After a number of desperately needed cups of coffee we met Susana
Palazuelos at an entrance to the market. She was full of enthusiasm and
ready to show us the varieties of good things to be had. Mexican markets are
normally divided into sections that are given to one category of product.
Fruits and vegetables, meats, fish, packaged goods, cheeses, and others are
the basic retail areas. For the immediately hungry, there are *fondas*. Literally
"inns," these are mini-restaurants and are often little more than counters
with cooking implements just behind. Clustered together, they are really the
original mall food courts. Each is family operated and serves homestyle
cooking. Each has its own specialty and each its regular customers. Watch-
ing diners banter with the proprietors reminds one of our own local diners,
only here the food is all handmade and usually fresh daily.

Immediately upon meeting us, Susana began the tour talking animat-
edly about everything we saw. We followed eating everything in sight. The
market's interior was lit with high ceiling windows and artificial light. A
warm light diffused by all the cooking smoke filled a large central space that
was divided up into a number of stalls. The aisles between them were so
narrow and the crowd of customers so great that we could hardly get
through, much less shoot the scenes. But we sacrificed. . . for the sake of
food. Even Dave and Ralph, with equipment in one hand held foods in the
other, munching and shooting simultaneously. Our first stop was a *tortilla*-
making stand; here they were made not by hand patting, but with a large
hand-cranked machine that looked like a pasta maker. The *tortillas* were
made quickly and were thin enough to be almost translucent. It was, said
our guide, the local style. Many of these were served within the market, and
the others were bagged in plastic for walk-in traffic. Ravenous now, we
moved on to a brightly tiled *menudo* stand. Sunday is traditionally the day

for this classic tripe soup, so we tried it. It was nicely spiced with some of Guerrero's characteristic chile, the *guajillo*. Since not everyone liked the idea of eating cow stomach, we moved onto to another colorful *fonda*, this one serving a delightful version of *quesadillas*. These turnovers were filled with squash blossoms, *epazote* leaves, and Guerrero string cheese and were served with thick fresh sour cream very much like a *créme fraiche*. Cream still dripping from our mouths, we passed on to a cookstand serving *cochinita*, marinated and roasted suckling pig. The meat was served in a hollowed-out *bolillo*, a Mexican-style roll, and topped with pickled *jalapeño* chiles. Delicious, of course, and familiar from North American versions of Italian beef sandwiches.

By now we were growing weary. Better food awaited us, however, if only we could carry on a little longer. We did and went on to the *cabrito* stands. Here we saw young goat, loads of goat set out in rows, great heaps of meat piled on the tables, and meat being pulled from the bones, especially the meat from the goats' heads under the horns. . . with the skull for decoration. A very Mexican decor, I thought. Marinated first in an orange-flavored sauce, the goat is roasted for some hours at low heat to bring out the flavors. When finally ready, the meat is picked apart or sliced, served on a banana leaf, and set in a piece of aluminum foil with a tangy green *tomatillo* sauce. Despite all our previous chomping, we all gobbled down this preparation. Barbecued goat is a prime example of the nature of Mexican food that Susana had discussed the evening before: the European/Indian mixture so typical of Mexico. Goat is Old World, but the delicious chile sauces are native American.

"Have a snack"

The banana leaves on which it is served come from Southeast Asia. As for the aluminum foil, that is strictly twentieth-century U.S.A.

Our guide led us deeper into the maze of stands. We were surrounded by stacks of wonderful things: banana leaves, piles of shrimp, and masses of herbs such as *papalo quelite* and *pipitza* or *pipicha* (similar and used in the same way as cilantro). Fruits of every kind appeared, from several kinds of *mamey*, bananas, *domínicos*, plantains (cooking bananas), grapefruit, oranges, lemons, and more. Then came stand after stand filled with *jícama*, a complete variety of swiss chards, fresh amaranth (*huazontles*), and all types of cheeses, such as *manchego*, Oaxacan string cheese, fresh *ranchero*, *cotija*, and *añejo*, among others. Everything was carefully arranged symmetrically to enhance the color of many of the foods and packages. One area was filled with chiles of every description from fresh to dried, bins of powdered chiles, and a score of ready-to-make *mole* pastes; that is, they were already mixed with that prime Mexican ingredient, lard. Each one of these was a different color, and the warm musty-pruney-spicy smell they gave off was delightful.

We now stood before a juice stand and were confronted by a variety of fruit preparations. Visitors to Mexico know that fresh fruit juices, squeezed or blended to order, are commonplace in "jugerías." This stand featured *zapotes* of several types. *Zapote* (the Spanish *zapota*, from the Nahuatl *tzapotlor*) is the sweet-fleshed fruit of a native Central American tree. It comes in several colors, from red to black, each with a slightly different flavor. "Try these," Susana said. "The black *zapote* is an ugly fruit, but it tastes delicious." She was right; blended up with some bottled water, it was sweet and refreshing. Standing next to the fruit was a container of bright green liquid. "Now you must try this. . . it's very good for you," said Susana. It turned out to be alfalfa. Feeling peaked, we all sampled the stuff. "It tastes like, well, grass!" I exclaimed. "Oh, but it's good for everything. . . picks you right up," our new friend declared, adding, "You know, many Mexicans are very health conscious and we like to use traditional, natural cures." We drank more.

Spurred on by healthful drinks, Susana then noticed that we had not tried some of Guerrero's real regional specialties, beginning with *pozole*. This is a kind of broth made from pig's head and feet and filled with whole corn kernels or hominy. Several regional variations are well known in Mexico, red in Jalisco and white in Guerrero, but the general outline of the dish is similar. Even so, it is a flexible dish, so one never knows exactly what the *pozole* will be from home to home or restaurant to restaurant. Everyone has their own recipe for making it, and in Mexico that means passed down through families, mother to daughter. The crew stepped up to a *fonda* dedicated to the dish, the "*Pozolería de Epe.*" There sat a customer, ready to dig into a large steaming bowl. Alongside were smaller bowls filled with ground chile and

Removing kernels from corn with a corn kerneler (olotetl *in Nahuatl*)

basil. Would he mind a camera over his shoulder as he prepared to eat the dish? "Not at all," he said, then sprinkled a good pinch of each flavoring into the broth and onto the plump kernels floating in it. It was nice and hot, and this was still morning. When it is said that *pozole* is the state dish, eaten morning, noon, and night, they mean it.

We went on. Famous *botanas, crab empanaditas,* appeared, then little *tamales* made with beans, and more. Interested in iguana or armadillo? Yes, indeed, but the *fonda* we stood before was out of iguana soup. Susana knew another place that was sure to have both. Armadillo is popular in the springtime, and iguanas are now raised commercially since the wild ones in the coastal areas are endangered. Or what about the excellent fish soup, made with lots of oregano and tomatoes? Both it and iguana soup are said to cure hangovers. Finally we cried, "¡No más!" Having been up at five and worked for six hours straight, all of us had to take a break. "You *gringos* have no stamina," Susana joked. "How could you not want to try delectable, spicy iguana?" We thought that we would get to eat iguana later on the trip, and, at least that day, we didn't need a hangover cure. Giving in to our evident weakness, Susana then suggested that we go to another place for a different food experience. "Very typical," she said. In addition, a place that we wanted to see was on the way: a *tuba* stand. We agreed to meet in the early afternoon for a trip down the coast. That small journey, as the market had done, reminded us of the complex history, food and otherwise, of the country that we had come to see.

Pozole

Pozole is a kind of corn-meat soup that is *the* regional dish of Guerrero, although versions are certainly made in other states. Its foundation is a staple of the pre-Columbian diet: hominy, or whole corn kernels. The hominy (*cachuazintle* in Nahuatl) of Guerrero is a special variety of corn with much larger ears than North Americans are used to eating, more like those grown for animal feed. When made from dried kernels, hominy must be soaked overnight, cooked, and then washed. Before each kernel is cooked, it must have the small "eye" at the base meticulously removed so that it will "blossom" when cooked. The process is laborious, so it is easier to use the canned variety, although the texture will not be the same. In Mexico, a whole pig head and pig feet are used to make the broth! Since most American markets do not stock whole heads—although pig feet are widely available—we recommend substituting the same weight of pork loin. When cooked, it makes a dish with which North Americans are more comfortable.

Soup:

1-1/4	lbs.	hominy
2-1/4	lb.	pig head (or pork loin)
2		pig's feet
1		whole onion, chopped
1/4		head of garlic, peeled

6	whole *guajillo* chiles, seeded and deveined
3	whole *ancho* chiles, seeded and deveined
	kosher salt, to taste

Garnish:

1	head romaine lettuce
1	bunch radishes
4	limes, quartered
1	avocado, peeled and sliced
	fried pork skins (*chicharón*)
1-³/₄ oz.	powdered chiles *pequín*
²/₃ C.	dried oregano
	tostadas

To *make soup*:

Place pork in a large soup pan and cover with water. Bring to a boil and reduce heat to simmer and cook until flesh comes off the head, or about 1 hour. When done, remove meat from water and set aside. When meat is cooled, remove all the edible parts from the head, or if using loin, cut into small chunks. It is best for the *pozole's* flavor not to skim the stock before using it again, though you may if a lower-fat *pozole* is the object. Place canned hominy and chile purée in the stock and return the meat to the pan. Return stock to a simmer and cook uncovered for 1 hour. When done, adjust salt to taste.

To *prepare chiles*:

While the soup is cooking, soak seeded and deveined *guajillo* and *ancho* chiles in 1 cup of hot water for about 20 minutes, or until soft. Place chiles, garlic, and ¹/₂ onion in the bowl of a food processor or blender and puree. When adding the hominy and meat to the stock before final cooking, stir in the purée as well. Cook as directed above.

To *serve*:

The oregano and *pequín* chile powder are added to each bowl by the diner, to taste. Remember, the *pequíns* are hot. The *pozole* is placed in each soup bowl, along with a portion of chopped onion, a thin slice of romaine lettuce and sliced radish, and seasonings to taste. Each portion may be topped with avocado slices and pork skin slices. Eat with *tostadas.*   *Serves* 6

Fish *botanas*, or snacks, are features of the Acapulco market. . . and of the city's restaurants as well. This one is a *ceviche* that can be made with shark, skate, kingfish, or red snapper filets. There has been concern expressed recently about the safety of fish "cooked" in this manner, that is, marinated in lime juice. Whether of not there is some factual basis for this concern, *ceviche* remains a glory of Hispanic cookery.

Tiritas *de* Pescado

1	lb.	shark, skate, kingfish, or red snapper, thinly sliced
1	C.	lime or lemon juice
½	C.	orange juice
½	t.	soy sauce
1–2		dashes white Worcestershire sauce
2	T.	vinegar
2		small *jalapeño* or *serrano* chiles, finely chopped
1		small purple onion, finely chopped
		kosher salt and freshly ground pepper, to taste
		romaine lettuce leaves
1		bunch cilantro, finely chopped

Squeeze lime juice into a glass or glazed ceramic bowl. Add fish and turn to coat thoroughly. Set in the refrigerator and allow to stand for at least 25 minutes. Remove the fish and lime juice from bowl. Drain the fish and discard the lime juice. Mix orange juice, vinegar, soy sauce, white Worcestershire sauce, and onions in the bowl. Season with kosher salt and freshly ground pepper, to taste. Return fish to the bowl and turn to coat thoroughly. Refrigerate for at least 10 minutes. When ready, serve on a bed of romaine lettuce and garnish with chopped cilantro.   *Serves 4*

Most fish recipes from the Guerrero coast are fairly direct. This is one Dudley found in a small town down the coast from Acapulco. It features the characteristic fish of the region, *huachinango.*

Pescadillas *and* Camaroncillas

1	lb.	red snapper fillets, steamed or sautéed and flaked
1		small onion, finely chopped
2		large whole Roma or Italian plum tomatoes, seeded and chopped
1	t.	dried oregano

2	cloves fresh garlic, finely chopped
12	small corn *tortillas*
½ C.	canola oil
¼ t.	kosher salt
¼ t.	coarsely crushed black pepper

Prepare the fish by steaming, poaching, or very gently sautéing in a small amount of oil. When done, allow to cool. In a glass bowl, mix the fish, onion, tomatoes, oregano, and garlic. Heat *tortillas* on a dry comal or skillet until soft. Lay out and fill each *tortilla* with the fish mixture. Use wooden toothpicks to secure the edges of the *tortillas*. Heat oil in a deep, heavy skillet over high flame. When hot, place *pescadillas* in oil and fry until golden and crispy. Remove from the pan and drain. Garnish with *guacamole*, red *guajillo salsa*, and fresh cheese.   *Serves 4*

The Acapulco Coast

Early in the afternoon, we picked up Susana and set out southward along the coast—the same *carretera escénica* we had taken from the airport. Again, we climbed the high ridges running along the ocean and looked down upon the scenic bay of Puerto Marquéz. Our escort talked about all the construction going on at Punta Diamante. It is a growing resort community complete with clubs where visitors and seasonal residents can eat, drink, and dance the whole night long. We learned that many famous and important personages have houses along this part of the coast. The area's development was an idea of the ex-governor of Guerrero, who was supported by the recently assassinated presidential candidate, Luis Donaldo Colosio. Be had been like a brother to the governor, Susana went on . . . . We understood a little of how things worked in those days. Interesting, some of us remarked, that the place had once been a hideaway for pirates that preyed on the *naos* that crossed the ocean to and from Manila.

Descending from the mountains, we came to the wide flat beach area where we had first landed. Sandy soil with scruffy patches of grass and tropical vegetation brought southern Florida to mind, but without the trucked-in topsoil and golf courses. The road passed through a moderately built-up area with shops, gas stations, and houses spaced along the way. Before long we arrived at our first destination, a small whitewashed building with a hand-painted sign inscribed *Tuba* above a small counter opening. When we first planned the program, Bob Ward, our consultant in Guerrero, mentioned that he had often passed this place en route to Acapulco. "Palm wine," he said. Right away we wanted to visit because we knew that it had come from the Philippines. I knew, too, that palm wine had been a favorite beverage in the civilizations of ancient Mesopotamia and was perhaps made in the same way today, so I was doubly anxious to try it.

Stretching out for several hundred yards behind the stand was a grove of coconut palms. It is from these that *tuba* comes, but the palm plantations of the region actually originated in Southeast Asia. In the later nineteenth and early twentieth centuries, entrepreneurs began planting palms to produce a most valuable crop, *copra*, from which came oil. Originally, *copra* was used to make soap. Late in the nineteenth century, hydrogenation, a way of stabilizing vegetable oils into solid form using coconut oil, was discovered. Margarine, once made with coconut, became a major food product. Thereafter coconut provided the world with most of its vegetable oil. Coconuts reigned until at least the 1950s, when new processes of hydrogenation came into use and vastly increased the use of soybean oils. Mexico was part of the international trade in these products and, to some small degree, still is. But the small palm plantation at the *tuba* stand has been used for something else.

Susana had never been to the place and did not even know what *tuba* was, but upon meeting the owner, Francisco Galeana Nogueda, she recognized him as an old, good friend of her relatives. In fact, he was a former government official who simply decided that running the stand would be a not very strenuous retirement activity. However, this was not because *tuba* is easy to make. *Tuba* is the sap of the coconut palm that has been allowed to ferment. To make it, first the tree must be tapped. No, first get a boy who can climb the tree and set the tap. This is done when the coconut just begins to bud. It is nipped off, an incision is made in the branch, a tube is inserted, and the sap is allowed to drip into a bucket hanging just below it. The bucket is emptied twice a day; it has to be, because in full flow a tree can produce one liter of sap per day. *Tuba* can be drunk on the first day but is usually allowed to stand two to four days. The longer it stands, the stronger it gets as the natural sugars ferment. The final liquid has the milky color and consistency of *pulgue* and *horchata* (the rice-based drink). We drank some two-day-old brew and found it to have a slightly coconuty flavor, with perhaps a little saltiness. We agreed that it is an acquired taste. Nonetheless, as I discovered later from Filipino informants, it is a favorite beverage in that country and is made in exactly the same way. Here was yet another example of the many influences on Mexican cuisine, this one related to the once world-wide Spanish Empire.

On down the coastal road, we came into more rural country. The road passed through more and more coconut plantations, only these had standing corn in front of and beneath the towering trees. It was an unexpected sight for us North Americans, since we hardly ever see the two plants together in the same context. The reason for corn became apparent when we came across a scattering of scruffy shacks that had been simply set down in a clearing. A few dust-caked, Indian-looking children were playing in an open space between the shacks and amidst some chickens. The structures were made of scrap wood, tin, cardboard, and some of Mexico's ever-present cinderblocks. We gaped at what seemed to be abject poverty in the midst of a natural, if ordered, beauty. In response, Susana told us that this was a squatters' camp. Homeless families, mostly poor farmers who could no longer make a living but could find no work, staked out land that might be state owned or even private. They lived on whatever meager income they could get from odd jobs and minuscule welfare moneys. The government seemed reluctant to move them out for many reasons, not the least being lack of adequate alternative housing or the jobs to pay for it. Furthermore, in Guerrero and Michoacán there had arisen movements on behalf of the long-repressed indigenous peoples of these states. Large demonstrations had already taken place in Mexico City, and not long before, an actual rebellion had broken out in Chiapas. It was a touchy situation for everyone. Nevertheless, the scene vividly illustrated the width of the social and economic gaps among the people of Mexico, indeed, in many parts of the world including our own.

Barra Vieja sits on a spit of sand with the ocean on one side and a brackish water lagoon, Tres Palos, on the other. The Beto Godoy restaurant is located just at the lagoon's edge, a short walk to the Pacific. It turned out to be a famous restaurant in the region. While it did have indoor dining areas, it was the outdoor section that interested us. The decor here was in the manner of a big *palapa*, with picnic tables and hammocks where more than one sated diner was taking a nice *siesta*. The whole area was open to the lagoon and the sandy beach. Pulled up on the shore were some small one- or two-man fishing boats with shrimp nets drying on racks nearby. Dave and Jan took one look and said that we had to shoot the shrimpers in the lagoon. While Dudley acted as translator, the two of them talked with one of the boatmen. . . about how it could be done while he discussed how much he would get out of it. His suggestion of one hundred *pesos* was eventually reduced to ten, since they were only going out about twenty yards from shore and the man himself would appear on television. Dave got some fine shots of how the shrimp hunters worked their small nets. Once again, though, the camera proved to be bad luck: nothing was caught.

That did not mean we had to go hungry. To the contrary, there was plenty of food and it was wonderfully prepared. For appetizers we gorged on some *sopes*, basically hand-made *gorditas*, sauced with red and green versions of *salsa*—the later made spicy with *pequín* chiles—and all topped with crumbled fresh cheese. Then we got down to the real eating. We began with *camarones al mojo de ajo*: huge butterflied shrimp, seasoned with garlic and *guajillo* sauce and then grilled. Overdone, but in Dave's words, "This is the best shrimp I've ever had." They were excellently flavored, even if we had to dig the flesh from the shell. The open-air grilling by the seaside and the sauce made the dish. We were ready to go on to the house specialty of whole fish when the manager asked us whether we wanted to see the cooking process. After a quick scouting trip, we had to get it on camera, and it proved to be one of the documentary's more savory sections.

Dudley had already explored the kitchen and discussed recipes with the manager when we arrived. The cooking area consists of two tiled rooms and a large bank of wood-fueled grills, open except for a simple roof. One room has tanks filled with fresh fish of several species. The customer chooses a fish that is quickly dispatched by a fish preparer who guts it, slices it open, washes it inside and out under running water, and then sprinkles it inside and out with sea salt. The salt, by the way, is gathered not far down the coast in natural salt pans. Filled with minerals, it adds to the flavor of the final dish. The fish is then sent to the cooks, serious women dressed in t-shirts and baseball caps, who marinate it for a short time in their special sauce. After about ten or fifteen minutes, the well-sauced fish is placed in a two-piece wire rack, set on the grill, and cooked until done. More sauce is added from time to time. The sauce, an original recipe of the house, is a mixture of three chiles—*guajillo* (again, the emblematic chile of Guerrero), *costeña* or *puya*, and *ancho*—vinegar, and herbs. It was spicy, mildly hot, and went perfectly with the wood-grilled fish. The final dish was somewhat overdone, but so flavorful that no one minded. A memorable food event, all of us agreed. We thanked our guide, Susana Palazuelos, profusely, and took our leave, hoping that her kindness to us would be repaid. (It was: Carol gave her new book a good write-up in her newspaper.)

Our long day drew to a close and so did our time on the tropical coast. We had quickly examined one environmental zone, albeit not in anything like its natural state. For us, the city of Acapulco itself stands not so much for its current status as a resort (that has happened only since the 1940s) but for a rich food zone and a symbol for an ongoing process in Mexican history: constant contact with the outside world, absorption and assimilation of new ideas, and at the same time, the sharing of Mexico's own indigenous products. Is that not human history as well?

Our journey began early the next day as we entered Guerrero's dry interior. That evening we gathered to discuss our plans and to talk about the next phase of Mexico's food history. The prehispanic period had already been chewed over; now it was time for the Spanish to appear on the scene, since so much of what we had seen and eaten came from across the Atlantic Ocean. Or, as we settled in for the next lesson, to mangle the words of Bertold Brecht, first comes the eating, then comes the moral.

For the eating part, the following are facsimiles of the dishes we ate on the Barra Vieja. It begins with shrimp.

Camarones al Mojo de Ajo

We had this dish grilled at the Betoy Goodoy restaurant. If you are preparing it this way, use the following as a marinade, but add 2 to 4 tablespoons of olive oil. Then grill. If you plan to sauté the dish, the following process works well.

½	C.	olive oil
1	lb.	medium shrimp, shelled and deveined
8		cloves garlic, coarsely crushed
1		dash Worcestershire sauce
		sea or kosher salt to taste

Heat oil in a large, heavy skillet until it begins to mist. Add shrimp, garlic, and Worcestershire sauce. Cook over medium heat, stirring, until the shrimp turn pink, about 4–5 minutes. Salt to taste.

Serves 6 as an appetizer

The shrimp can be eaten as they are, but a nice coastal sauce goes wall with them. This one hails from the same source.

Salsa Costeña

6		*puya* or *guajillo* chiles, seeded and roasted or toasted
8 (½ lb.)		*tomatillos*, peeled and simmered
1		clove garlic
½		medium onion, chopped
⅓	C.	chopped cilantro
		sea salt, to taste

Roast or toast the chiles on a heated griddle. While they are cooking bring a medium pan of water boil, add the *tomatillos*, reduce heat, and simmer until they are soft, about 10 minutes. Set aside the water. Place all the ingredients except the cilantro and onion in the bowl of a food processor or blender and purée. Add the *tomatillo* water as necessary to thin. Remove the sauce from the processor and stir in the cilantro and onions. Adjust salt to taste. Serve warm or at room temperature.

Makes about 1 cup

The *pièce de resistance* of our coastal trip was *huachinango* (red snapper) in the sauce mentioned above. Unless you cook completely fresh fish on a wood-fired grill on an ocean beachfront, the flavor will not be the same, but it is worth a try anyway. Dudley reminds us that a shot of *mezcal* goes well before eating this dish. (That or *tequila* always makes cooking more enjoyable, he says). Serve with fresh corn *tortillas*.

Huachinango a la Talla

1-½	lbs.	red snapper fillets
1-½	T.	sea or kosher salt
2		whole *guajillo* chiles
1		whole *ancho* chile
1		whole *costeño* or *puya* chile
2		whole tomatoes, chopped
2		cloves garlic, peeled
1		whole clove
¼	C.	chopped onion
½	t.	vinegar
¼	t.	of cumin powder
¼	t.	of dried oregano
¼	t.	of dried marjoram
¼	t.	of dried thyme
½	t.	freshly ground pepper
1–2	T.	canola oil

If purchasing the fish whole, have the fish merchant butterfly the fillets but leave the scales on them. Rinse the fish, pat dry, and set aside. Prepare the sauce (*salsa costeña*). Soak the chiles in hot water for 10 minutes. Drain and place them in the bowl of a food processor or blender along with the tomatoes, garlic, clove, onion, vinegar, dried herbs, and freshly ground pepper. Set aside the chile water. Process until a smooth purée is formed. Add chile water to thin *slightly*. (The purée must be thick.) Heat the oil in a deep, heavy saucepan. Add the purée, bring to simmer, and cook for 10 minutes. Place in a large, shallow dish and allow to cool. Have ready the snapper fillets. Sprinkle 1–1-½ tablespoons of sea salt over the fillets. Place the fillets in the chile sauce and allow to marinate for at least 20 minutes. Turn the fillets in the marinade from time to time. Heat a charcoal grill and lightly grease the rack. Place the fish fillets on the rack, set the rack over the hot coals, and grill the fish,

Making fish in totomoxtle (wrapped and steamed fish)

scales downward, for about 15 minutes. Baste the uncooked side of fish and then grill that side for a few minutes, until done.　　　Serves 3–4

Note: The fish may be cooked under a broiler following the same procedures outlined for grilling.

Wrapping and steaming are pre-Columbian cooking techniques that are widely used in Mexico today. The following recipe can be found in any town or village throughout Guerrero and Michoacán, anywhere that fish, corn, and cactus are found.

Filetes de Mojarra en Totomoxtle

(Porgie Filets with Nopalitos in Corn Husks)

12	porgie filets (or red snapper), 4-6 oz. each
6	*nopales* (cactus leaves), cooked in water, drained and finely chopped
½	medium onion, finely chopped
1 t.	oregano

1   t.   salt
1   t.   olive oil
6   *totomoxtles* (corn husks)

Spread fish filets flat. Mix together the nopales, onion, oregano, salt and olive oil. Place portion of mixture on each fillet, then cover with another fillet. Wrap each in corn husks. Set wrapped fish in steamer rack and steam for 30 minutes. Unwrap fish when ready to serve and cut into appropriately sized pieces. Serve with Molcajete Sauce (see 248). *Serves 6 or up to 24 as appetizer*

The Coming of the Spanish

A Background on Spain

In the summer of 1519, native peoples on the east coast of Mexico, near what is today Veracruz, were amazed to see "mountains floating on the sea" with billowing white clouds above them. On them were strange white men. . . . Perhaps the ancient prophecy of the return of the god Quetzalcóatl was about to be fulfilled. The men were not gods, but Spaniards. Within two years, the great Aztec Empire of central Mexico would be destroyed. . . and the Spanish religion and culture would be imposed on all the native peoples of Mexico. Eventually the Europeans and Indians merged into something new: the peoples of Mexico.

The Spanish conquest ended 3,000 years of regional cultural traditions centering on politics, society, and religion. These were not discrete traditions. To the contrary, partly due to trade, from conquest, and certainly due to various migrations, the peoples of the ancient Americas had a history of cultural intermixing long before the Spanish ever arrived. By estimate there were about 400 different ethnic groups and dialects within Mexico. Yet, as we have seen, most shared common ways of life, religion, and political organization. Ironically, it was these similarities that allowed the Europeans to conquer and rule Mexico. Much would be swept away by the Spanish, but, like the immutable landscape and climate, much remained.

Hernan Cortés, the conqueror of Mexico, "as born in Medallín, Spain, in a hard, poor region called Extremadura in 1485. He sprang from an impoverished but noble family who managed to send him to the University of Salamanca. There he was to study the liberal arts—not our modern ones, but their medieval predecessors: canon and civil law and theology. Cortés never finished school, but instead sailed to the Americas, the Caribbean, where he became a minor landowner and gentleman farmer, a minor official, and the eventual conqueror of the Aztec Empire. These facts represent more than just historical data; they are representative of major events in history and of the workings of historical processes. Cortés's life tells us something about who the Spanish were and, at least for the purposes of this book, about their food and culinary background. That history was rich, with roots even deeper than those of the New World. Let us briefly begin at the beginning.

Well, almost at the beginning. Approximately 8,000 years ago, the Iberian Peninsula was mainly covered in forests. The remains of the last Ice Age had withdrawn into the higher reaches of the Pyrenees Mountains, leaving behind a lush landscape. Here dwelt small bands of hunting and food-collecting peoples who lived in very much the same way as the peoples of Mexico did during the same time period. Deer and smaller game, fish from the coasts, wild fruits, berries, and some grasses were the staples of their diets. For small populations scattered across a wide landscape, this would have sufficed to sustain them. But when populations grew too large for the land to support, other more reliable ways of getting food had to be found. Fortunately, that source was at hand.

Sometime in the sixth millennia, new peoples from the east entered the scene. At least 1,000 years or more before, farming villages had appeared in the eastern Mediterranean regions of Europe—what is today Greece and the Balkans. Small communities with populations of perhaps fifty to no more than several hundred people lived with their domesticated animals and practiced something that was closer to horticulture than full-scale farming. Their tools were not plows (not until the fourth millennium), but digging sticks, not metal tools but polished stone, and locally made pottery for cooking and storage. Archaeologists call this era the Neolithic Age, and, except for the wider range of animals, life was not very different from that in the early villages of Mexico. In terms of technology, and social and political organizations, the New World and the Old were on parallel tracks for many thousands of years.

Neolithic villagers—we do not know their names, much less their languages—began to migrate from their home areas into the rest of Europe. One route of travel was along the Mediterranean coast. The territories they entered were not vacant. Hunter-gatherers lived in the forests where plenty of food was available to them. There had been a long period of contact among foraging peoples such as those who lived on marine resources, for instance, and who moved back and forth between the areas of the farming villages and the forest hunters. These folk used pottery and kept some domesticated sheep, but did not domesticate plants. Slowly, it appears, foraging peoples used and came to rely on domesticated plants and animals as more reliable food bases. Eventually, over long centuries, all three groups mixed together to form new mixed farming communities across the western Mediterranean region. By roughly 3000 B.C., Spain had small farming communities scattered across its landscape.

What the early farmers planted were seed crops, several kinds of wheat—some for boiling in porridges, others for grinding into flour for breads—barley, lentils, garbanzos, and peas. If sheep were the first farm animals brought to the west, along with dogs, then cattle and pigs were not far behind. All across Europe cattle became the chief source of animal protein, which came from meat and milk. (The ancient farmers made cheeses.) We know, too, that farming peoples lived amidst forests, and, in more temperate climates, they kept pigs, since these are forest-adapted creatures. Five thousand years ago, then, most of the foundation for traditional Spanish foodstuffs had been established: bread, garbanzos, gruel, and some cheeses. Two more additions remained: olives and wine. Archaeologists and historians are not sure about the exact date of their introduction to Iberia, but sometime around the first millennium seems likely. That is when Spain received colonies of Greeks and Phoenicians, both of whom had had thousands of years' experience in growing both crops. The origins of the famous Spanish olive oils and wines are in that era. Thus, by the time Rome took Spain as one of the jewels of its empire, after 202 B.C. (when it won a war for the empire with Carthage), even more of the pattern of what we think of as typically Spanish food today had been set.

Another historical force what went into the making of Hernan Cortés and his era began in the early eighth century A.D. There are two aspects to this force, one having to do with food and the other with ideas about the world, religion, and warfare. In 711 Islamic (usually called Moorish) armies from North Africa began to overrun Spain and set up a kingdom they called Al-Andalus. Early in the century, the Umayyad Dynasty established a capital at Córdoba. Moorish Spain would last for almost 800 years and was not extinguished until 1492. At its height, Al-Andalus was a brilliant cultural center. A state tolerant of cultural diversity, it permitted Jews and Christians to live and prosper alongside followers of Islam. Its cities grew wealthy, its crafts were world renowned, and science, medicine, trade, fine arts, and especially agriculture flourished. Here would be yet another building block of Spanish food in at least two ways: the introduction, or at the least expansion of, new crops, and the basic outlines of culinary techniques and flavoring.

In these times, citrus fruits became well established in Spain and in its cuisine. . . and later in Mexico as well. Domesticated oranges and probably lemons originated in northern India and slowly made their ways east and west. Romans knew of them and began to plant them in North Africa, but only as luxury foods. Citrus trees may have been planted in Spain during the Roman period, but their expansion into all fertile parts of the peninsula was done in Moorish days. Rice, also an Indian import, was known to ancient Greeks and Romans, though not used much, and may have been grown in Italy and Spain in very small quantities before Al-Andalus was formed. Middle Eastern cuisine uses plenty of rice, so its appearance as a cultivated crop in Spain was only a matter of getting the appropriate agricultural systems in place. Today, if fact, rice is widely grown in the extensively irrigated land in the Guadalquivir River basin just below Sevilla. Need we point out that rice is a staple of Mexican restaurant food, either on the plate with entrées or, as usual in Mexico, as a *sopa seca* or dry soup that is served as a separate course before the main entrée?

These are not the only elements of Spanish fare that came from the east. Flavor profiles indicate it has something to do with Baghdad and Persia as well. As Professor Susan Tax Freeman of the University of Illinois, Chicago, has observed, early Spanish culinary literature is Arabic in flavor and in fact.[17] The earliest cookery manuscript found so far dates to the thirteenth century and is in Arabic. (It was found in the palace at Valencia and was not translated into Spanish until the 1960s.) What were those flavors? They show heavy use of sweet fruit in meat dishes and huge infusions of herbs in most dishes. Nuts and both fresh and dried fruits were widely used in many dishes. Once these were universal ingredients, but now they are more regional, for example, in Catalonian cookery and its Sicilian relative. Techniques included using ground nuts, bread crumbs, and egg emulsions as thickeners. In short, the flavor profile of medieval Spanish *haute cuisine* was highly aromatic and sweet with some spicy flavor that came from black pepper. We know that black pepper appeared in many recipes from the Roman period through the Middle Ages, but how much was used—how much "heat" was in the dishes—is not yet known.

Spain was not alone in being influenced by the Arabic world, for even a cursory glance at medieval cookery literature shows the same trend. Baghdad and Persia were the meccas of *haute cuisine* in the Middle Ages. All the spices that rich Europeans sought came through the Middle East, including cinnamon, pepper, cloves, and nutmeg, and they all appeared in many dishes, sometimes all at once. Vinegars made from varieties of sources were used to make characteristic medieval sauces (such as verjuice and eisel) and were often mixed with spices and other bold seasonings. The cuisine is said to have been one of addition, rather than infusion: the more (costly) ingredients, the better the dish. Recreations by modern researchers of some of the medieval dishes turn out to be surprisingly tasty, not just a garbled mass of noncomplementary flavors. That will come as no revelation to those who have had the pleasure of eating the marvelous multiseasoned cuisine of Persia. There, too, a distinct sweet-sour flavor profile is preferred. Interestingly, something of this tradition is preserved in Sephardic Jewish cookery, and why not, since many Sephardim came from Spain after they were expelled from the country along with the Moors in 1492.

It is not an accident that Europeans should crave sugar. Human beings have always had a sweet tooth and they satisfied it with fruit and honey before the advent of sugar. Arabs began sugar production in the west and tried to control its trade in the Mediterranean in competition with the Christians, who made Cyprus into a major sugar-producing area. Indeed, the whole sugar confection tradition in Europe comes from Arab kitchens, likely via Spain. Our word "candy" comes from Arabic words for both sugar and confections. That sugar should have translated to Mexico can come as no surprise. *Piloncillo*, the brown sugar, the upside-down cones in which it often appears in Mexico, take the same form as they did in the Middle Ages. Nor is it by chance that Europeans founded sugar plantations in the New World as soon as they could. Sugar was every bit as valuable a commodity as the spices from the Orient.

As for common folk in Medieval Spain, we can be sure that they ate simpler fare. The cooking manuals of the time were entirely class bound and made for the elites. Peasants everywhere in the world ate grains: porridge or gruel in Europe and corn-based dishes in America (and rice and millet in China, incidentally). Not much sugar for these people, or cinnamon and other spices. That many herbs went into those porridges is also likely, but there is simply no record of them. We do know what the common Spanish seamen ate when they went out on voyages of conquest and trade: salted beef, pork, fish; garbanzo beans; olive oil; garlic; bread—usually hardtack— and as many fruits and vegetables as they could take. The standard on-board meal would have been a stew or *cocido* made of these foods, or at extremes, hard bread soaked in water (wine if they had it). It was not unlike peasant fare at home and the menu has a long pedigree.

While some elements of Arabic cookery remain in the Spanish cuisine, many have disappeared or the main ingredients have changed. One obvious reason for this is the introduction of New World foodstuffs. There is another cause for the change and one that greatly shaped Hernan Cortés's ideas: the Reconquest of Spain. This is the name given to a long, long series of wars between the Christian kingdoms of northern Iberia and the Islamic state(s) of the south. The two major Christian kingdoms involved were Aragón on the east (including Cataluña) and Castilla in the center and west. The rulers of Castilla, by which the later Middle Ages was usually called "Spain," were rigorously religious, so that their war against the emirate of Granada, the last

Moslem stronghold, was something of a crusade. Eventually the two kingdoms united through a fortuitous marriage between the heiress to the throne of Castilla, Isabella, to the successor to the throne of Aragón, Fernando. When the thrones of both kingdoms fell to them, Spain was united under the famous "Catholic rulers." The only institution they had in common was the Inquisition, the enforcer of religious and political orthodoxy. That arm of the Church—it can only be described as fanatical—has colored outsiders' perceptions of Spain. With monarchical and religious passions burning, Spain finally drove out the Moors, along with any number of "heretics," in the fateful year of 1492. With the Moors went Jews who, if they did not convert to Christianity, had to give up all of their possessions.[18] Most went to far more tolerant Moslem countries where they could live mainly in peace.

Food plays a role in all of this. When the Moors and Jews were expelled, priests, monks, and local secular leaders were intent on extirpating all vestiges of their ideas. That meant foodstuffs as well. Condiments also changed, because all those "eastern" elements had to go. That may be one of the reasons for the fairly uniform and increasingly simple condimentation of Spanish fare, which includes many wild herbs such as oregano, thyme, and basil as well as garlic, onions, and olive oil. Rice (also an Arab import) would be flavored with these ingredients as well as saffron. Lastly, and most importantly there was pork. That meat is, of course, forbidden by Jewish and Moslem law, therefore eating it became a test of Christianity. Inquisition documents show that pork was a confirmation of Christian orthodoxy. Pork had to appear everywhere in kitchens, in everything from wineskins to other dishes such as vegetables. (Might this be the origin of pork and beans?) A specialty since the Roman era, the sausage tradition grew even stronger in Spain, as it became mandated by governmental and religious laws. Pork, now the paradigm of Spanish dishes, was to become central to cuisine in the colonies as well.

Hernan Cortés was born into this world of war, conquest, and religious orthodoxy and into a Spain whose outlook and institutions were largely medieval. By the time Cortés was old enough to fight, Europeans had been doing just that for many years. Italy was the cockpit where the Italian powers and European monarchs fought for glory and power. Most of the armies were mercenary. They fought for money and what it could buy them as individuals: power and prestige. The Reconquest had forged fierce soldiers, and the Italian war honed their skills and their greed. Add to that the gloss of education given the son of a minor noble family along with a certain formal piety, and there is Hernan Cortés. Interestingly, common Spaniards were not nearly as orthodox as we might think and were certainly not obedient to every dictate of their churchmen. Cursing, swearing, and taking the Lord's and every other member of the heavenly host's name in vain was common practice. Many ordinary Spaniards cast cynical eyes upon the clergy, although they might not do it overtly. Cortés himself dictated church activities as he saw fit, not unlike that most pious of monarchs, Felipe II (Basil Rathbone in the movies!). Had the conquerors been more obedient to the good churchmen who came to the Americas to minister to the natives, untold suffering might have been averted, as well as countless deaths.

The Conquest

"The Spanish conquest of Mexico was not merely a political act; it was a biological conquest."—from the documentary "Hidden Mexico"

The story of how the Aztec Empire fell to a small group of Spaniards (about 600 initially) backed by a large army of native peoples who hated their imperial tribute takers has been told many times. The political act was sudden; in 1521 the capital, Tenochtitlán, was captured and destroyed. The Emperor, Moctezuma Xocoyoltzin had been murdered, his place taken *de facto* by none other than Hernan Cortés. The conquest of the rest of Mexico is far more complicated and took much longer, maybe extending even into the present day, if that is the meaning of the recent Indian protests and rebellions by *indigenas*. Although the immediate result was that some of the *conquistadores* made themselves rich (most actually died young or in poverty), a secondary result was the creation of the first genetic mixture that would eventually become the majority of the Mexican population: the *mestizos*. Cortés's letters to the king of Spain belie his famous toughness and ruthlessness, since he did have admiration for native peoples and even left moneys in his will for a college in which some might be trained in law and theology. Certainly he was amazed at the magnificence of the capital city he was about to destroy and the lifestyle of the imperial court. That brings us back to food.

One of the men accompanying Cortés on his first journey to Tenochtitlán wrote some thirty years later about the events he saw. Bernal Díaz del Castillo is one of our main sources for recreating the history of the Conquest. His account also tells us about the Aztec's food and daily lives. In a celebrated paper, Sophie Coe[19] compared two meals that Bernal Díaz witnessed. One was an ordinary meal taken by Moctezuma in 1520, and the other was a banquet put on by the Viceroy of New Spain in the same place, only now called Mexico City, in 1538. Nothing served to show better what was happening to food and foodstuffs in Mexico. He describes a meal composed of wattled fowl, pheasants, native partridges, quail, domestic and wild ducks, deer, peccary, reed birds, doves, hares, and rabbits, among other native animals. Coe supposes, on very good grounds, that these were cut into small pieces and served in a chile-flavored sauce. There were more than two thousand jars of chocolate as well as fruit without end. As he ate, Moctezuma was served by two very graceful women who made *tortillas* kneaded with eggs and other nourishing ingredients. The *tortillas* were very white, as was another kind of bread that was made like long rolls and kneaded in another manner with additional ingredients in it. He also ate a kind of wafer called *pan pachol*. Whether it was baked crisply or fried, as the Spanish would have done it, is not known.

In contrast, the banquet of 1538 was a blowout in the grand medieval tradition. In a condensed form, the menu included salads, roasted kids and hams, pies made of quail and doves, stuffed fowl and chickens, *blancmange* (pudding made with almond milk), *tortas*, chicken, native partridges, and quail in vinegar (*escabeche*). That was the first course! The next had many pies made of birds, game, and fish (none were eaten, but done for show), and cooked lamb, beef, and pork with turnips, cabbages, and garbanzos. Fruit of many kinds came in the middle of the feast, followed by whole cooked native fowl with their beaks and feet silvered, whole ducks with gilt beaks, and heads of pigs, deer, and calves, for show. The diners also got courses of olives, radishes, and cheese as well as cardoons, and native fruit. Fountains of red and white wine flowed freely. As if all this were not enough, Díaz says that the lesser lights among the Spanish had whole roast young cattle stuffed with chickens, quail, doves, and bacon. Our witness and participant says that everyone ate to the point of bursting.

What does the comparison tell us? That the Spanish elite and would-be elite insisted upon eating European food, at least in official settings. Everyone wanted meat. The Europeans had come from a continent in which only the rich ate much meat (rather like the situation among the Aztecs), and now they wanted all they could get. Their pigs and cattle came right away; the first pork butchering operations in Mexico City were in place by at least 1525. Sweets were also imported quickly. (In this banquet, ladies were served several kinds.) Spanish landlords quickly set up sugar-growing and processing operations, and even imported African labor into Mexico to run them, as they, the French, and English had done in the Caribbean. Pies were a European standard and they required wheat flour, eggs, and butter for their crusts. Unless wheat was imported, then it was planted quite soon after the Conquest. There are many more conclusions to be drawn from this interesting comparison (including a glimpse into what seems to us to be the horrendous hodgepodge of a medieval banquet), but this much is clear: the Spanish intended to be as Spanish as possible in their new land.

There is a truism among historians that colonial societies retain more traits of the countries that founded them than remain in those countries' original homelands. That is certainly so among colonial elites in Mexico, as the 1538 banquet shows. There are no native dishes on the menu—only native Mexican ingredients prepared in European ways. Mexican cookery, then, still retains some of the medieval Spanish practices. Throughout the Colonial period there was good cookery, and it passed down the social ladder into ordinary homes, especially in cities. What are some of these old ways? One is the great amounts of spices and herbs used to prepare certain dishes, particularly meats. The kinds of spices used, cinnamon, for instance, is also a tip-off. Few European dishes utilize this spice except for desserts. (Our apple pie is thoroughly medieval.) Thickening agents routinely included breadcrumbs, based on a technique used by the first star European chef, Taillevant, at the end of the fourteenth century. This practice remained current until the seventeenth or eighteenth centuries. (We use *roux* or vegetable starches today.) *Adobo*, vinegar-based sauces or marinades, are nothing less than the medieval standards mentioned previously: verjuice or eisel. Even the meats and the ways that they are cut for some dishes is antique: for example, the whole chunks of pork used for *carnitas*. Garlic and onions in everything. . . the kinds of cheeses routinely used in Mexico. . . these are but a few old Spanish ways that remain embedded in Mexican cookery. Once again, Mexican cuisine is a rich blend of the Old and New Worlds, but we should not forget the role that medieval Europe had in developing it. And, if there is one dish that demonstrates this fusion, it is *mole*. More on that later.

This being said, it would be instructive to know what the Spanish ate in ordinary meals when indigenous servant women did the cooking. They probably ate things we would recognize as Mexican food, such as European meats mixed with chile sauces on a corn *tortilla*. Perhaps this was so originally, but European plants and animals came to dominate the food scene. It has been estimated that of the roughly 250 plants cultivated in the New World, only forty-five are clearly indigenous. Those are crucial plants, as we have pointed out, but they are still relatively few compared to those eaten before the Spanish arrived. New World plants include wheat, rice, barley, oats, alfafa (these latter two for fodder), sugar cane, coffee (a later product), wine grapes, bananas, mangoes, peaches, oranges, lemons, chickpeas (garbanzos), onions, melons, apples, cilantro, basil, oregano, tarragon, thyme, chicory, cinnamon, cloves, pepper, nutmeg, anise, cumin, and many more. Some will be recognized as Arabic introductions to Spain. As for food animals, pigs (not our modern ones, but more like the wild razorbacks that now live in many parts of the Americas), cows, sheep, goats, and chickens remain at the foundation of the Mexican kitchen. The turkey, one of the few Mexican domesticates, went eastward to Europe and then returned to North America, where it has become the food symbol of one of our national holidays. European grasses, as well as other plants and animals, supplanted native species and colonized the Americas. The conquest was as much in the realms of botany and zoology as in anything else.

Not so incidentally, foods sent from the New World became major players in changing the basic cuisine of Spain. As Professor Freeman points out, products of the New World became increasingly central to the definition of Spanish cuisine. For instance, the *tortilla española* is made with potatoes (from Peru). Stuffed peppers are made with European techniques but by using Mexican plants. And what about the *gazpacho* with its tomato base? (The original was merely crumbled bread "soup.") There are many more examples, including especially the tomato, whose use may have spread via Spain. And we cannot leave out corn. It became a fodder crop for the famous Spanish pigs, as well as for poor folks, just as in other parts of the world. The influences running between Old Spain and New Spain were not all one way.

That the Spanish and their animals were a disaster for the indigenous peoples need hardly be said. The Spanish crown gave Cortés and his men *encomiendas*, large tracts of land with native villages on them. The Spanish landlords had absolute power over the subject peoples who paid them tribute in the form of labor, produce, or any other possessions of value. The Spanish abuse of the indigenous peoples was so appalling as to prevent its detailing. The legend of Spanish cruelty, the "Black Legend," has its foundation in reality. Several important churchmen such as Fray Bartolomé de Las Casas argued against *encomiendas*, to no avail, for the *encomienderos* were laws unto themselves. In fact, these plantations were familiar to the Spanish because they duplicated the system back home in Castilla, an essentially feudal estate. The *encomienda* system eventually declined at the end of the sixteenth century. But by then great damage had been done.

By the seventeenth century disease, atrocious working conditions, and overwork had destroyed much of the indigenous population. It is estimated that by 1700 only about 1 million native people survived from a population of about 11 million at the time of the Conquest. Huge cattle and sheep herds were allowed to trample the good arable land of the native farmers and they were denied water rights. Because it was impossible for them to live under this system, many *indigenas* retreated to poorer lands where they became dirt-poor farmers. Others moved to *haciendas*, which were essentially self-sufficient estates where they worked as share croppers.

Eventually Mexico recovered. By the eighteenth century the population began to grow again, only now there were an equal number of *mestizos* and Indians, with the Spaniards making up less than twenty percent of the population. By then, however, 200 years after Cortés, Mexico had become a new society, something we can recognize as modern. The outlines of its cuisine had been set and needed only a few more additions to fill out what is today's complete picture. Indeed, by 1800 Mexico was ready to become a nation. . . but that is a later story.

To provide an example of cross-Atlantic influences, our friend, the eminent Spanish (Andalusian) chef and restaurateur Emilio Gervilla, gave us a recipe that he thought showed elements of archaic Spanish country cooking with New World additions. It is a bean dish rather like the classic southern French dish. There are tomatoes, of course, and beans. In pre-Columbian times the beans would have been broad beans: *favas*. Navy and all other varieties were American domesticates.

Cassoulet

2	T.	olive oil
1	t.	chopped garlic
1		small onion, chopped
1		small carrot, diced
2		fresh ripe tomatoes, seeded and chopped
4	oz.	boneless shoulder lamb, cubed
4	oz.	boneless pork shoulder, cubed
1	lb.	navy beans
2		quarts chicken or veal stock
4		whole duck legs
4		small pork sausages (Spanish *chorizo*, if you can find it, is most authentic)
		salt and freshly ground pepper, to taste
		breadcrumbs mixed with butter, for topping

Heat the olive oil in a large heavy skillet or Dutch oven. Add the garlic, onion, carrots, and tomatoes and sauté for a few minutes, until the onion turns transparent. Add the lamb, pork, beans, and stock. Salt and pepper to taste. Bring the liquid to a boil. Reduce heat, cover, and simmer for 1-½ hours, or until beans are just tender. Add duck legs and sausage, cover, and simmer for about 1 hour, until legs are tender and done. Adjust seasonings. Pour *cassoulet* into a casserole and top with the breadcrumb mixture. Place under preheated broiler and brown. Serve at once.   *Serves 4*

Once the Spaniards settled into their new domains, both their genes and foods mixed with the native peoples'. The following recipe is one of many illustrations of this point. Consider the ingredients. Red beans and *guajillo* chiles are native. The kinds of garlic and onions used in Mexico are European, but there were and are native versions that were used in prehispanic cookery. Old World oregano took root in Mexico, developing into a number of varieties with different flavors. *Chorizo*, Mexican sausage, has its roots deep in Europe, where sausage-making traditions date to prehistory. Pork is from across the Atlantic and the hot spicing is native. Then there is the *tequila* or *mezcal*. It is the juice of the Mexican *maguey (agave)* plant used by the indigenous peoples to make a fermented drink. The Spaniards brought distilling with them, applied it to *maguey*, and Mexico's most famous beverage was born. This bean dish, which might be considered a kind of Mexican *cassoulet*, is truly *mestizo*. The recipe is prepared in three stages—beans, *chorizo*, and *adobo*.

Frijol de Novios

(Sra. Fausta Guevara, Chilapa, Guerrero)

2	C.	dried red beans, soaked (see directions on p. 244)
3/4		small onion, sliced
2		bay leaves
1/4	lb.	*chorizo* (Mexican sausage), removed from its casing and crumbled
1/4		onion, chopped
1	T.	olive or canola oil
1		*guajillo* chile, toasted, soaked, deveined, and seeded
1/4		small onion
1		clove garlic, finely chopped
1-1/2	t.	finely chopped fresh oregano
1/2	t.	*mezcal* or *tequila*
		a pinch of chopped fresh oregano
		kosher salt to taste
1/2	C.	*queso fresco*, grated, or ricotta cheese

To prepare the beans:

Place the soaked beans, 3/4 of an onion, and bay leaves in a large pan with enough water to cover them plus 1 inch. Bring to a boil, then reduce to a simmer. When almost done, add kosher salt to taste. Remove the beans from the pan, reserving some of the liquid, and place them in the bowl of a food processor. Purée, adding reserved liquid as necessary to create a fine sauce.

To *prepare the* adobo:

Soak *guajillo* chiles together with $1/4$ of an onion and garlic in warm water for 10–15 minutes. Drain and place them, together with the oregano, in the bowl of a food processor and purée. Blend in *tequila* or *mezcal*. If more water is needed to achieve the right consistency, use reserved chile water.

To *prepare the* chorizo:

Heat 1 tablespoon of oil in a deep, heavy skillet. Add $1/4$ of an onion and *chorizo* and sauté until the *chorizo* is cooked through and the onions are lightly browned. Remove from the skillet. Add 1 teaspoon of oil to the skillet. Pour in the bean purée and the *adobo*. Sauté gently until the mixture bubbles up and begins to get crusty on the bottom. Taste and add salt to taste. Move the pan back and forth, flipping over the beans until all sides become somewhat crusty. Remove from the pan and place on a serving dish. Sprinkle oregano and cheese on top. Serve with the *chorizo* and onions in a separate bowl. To eat mix, the *chorizo* and bean mixture on individual plates.   *Serves* 4

3

TAXCO

The Journey to Taxco

"Just over the hills surrounding Acapulco we entered the arid interior of the state." —from the documentary "Hidden Mexico"

"¡*Basta*!" the crew cried in unison. "Enough history!" We had climbed into two large Chevrolet Suburbans that the tourism authorities had laid on for us. Mercifully, the cars were air-conditioned, since the temperature was ninety-plus degrees as we drove up into the hills above Acapulco. Our next destination was to be Taxco, where we would shoot Easter celebrations. Looking down on the superb coastline, Jan yelled for the drivers to stop. This is how we have always shot when on the road. When something scenic or material to the program's direction came into sight, whatever drivers we had were required to stop. Most were happy to do so—it was a welcome break from dodging Mexican trucks, anyway—and they often gave suggestions for subjects to the cameramen. Unfortunately, shooting like this is time consuming, but it's a necessary process. These particular drivers were not so keen on stopping at every hilltop and were certainly not pleased to have to obey a woman "boss." But Jan has never been one to suffer opposition when she is convinced of the justice of her cause. So, we often stopped. . . and discovered some interesting things.

Our first destination was Chilpancingo, the capital of Guerrero. We got onto the brand-new expressway connecting Acapulco to Mexico City that happens to pass through the city we intended to visit. We had arranged beforehand to have the toll taken care of because we were told that the cost from end to end is about $70! Needless to say, the road was virtually empty of vehicles, so we zoomed along on a highway that looks like any U.S. Interstate route. As we learned from other more twisting and circuitous roads in central Guerrero, this one may have been a little dull, but it saved more than time—it also saved our breakfasts!

We emerged at Chilpancingo just in time for a trip to—where else?—the market and the artisans' shop. Bob Ward, our expert in the arts and crafts of Guerrero, knew the shop well and told us that it would give us a good overview of what the village artists of the state could do. Chilpancingo, with a population of about 70,000, is not a tourist magnet, except for visitors interested in seeing the state capital, the university, or the locations we visited. Anthropologists find the place of greater interest because the small city is the center for many indigenous towns and villages in central Guerrero. The capital serves as the center for the ethnological work being in the region.

Unprepossessing as it may seem, Chilpancingo did play a role in the story of Mexican nationhood. In 1813, during the struggle for independence from Spain, the leader of the rebel forces, José María Morelos y Pavón pulled together a congress of patriots in Chilpancingo. The group set forth a declaration of independence and would have written a constitution, but Spanish troops arrived and captured the town. The congress moved to the nearby village of Apatzingán, where the first of a number of Mexican constitutions was agreed upon by the delegates. It was, incidentally, modeled on the first French Republic rather than the United States. It was never put into effect, however, for not long afterward Morelos was captured and executed, thus passing into well-deserved glory in Mexico's official mythology of nationhood. Today, nothing but murals in a public building hint at Chilpancingo's heroic past.

We were there for less heroic reasons and so dived into the market located near the city center. It looked like any other such place in Mexico: a warren of retail stands more or less divided into areas of specialty. The market's interior was designed to be cooler than the outside temperatures, although this was not enough to prevent the odors of aging meat and fish in the relevant sections. There were, however, products and preparations we had not seen before. Dudley, spying all sorts of interesting things, began dragging the camera crew and me to first one stand, then another. We walked to a stand at the market's entrance. The López family had large displays of flowers. To us they resembled ordinary flowers, but Dudley said they were something else. A display of bright yellow marigolds interested us. "*Cempaxuchitl,*" said Mrs. Lopez. Dudley knew that these were the famous pre-Columbian "flowers of four hundred petals" that were used in many rituals. They always appeared on tombs and on altars dedicated to departed ancestors and in rituals tied to the corn harvests. They still are, said Dudley, adding that they are also fed to chickens to make their egg yolks yellow. We were to see them again during the Easter celebrations in Taxco.

Next to the flowers was a charcoal brazier on which large ears of corn were roasting. This treat, called *ezquites,* is found wherever Mexicans gather. The roasted ears are eaten from the hand and flavored with lime, chopped *epazote,* and crushed *pequín* (hot) chiles. Dudley had to have one, since he regarded it as his obligation to eat everything, and everyone else sampled some as well. *Ezquites* bears only a superficial resemblance to our corn on the cob: the corn is the large-kerneled variety that Mexicans favor, not sweet but starchy, and is prepared highly seasoned. Apart from the lime, this is no doubt what shoppers in the great market at Tenochtitlán, or a much earlier Teotihuacán for that matter, ate while strolling among the vendors.

Making salsa

The Chilpancingo market was loaded with neatly stacked piles of fruit, including some varieties we had not seen before. *Tejocotes* (they look like a small apple, have a sour-apple flavor, and are used in preserves), *chirimoya* (the delicious green-skinned, sweet-sour fruit), its close cousin the *guanaba*, locally grown *granadas* (pomegranates), *nanches* (similar to a small yellow cherry), and many more were in abundance. One fruit was particularly intriguing. It looked like a small bean covered in a cotton-like fiber, something like cotton candy. Upon opening one up, Dudley smiled with pleasure, calling it *huamuchitl*, or "small cotton fruit." It turned out to be very sweet and very delicious. Later, we stopped along the road at some trees that were loaded with them and gathered some for the rest of the trip. That is how common *huamuchitl* is in Guerrero.

Dudley navigated through the market, and the crew, with camera and equipment in hand, followed closely. He had discovered the *fonda* section and searched it in hopes of finding iguana. There was none, but we did find a neat little *fonda* run by Elena Alia. It looked like many others: a tiled counter, a few chairs, a barrel-shaped fire receptacle covered with a flat metal plate or *comal*, and a small work surface. What made this *fonda* different was the *masa* (corn dough) she used: blue. We knew Mexican farmers grow many colors of corn, but it was still something of a surprise to see blue corn *quesadillas*. They are something we North Americans usually associate with New Mexico. Here they were filled with pumpkin blossom, *epazote*, and the wonderfully textured Oaxaca string cheese. Lively and cheerful before the camera, the cook patted out the *tortillas* by hand, quickly toasted them on her *comal*, filled each with the mixture, folded each *quesadilla* over, and finally fried them in oil. Served with very tasty red (*guajillo*, of course) and spicy green (*tomatillo*) sauces, these *quesadillas* had both visual and savory appeal.

By now Bill Goldman and Bob Ward, our art experts, were anxious to get on to the *Casa de las Artesanías* to examine the latest regional artisans' works. Bob knew the director, who promised to give us a tour of the shop. There are shops such as these all over Mexico; some are government-owned, others are privately run. The staffs regularly go out to villages and collect the artisans' work for sale. The shops are good venues for artists and villagers whose work might not reach wider audiences. Marisela Miranda took us through the large store. The place held wonderful things, from hand-carved furniture to masks, pottery, *rebozos* (shawls) and other village-made clothes, and especially lacquerware from Olinalá and the villages near it. As we examined window cases filled with it: intricately decorated wooden boxes, trays, dishes, and even large trunks. Bill, who knows the art well, explained how they are made.[1] Pine and a local sweet wood called *linaloé* are carved into whatever the vessel will be. The piece is then coated with two layers of different colored lacquers and allowed to dry. Designs are then etched into the piece with a thin stylus or needle and the surrounding layers are shaved off. The result are designs in relief with subtle mixtures of color and interesting natural and geometric designs. Lacquer work was done in pre-Columbian days and was used mainly for gourds that held liquids. The technique used in Olinalá is partly ancient and also part of an evolving set of artisan techniques. Needless to say, the mad shoppers among us—Dudley, Bill, and Bob—had to have the best and most original designs they could find. Bob hesitated a little in this section because he had spied some of the masks that he loves and knew that later on he would get even more of them from one of the best artists in the state.

One mask was that of the tiger. A jaguar in reality, this ritual figure dates back to Olmec times. Today it remains important in village dances. One of the most famous village dances held in Mexico is in the Guerrero village of Acatalán. We had hoped to go there and have the villagers recreate the dance for us. (It was the wrong time of year.) Having failed to get it arranged from Chicago, we hoped that Marisela could do it. It turned out that she could not, but she did help us arrange for something special, a meeting with a friend of Bob, a fabulous mask carver, and a tour of his village, Xalitla.

We left Chilpancingo and headed north toward Taxco. The landscape was ever more desert like as scenes of dry river beds, dried brush, dead trees, and cacti surrounded us. Then, just at the side of the road to the right, we saw two old huts near a spectacular stand of candelabra cactus. Down to the left below the road was a wide scree of pebbles left by a desiccated branch of the Río Balsas. In unision, almost, all of us yelled to the drivers to stop. One driver looked puzzled and began to speak, but Jan and Dave were not listening to anyone: the vistas were too good. Camera at the ready, we leapt out to inspect the scene. The huts looked wonderful—the perfect place for an on-camera discussion of peasant huts. The whole thing looked like a set from a spaghetti western, lacking only "the man with no name" appearing before our very eyes. We had wanted to shoot something like this in Acapulco at the squatters' shacks, and now we had the chance.

First, Jan, Dave, and Ralph headed into the cacti. These were giants, their multiple arms held close to their bodies and stretching up as if in prayer. Such a large stand made it appear like a deliberate plantation. As usual, shooting took a long time and the rest of us stood perspiring in the dry heat. Meanwhile, I explored the huts. They were crudely constructed of woven branches with poles for uprights and roof braces. A few clay pots hung by wire from several crossbeams, and on a crude wooden table stood a few cracked pottery cups. In one corner there was a clay cookstove measuring about four feet long and about two across. It had a firepit on one side, an open space on the long side for stoking, and an open firehole on top. Ashes remained in the pit and a metal plate, the ever-present *comal*, lay ajar at the top. The stove was exactly the kind found in any village house, or even in any prehistoric village. What a find! This hut was obviously used by cattle herders in the post-rainy season when there would be enough grass to feed their stock. It was a perfect model of a house in an early farming village. The crew returned and we shot the scene, making the same observations on camera, for a segment on continuities in village life that we like to put into documentaries.

Just as we were getting into our vehicles to resume the journey, two large tourist busses pulled off the road near us. A stream of mostly middle-aged people speaking German emerged and promptly marched up into the cactus patch. What was this, we asked, the site of a tourist location? "Oh," replied one of the drivers, "I was going to tell you that this *is* a tourist attraction. . . . It was a set for some Cantinflas movies!" So much for the on-camera discussion of the place! I argued that even though it had been a set, it was used by real herders now, but to no avail. At least we got scenes of the dried river bed and the scorched country.

We drove on through the fairly level terrain that is part of the Balsas "depression," past the town of Iguala, where the first effective declaration of Mexican independence was signed in 1821. The first Mexican flag was made here as well. For travelers, Iguala is merely a large traffic rotary on the highway to Taxco. Traveling north, we began to ascend into the volcanic mountains. The road twisted and turned, dipping into small valleys then ascending ever higher. We passed old Taxco, a small early settlement, and finally, as we climbed to the top of another mountain, there crowning it was Taxco. After a long, hot day, we were delighted to arrive.

Taxco is a small city, really, with about 40,000 inhabitants, and is now promoted by the country's tourism board as one of the country's better preserved colonial cities. It is a national monument by federal decree. Taxco has an interesting history to go with that designation. When the Spaniards first came in 1529 to Taxco, or a small town near the current location, it was already occupied by Nahuatl speakers, who called it either "small hill" or "place where the ballgame is played." (No ballcourt has been found yet.) The Spanish had come under orders from Hernan Cortés, looking for metals, and they eventually found huge veins of silver. By 1534 engineers had built a mining works that included an aqueduct, a water wheel, and a smelter. Ruins of the original aqueduct—old arches—still stand along the road to Mexico City. After being deserted for some years when the first silver lode was exhausted, Taxco had its first revival in 1743 when Don José de La Borda, a Spanish miner, discovered another immense vein. Borda became commensurately wealthy and spent his fortune creating fine buildings, in particular the Cathedral of Santa Prisca. The mines brought many other fortune-seekers who were responsible for most of the now-picturesque buildings in the city. Needless to say, most of the labor in the mines was provided by the indigenous peoples and *mestizos* who lived in small villages in the vicinity. But, once again, the silver ran out and Taxco's fortunes sank. Then, in 1932, William Spratling, a North American professor with a love for Mexico, came to town. The United States ambassador at the time, Dwight Morrow, had planted the idea of reviving silver work in this once-major silver-producing center. He did just that, and before long factories and shops sprang up everywhere, numbering at least 300 today. With all the new silverwork shops, Taxco has become a tourist attraction. On almost any day tourist buses make their ponderous way into the city to disgorge hordes of customers who come, buy, and mostly leave. Few foreigners stay for the real life of Taxco—the religious life we had come to see.

Taxco is every bit as picturesque and quaint as guidebooks say. Built on a 5000-feet-plus mountain top, it is all cobblestones, narrow streets, and small squares. Houses and commercial buildings, most with balconies, line the streets, and many are several hundred years old at the least. Our vehicles wound their way through the narrow streets amid crowds of people who were beginning to celebrate *Santa Semana*, or Holy Week. That night the masses would be said in the parish churches of Santa Prisca and San Sebastián, followed by a Procession of the Virgins to be presided over by an image of the Virgin of the Nativity. That image, taken from Taxco's church of the Virgin of Guadalupe, is the symbol of the common people of Mexico and is much older than the arrival of Christianity in the country. We were to learn more about its religious history that very night.

Our hotel turned out to be completely charming. It was the Hotel Los Arcos in Juan Ruíz Alarcón, just a short distance from the small *zócalo* that stands before the city's cathedral of Santa Prisca. It is three stories and is built around an open courtyard that is decorated simply with plants. Built in the early seventeenth century, the hotel was originally a convent. Like so many other *ex-conventos* in Mexico, it was secularized during one of the several periods of Mexican history when Church properties were confiscated by the state. The rooms are plainly furnished with good local wooden furniture and are quite comfortable. Evidently, the place has been undergoing renovation for some years and the work was still in progress when we were there. The dining room was not in operation, so we had to find our morning coffee elsewhere, in the nearby market as it turned out. Since Los Arcos is close to the center of town, we were well located for shooting the many processions. Unfortunately, right around the corner behind the hotel, in a wide space at the junction of two streets, a new bar had been opened. . . playing ultra-loud disco music well into the night. How the Taxco authorities allowed that during Holy Week puzzled us, but we were told that there was little they could do to a private business. Since no one ever seemed to be in the place, though, all of us looked forward to its eventual demise. Ah, the joys of free enterprise!

Our first night in Taxco gave us an introduction to some of the meanings behind the processions we were going to see. Dinner had been arranged at a restaurant named Los Balcones that was located in a little plaza near the city center, the Plazuela de los Gallos. The dining room was on the second floor with, of course, windows opening onto small balconies. From there we witnessed the first of many processions. Dinner began with a Taxco specialty, the "Berta," a drink invented by the local bar of that name. It is something like a margarita and is made with lime juice and tequila, with honey substituting for orange liqueur. In some versions, grenadine is added. We all needed one at that point. The next course was the best of the evening, *sopa fabada*, a soup made from dried lima beans, the Mexican version of *crème fraiche*, bechamel, and lots of cilantro. The rest of the meal was more mundane, but very Spanish—roast loin of pork stuffed with raisins, garlic, and almonds. Carol mused aloud that the dish seemed Arabic in origin. "Quite so," we historians replied.

By the time the meal ended, about 10:30 P.M., the first procession was passing along the street beneath us. A man we thought was one of the restaurant's owners joined us as we packed the balconies. When we returned inside, he introduced himself as Dr. Rodolfo Juárez Castro, not a restaurateur, but the brother and son of the proprietors. A large, serious man with a good sense of humor and halting but good English, he asked what we were doing in Taxco. Informed of the project, he asked if we would like more information on folklore and its relationships to indigenous foodstuffs. We said we would and he explained that he was an ethnopsychiatrist who worked at Taxco's Adolfo Prieto Hospital and also in Chilpancingo, with indigenous groups in the state: Nahuas, Zapotecs, Tlapenec, Zamusgos, and others. His work involved a fascinating mixture of psychology, anthropology, medicine, art and literature, culinary practices, folklore, history, and religion. In short, he knew a very great deal about the inner lives of the peoples among whom he worked, and, because he had been raised in a culinary household, about how food related to everything he was studying. All of us were riveted by his accounts and, drinking a few more Bertas, we listened intently. Dr. Juárez Castro began with comments on the foods we had seen.

Cuisine, he declared, has no beginning or end; it is continuous, a living thing, filled with action and movement, as are all components of any culture.

Cuisine is an art form related to others such as storytelling and the graphic and plastic arts. The same women who cook at home, who think about flavors and ingredients, also make and decorate pots. All are expressions of culture. Perhaps, then, eating such food is a way of experiencing other conceptions of the world. Pre-Columbian people thought so because to them all food had a ritual and religious meaning. More about this later, said our informant.

"When it comes to Guerrero," our new friend said, "I think that we have a generic pattern in our foods, in spite of the fact that the state is so varied in its environments—both coast and mountain." He went on to enumerate corn as the most important food, then beans, vegetables, and different Mexican herbs, some that are found nowhere else. Guerrero, he said, has more than 6,000 indigenous communities so that, despite a certain uniformity, there is an enormous and rich culinary heritage, just as arts and crafts differ from people to people and from village to village.

All the indigenous peoples ate, and still do consume, fish, rabbit, armadillo, chicken, doves, and *pijije* (a small bird). Of course, *pozoles* and *clemole*, or "pot *moles*," are old standards. So popular is *pozole* that it has been institutionalized. From the coast to the mountains, from village to city, *pozole* is a traditional social ritual in two ways and on two days. The first is something everyone knows: Thursday is *pozole* day. We had already discovered this when asking for the dish in Chilpancingo; none was to be found, because it wasn't a Thursday. So, this ritual is about the family at home eating a traditional food. The second *pozole* day is not so well known. In the real back country villages, there is little sense of the modern calendar or even of modern clock time. Life's rhythms are of nature and farming. Therefore after a long week of daily hard work, Saturday evening is for *pozole*. That tradition might be pre-Columbian, but was more likely created in the Christian era when people had to learn that Sunday was the day of rest and prayer.

Guerrero has two types of *pozole*, green and white, the lecture continued. Green *pozole* is made with *pipián*, or pumpkin seeds, which give it the consistency and texture of green *mole*. White *pozole* is more characteristic of Guerrero. The difference between this preparation and those of other states, said Dr. Juárez Castro, is that "we" use onion, pork skins, avocado, lime, oregano, and diced chile as condiments for the basic dish. Incidentally, Dr. Juárez Castro warned us, when making this dish using dried hominy (not canned), leave the "head" of the corn ear in because it has been proved to be of value by the Nutritional Institute of Mexico. (This is more or less akin to leaving the skins on many fruits and vegetables to add to their nutritional value.) Since pork was introduced by the Spanish, the best *pozole* is cooked with pig's head, something that is found in all of Guerrero's markets but is not so common in other region's markets. Pig heads have many uses in traditional cookery, such as brains for *Tacos con sesos*, which are excellent when made with onions, chopped fresh peppers, *epazole*, and good crispy shells. For that matter, pig brains give a good flavor to *pozole* as well. (We did not test this assertion, but Dudley and I agree that calf and lamb brains are eaten for texture, not flavor; perhaps pigs, being far more intelligent animals, have more tasty organs of thought.)

"Pigs were among Spain's greatest contributions to the Americas," Dr. Juárez Castro went on. "We use every part of the pig. The head serves not only as a condiment, but also as the main flavoring ingredient. In some parts of Europe they use the pig's head for sausages and many other cold meats, but here in Guerrero we prepare the whole pig because we have to share it with the whole town. When we cook pig, it is a tradition with social significance. This is another culinary manifestation. The pigskin can be sun-dried for at least two days to acquire just the right consistency when it is fried for *chicharrón*. The kidneys can also be well prepared with *mezcal*, and the pig's feet are also very good prepared à la vinaigrette. And, oh, did I tell you that when eating *pozole*, the first thing on the table is a good *mezcal*, which can be white or sour. The sour *mezcal* is aged and infused with *damiana*. *Damiana* is an aphrodisiac with medicinal values. We drink this *mezcal* with sea salt and *lima rey*, which is a greener lime than the others." Dr Juárez Castro had said all that without taking a breath. By then, we had all tried a *mezcal*, or two.

"You know, there are other things we eat that North Americans don't or, at least, hardly ever do. Have you tried them yet?" Dr. Juárez Castro asked. He mentioned iguana, turtle (some of us knew turtle soup, at least) and something really unusual, the pijije bird. This small bird inhabits a region of the Guerrero coast called the Costa Chica. Their season is from September to March, before they migrate and after the corn harvest. When the corn is taken in, the tiny birds descend on the fields to scavenge what ears might have been left. The unlucky ones are caught in nets and prepared for cooking. The birds are not eviscerated or plucked, simply covered in clay, then set into a bed of burning charcoal for at least one-half hour. When they are done, the clay cover is cracked open and the birds are served with fresh cheese and *tacos de frijoles*. No other seasoning is used because cooking in clay seals all the juices, especially the bird's salty blood. Dudley, who had eaten the dish, agreed with the ethnogourmet that *pijije* cooked this way are delicious. Too bad we were too late in the season for them, since Dr. Juárez Castro told us that it was the great dish of the higher sierra regions. On the coast, iguana fills the same function, though it is not cooked the same way. Iguana is prized not only for its meat, but for its blood, the drinking of which, folklore holds, makes people very strong and resistant to disease.

"Would you care to visit Los Balcones's second floor?," Dr. Juárez Castro asked. Several of us who had survived the rigors of the day followed our host. The second floor was a large glassed-in area that gave us a panoramic view of Taxco. The city's hilltop topography is such that many houses have similar views from their upper floors. Above us spread a vast carpet of stars. A full moon, brighter in the clear dry air than I had ever seen it, illuminated a full sector of the sky. The setting gave an immediacy to our guide's magical mystery tour of religion and food, both past and present. "You know," he said, "that we Mexicans are the products of two great traditions, which we can see in religion, art, and gastronomy. It is all very complicated." (Later, he wrote this to us, paraphrasing Octavio Paz: "The history of Mexico is like men who search for their affiliation, their origin, successively Hispanic, Francophiles, Indigenes, some mixtures. . . and we cross the history like a comet of jade that from time to time lights the sky.")

"Like everything else in Mexico, it seems, religion finds expression in food, or the other way around. Easter time in Taxco is a perfect place to see it," Dr. Juárez Castro continued. "The Franciscans and Augustinians, Spanish monks who came to convert the indigenous peoples after the Conquest, took care to transform all the old deities. We may celebrate the Christian symbolism of the holy cross, but there is a secret within it, the indigenous ideas of the sacred. For example, on September 29th we celebrate the festival of San Miguel Alcalde on the same day as the ancient festival of the sun. We eat breads, marmalades, and especially corn boiled with salt. It is not salt, though; instead of regular salt, we use a thick block of a naturally salty mineral found in sandy and rocky terrains that gives the corn a dark color. The mineral is called *tequesquite* and comes from the central, higher zones of Guerrero. It has long been used by villagers, especially during the pre-Columbian times when access to salt from the coast was limited. Now *tequesquite* gives boiled corn an excellent flavor, particularly since we do not use butter in much of our cookery. The flavor comes from the mineral, *epazote*, chiles, and limes. That is all. Butter came from Spain, so here is an ancient food practice that appears in a Christian festival. But there is more. *Tequesquite* also means *Acatlicue*, or 'mother earth.' Salt, minerals, and corn come from the earth itself, the great mother, the ancient goddess."

We recalled the myth of Coatlicue enshrined at the great temple in Mexico City that we had visited on our first day in Mexico. Dr. Juárez Castro replied that, yes, it is all related to that. "Therefore," he concluded, "our cuisine is complex in more ways than flavors and textures, but in being the union of cultures." We would take this as our text when viewing the celebrations in Taxco and certainly when eating the special foods of the season.

"One last thing," Dr. Juárez Castro said pointing to the night sky, "natural phenomena, celestial objects—the sun and moon—were all pre-Columbian objects of worship, and this passes on down to modern folk practice." One of the most important of all the pre-Columbian gods was the feathered serpent, Quetzalcóatl, who was the god of spring renewal—of the rebirth of the growing season and the harbinger of the coming rains. Ancient Mesoamericans had many gods like him with similar attributes and all associated with the planet Venus. What became Easter was Quetzalcóatl's season. The Procession of the Virgins to Santa Prisca, Dr. Juárez Castro said, replicates prehispanic pilgrimages in honor of Quetzalcóatl. The god's color was green, like the planet; therefore, spring greens were eaten in his honor. *Epazote* and fresh amaranth were especially used, the first being a critical ingredient in Mexican cooking, particularly in the drier, less verdant uplands. Green amaranth remains the symbolic Easter dish, so consuming it is more than simple alimentation—it is an act connected to the sacred. The Spanish missionaries knew all about this—after all, the bread made in some parts of Mexico and given at Mass and Easter is Christian—and tolerated the use of these plants in folk practice.

As we heard this, Dudley and I had similar thoughts about Mexican food. First, this is one of few native cuisines in the world where green is so important. *Tomatillo* sauces are just one of many green dishes one finds in the Mexican kitchen. In fact, sometimes green food coloring is used to ensure that a sauce is green enough. Just then, we realized we could link the climate and landscape to this interest in green: a long dry season, then rains and a suddenly lush countryside, with any watered valley green in contrast to the tan-gray country around it. European cuisines of the sixteenth century, or even thereafter, hardly feature green coloring. Only certain vegetables are allowed their natural green color and it is usually a very deep green at that. (Spinach and deep green broccoli come to mind, although peas have a bright green hue.) The basic ideas behind green foods differ in the two traditions; one has to do with a relatively modern and "natural" idea about foods, and the other with a deep religious tradition.

If foods have religious significance, perhaps this is one explanation for two key elements of Mexican food and life. One is the preoccupation with food in and of itself and the varieties of subtle flavors and textures found in the cuisine. We have already noted how much of Mexican life centers on food—perhaps some of this has to do with its very ancient sacred qualities. The second proposition goes like this: a polytheistic religion means sundry deities, their manifestations represented by certain foods, so the varieties of food today might just represent the many displays of the sacred. Standing under the stars in just that place made this explanation seem reasonable.

It was well into the night when we finished with the wonderful Dr. Juárez Castro. We departed, weary, but now armed with information and new perceptions of the events that we had come to witness.

Among the many things Dr. Juárez Castro told were the names of the best cooks in Guerrero. He and others claim that title might go to residents of Chilapa, a town located in the mountains to the east of Chilpancingo. What makes its cookery good, our informant said, is that the dishes are more "authentic" than in other areas. One thing we would learn is that the recipes we got from that town were very much like a meal we had later on in Ameyaltepec at the house of Nicolás de Jesús. The following is something like the food we ate at that meal.

Chiliajo de Pollo

(Sra. Ofelia Apresa de Aguirre, Chilapa, Guerrero)

4		chicken thighs, cooked
7		*ancho* chiles, toasted, soaked, deveined, and seeded
6		*guajillo* chilies, toasted, soaked, deveined, and seeded
10		whole black peppercorns
1		whole clove
1		stick cinnamon
½	t.	chopped oregano
2		cloves of garlic
½	C.	bread crumbs
4	t.	canola oil
2	qts.	chicken broth (from the chicken thighs)
		kosher salt and freshly ground pepper, to taste

Place the chicken thighs in enough water to cover. Bring to a boil, reduce heat and simmer for 1 hour. Remove the chicken and drain and reserve the chicken broth. Toast chiles lightly using a frying pan or *comal*. Soak chiles in enough hot water to cover plus 1 inch for 10 minutes or until soft. After seeding and deveining, place the chiles in the bowl of a food processor or blender and purée. Grind peppercorns, clove, cinnamon, cloves, and oregano until fine, using a grinder or *molcajete*. Mix this into the chile purée. Heat canola oil in a deep, heavy skillet over medium heat. Add breadcrumbs and sauté until golden brown. Add the chile mixture and bring to a simmer. Simmer until the mixture reaches a medium consistency. Incorporate the chicken broth slowly, mixing well. When all is simmering, stir in the chicken pieces. Season with kosher salt and pepper to taste.   *Serves 4-6*

The Artists' Village of Xalitla

One of the reasons we had come to Taxco, apart from the Easter ceremonies, was to visit artists' villages south of the city including Ameyaltepec, home to a whole school of artists and our old friend Nicolás de Jesús. We had made arrangements to meet him there the next day. Today we would drive to the village of Xalitla to find one of the best mask makers in the state, Livorio Celestino. Dudley and I did not know him, though we had seen his work at Bob Ward's house. Based on that and Bob's strong recommendations, we had written him into the documentary's script. But first we had to find him. Livorio has a small farm in the village, but to make ends meet he works part time as a janitor in the classiest hotel in Taxco, the mountain-top Hotel Monte Taxco. Being an artist, though, he is also in the process of painting murals in the hotel. He was not in Taxco when we inquired, so we trundled into the vehicle provided by the state tourism authority and set out for Xalitla, back along the route to Acapulco.

Before leaving, we took inventory of ourselves and had some coffee. I, for one, cannot even think about moving in the morning without a dose of coffee. Since our hotel did not have a restaurant, we inquired at the desk where we might find some. The charming young women, definitely Nahua by the way, directed us to the nearby city market. Ralph and Dave had already found a place the night before, a bar called "L'Esquina de la Abuela." They had gone out to explore the city after our dinner at Los Balcones and became instant friends with the proprietors, whom they taught to play pinochle. Though neither knew Spanish, Ralph is a teacher of Italian, which is close enough to Spanish to make communication possible. The two are so congenial that everyone got along famously, and this contact would prove to be invaluable when we shot processions the several days later. Dave and Ralph did not know whether their new friends' café was open yet, so Dudley and I walked to the market for a little food shopping.

We found one of the more interesting markets we had come across, which we will discuss later. Passing through another labyrinth, we found our way to the *fonda* section, where a sunny dispositioned vendor, Señora Ruíz, stood before large enameled pots of *atole* and *café de olla*, or pot coffee. It is a version made with lots of brown sugar, cinnamon, and other spices, more of a dessert than one's usual morning eye opener. We got large containers of it for our colleagues anyway. The stand was next to the fresh baked goods stands, and we quickly bought *bolillos* (rolls made with a slightly sweetened bread dough), *pan dulce* (sweet breads with sugar sprinkled on top), and some of the crisp pastries that Mexicans love. Back in the hotel, all of us managed to get the coffee and baked goods down, though not gladly. Such sweet stuff was not the best way to start the kind of drive we were about to take.

Our vehicle was a Volkswagen bus made to seat eight people at the maximum. We were nine in number plus equipment. The only way to squeeze everyone in was to put one of us into a small space in the back, over the engine, where a shelf was normally. The only way to get into the slot was through the bus's back hatch. We all eyed one another, waiting for a victim to volunteer for the back. Finally, Dudley, in a fit of *machismo*, stepped forward. He thought that as a native he should be able to cope with anything the country had to offer. To date, he had not suffered any of the usual gastric distress associated with visits to Mexico.

Xalitla is only about thirty-five miles from Taxco, but mountains and winding two-lane roads make the journey much longer than a simple glance at the map suggests. Also, we were in Mexico, where the pace of life is considerably slower, as we discovered throughout our trip. By mid-morning the temperature had already reached into the 80s as we spiraled our way down a mountain and then up again. The bus, never highly powered to begin with, moved as if through gelatin with Edgardo, our driver, bashing the gear box to get the thing up hills, then barreling down hills, his brakes screeching with every application. We all held on, prayers on our lips. After a while, we began to hear moans from the cramped space in the rear. "Dudley, are you alright?" we asked. "I don't know," came the muffled reply from the rear. After some more rolling, rocking, and groaning, we inquired, "Dudley, what's the matter?" Then came the chilling reply: "I theeenk I'm going to be seeeek." "How sick?" Jan demanded. "I theeeenk I'm going to vomeeet." "Stop the bus!" we all shrieked in unison, nausea spreading among us like a miasma. Edgardo pulled over onto a wide part of the road in a swirl of dust. We had stopped under yet another hill, this one with a house on it. Our driver jumped from his seat, raced around to the back of the bus, and unlocked the door. Dudley staggered out, collapsed on the ground, and, I am loath to report, began to retch convulsively. At just that moment, a lanky brown dog raced down the hill, came right up to our friend and, as we watched in horror from the bus windows, began to eat Dudley's late breakfast. With some help, the chef staggered away from the point of his distress. Fortunately, we carried plenty of bottled water. With healthy swigs and a little rest, Dudley willingly climbed into the back and we made our way to Xalitla. All he could say about his misfortune was that he knew now why he would never eat a dog.

Xalitla turned out to be a village just off the main road. On the road's frontage there is a small general store and gasoline pump. Down an incline to the rear the village spread out below. One main dirt street running uphill and a couple of cross streets compose the thoroughfares. After buying a cold drink, we all walked down the slope toward the small post office/village center near the bottom of the main street. The houses are really small farmhouses: rectangular, mostly made of cinderblock, with roofed square porches. A blast of Mexican pop music assaulted us as we got to the top of the main street. There on a porch sat two teenagers blasting their boom box, no doubt to entertain their fellow villagers. As we walked to the bottom of the road, we noticed farm animals in house's fenced-in yards. The chicken-wire was hardly a barrier, since chickens and piglets scurried into the road, squawking and squealing respectively. Being very fond of pigs, I found it difficult not to tuck one of these little critters under my arm. Xalitla turned out to be an interesting rural community that was also connected to the outside world.

Marisela Miranda from the Casa de las Artesanías had arranged for one of her colleagues who worked with artists in the area's villages to meet us at Xalitla and introduce us to Livorio Celestino. The crew gathered at the post office, a small building with a counter window that was the appointed meeting place. Bill and Bob went off to the opposite end of the village where they knew of a workshop. We waited and waited as our director grew more and more impatient by the quarter hour. When our guide had still not shown up, Dudley and I remained behind at the post office while Jan, Dave, and Ralph went off to shoot some background scenery. We wanted to telephone Nicolás, whom we knew was in Ameyaltepec, to arrange for our meeting the next day. Village telephones work in interesting ways. Most have just one, at the post office. When a call comes in, whoever is in the post office takes it and then summons the party in question via loudspeaker. That is why we had to wait at the post office to talk with Nicolás his village has the same system. While we waited, an old man sat down on the bench located at the post office's entrance. Dudley and he fell into conversation. We soon discovered that Roberto de la Cruz was himself a painter; indeed, he is one of the originals of the school that had grown up around Ameyaltepec. He is originally from Ameyaltepec but lives in Xalitla because he married a woman from there. De la Cruz had learned to paint in his home village, originally on pottery, and then on the special paper they developed when the painting tradition began in the 1960s. The same paper is used to this day. Later, after moving to Xalitla, de la Cruz and Nicolás's father, also an eminent painter, taught the people of Xalitla how to do this style of painting. That, he said, is how Xalitla became part of the *amate* painters school. Would we care to see some of his work, he asked. Yes, indeed, we replied, as soon as everyone returns.

De la Cruz began to tell us about the history of the local villages and mentioned that Xalitla's real name is Xalatlán, "the place where there is water and sand." At that point everyone returned. Bill and Bob went off with Señor de la Cruz to see his work, some of which, they reported, was quite interesting but they, for once, refrained from buying any. We still waited for our guide, but the pitying postmistress had sent a message to the Celestino house and one of his daughters turned up. Her father happened to be in the fields, and she said she would take the crew to him. We all agreed that we should have shots of Livorio the farmer as a background to his artistic work. The three took the bus and set off for the fields, promising to return soon. They did, three hours later. Meanwhile, Carol, Dudley, and I waited expectantly at the small general store. When they finally returned they were full of moans, groans, and sunburn. It turned out that the fields were about a two-mile hike in 100-degree temperatures from where they parked. But what they got on tape was worth the wait and the effort of getting it.

Livorio's farm is right along a branch of the Río Balsas. But after months of drought, the river was only a shadow of itself. Livorio's dog splashed in the shallow stream as Livorio drank from the precious current. He is a fine-looking middle-aged man, bronzed, with graying hair brushed backward. In the documentary he is seen cutting a channel into the earth from the stream to his fields and orchards. It is a simple water supply system, the oldest type known, but water is so scarce that he can irrigate only once every eight days. He and his wife walked through their orchard, filled with mangos and limes, cutting branches and harvesting. Other shots, just a hundred yards away, showed something different: dry land, scrawny cattle (the cattle everywhere were the boniest I had ever seen), donkeys, and turkeys. It was all vivid testimony to the value of water in the dry lands and those scenes from the documentary linger in the mind.

A couple of days later, Livorio came into Taxco for a session where we taped him actually carving a mask. As he carved, he spoke in his native Nahuatl to tell us what he was doing. He then held up some of the finished masks that he had brought. His masks are used in traditional village dances. Most of them represent *nahuales*, or were-animals, people who have taken on animal spirits. Some of these spirits are good, others bad. We later saw many illustrations of *nahuales* in paintings at Ameyaltepec; they represent popular beliefs in rural areas. Livorio held up one mask, then another; most were "little animals," or *caltzín* as he called them, "figures that come from my ancestors." First a fox face, then a narrow-nosed wolf, a bat ("bloodsucker," he said), a lizard, a cat with spots (*mistón*, which "comes from my mother, a dance for my mother and the Virgin of Guadalupe—from this village"), an old man ("my father, he was ninety years old"), a *burro*, and a little dog ("that protects against *nahuales*"). Of all the animals, the *tigre*, really a jaguar, that Livorio carved for us on camera is the most powerful animal spirit of all. . .

The kitchen

and has been since at least Olmec times. The masks are gorgeous, not because they are brightly painted or even elaborately carved, but because of their power, a force that grows from the simplicity of form and dark subtlety of the coloring. What Livorio does comes from the heart of a village life that runs deep in Mexican history. Need it be said that when he was finished, all of us bought up every mask he had, including the unfinished one, a rare find.

After we had finished with the farm shots, our long-awaited guide finally appeared. He apologized profusely, saying that he had been away from home when the message came and had rushed over upon hearing that we were in the village. We walked through town, up the main street to the very end, with Pablo Nicolás. He told us that he had been to Chicago for an exhibit of his and other *amate* artists' work at Marshall Field's department store. When there, he had stayed with his good friend Nicolás de Jesús from Ameyaltepec, who was living in Chicago at the time. Did we know him? When we told Pablo that this was the person we had come to see, he quickly invited us into his house and offered us some snacks. Seeing that here was an opportunity to shoot a typical village house, we agreed and walked into the kitchen. It was made in two parts, one small area with a table for sitting and eating indoors and an open area where a *molcajete* rested on the dirt floor. The sink and water pipe were outdoors. Nearby, the family pigs and chickens foraged in the yard. Señora Nicolás quickly made a *salsa* by blanching some tomatoes, chiles, and onion on her small stove. She peeled the tomatoes, threw everything into the *molcajete* together with some garlic and cilantro, and ground them all up. Naturally, we had to shoot the process because it was the first time we had seen it, although we would again, many times. For taste and texture, this is the best technique for creating sauces.

We then moved on to Pablo's workshop, where he was working on a large painting. It was in the style we had come to expect of the region—a native style, with figures in solid outline blocks of bright colors, and floral or geometric borders. As the artist painted, he described the scene's meaning. There was a village and its surroundings, where we see people working hard in their fields. Some were bringing food made by women who worked in home kitchens making *tortillas*. We also see people going to church to leave offerings to the saints. Near the center were three sick people, two of them in bed. Witches or medicine women attended the patients with herbs and spells for their recovery. In the lower left people were depicted assuming animals' shapes, for they are *nauhuales*, the spirit animals. The explanation was that people can become ill through the evil doings of bad animal spirits. The cure is counteraction: to summon up good animal spirits to combat the harmful ones. With the help of secret formula of herbs and roots, the good spirits can cure the ill. How can these spirit animals be seen, we asked. Pablo replied that medicine women and men have visions or trances in which they can see the person (whose spirit has become a *nahuale*) or the external spirit who is responsible for the problem. Hearing this story, Livorio Celestino's masks once more came to life. Clearly, the masks were used in dances that had to do with good and evil spirits and with people turning into the animals that represented those spirits. Once again, we were seeing ancient themes carried through into our own time—if these villages truly are in our time.

We then walked down the street to the workshop that Bob and Bill had found earlier in the day. It was basically a wooden shed in which Ramiro Nava Larios, another mask maker and general woodcarver, worked. A large workbench stood in the center and the rest of the space was filled with raw materials, pottery, and gear of all kinds; in short, it was a real workshop. He had finished carving a large crucifix which he was in the process of painting in pinkish flesh tones. Nava explained that the piece had been commissioned for the festivities in Taxco and would be carried in the big procession on Thursday night. We decided to shoot that as well. His creations and various pieces from other villages covered the walls. And there, standing out from all the rest, was a complete jaguar costume like those used in the dance at Acatlán. Hand made and fairly crude, created from a rough cloth smeared in yellow paint and dabbed-on black spots, it was the "authentic" thing. . . and Dudley had to have it. After a little negotiation he got it, rationalizing the purchase by saying that it would be displayed in the restaurant. We knew better and teased him mercilessly then, and we still do. But it *is* a handsome costume.

Cuco's Club

Mercifully, the trip back to Taxco at the end of the day was less eventful than the morning's. We returned tired and hungry and were rewarded by a fine meal with someone who was to become a friend. Passing through the Plaza Borda, the *zócalo* just in front of the cathedral, we walked along Avenida Guadalupe toward the small Plaza San Juan. Both plazas were filled with people going in and out of the many restaurants and shops that were still open. The atmosphere was festive as everyone awaited the processions that would begin at 9:30 that evening. Passing through the smaller plaza, we walked up (almost every street in Taxco is up and down) Calle Carlos J. Nibbi to what appeared to be a private residence. An iron gate stood before a parking area and behind it was a house. Assured that this was, indeed, a restaurant, we walked through a set of French doors into a small dining room. It was quaint and comfortable, obviously a house whose ground floor had been converted to a small restaurant. On one side of the room was a china-filled buffet with a mantlepiece next to it. A large table set for all ten of us stood in front of it. Three other small tables occupied the other side of the room. To one side of the smaller area, we saw a doorway leading into the small kitchen. It was not what we had expected in a city filled with restaurants.

Although we had a set meal that night, menus were laid on the table. The restaurant was named "Cuco's Club," and before a few minutes were gone, the proprietor, José Refugio Alvarez Quinto, or "Cuco," himself appeared. Roly-poly and smiling broadly, he looked like our image of Dickens's ever optimistic and goodhearted Mr. Fezziwig, especially since he carried a large tray filled with margaritas. When they proved to be excellent and made with high-quality tequila (Herradura, Cuco said, the best) and freshly squeezed limes, we liked him all the more. The meal, prepared by Cuco and his sister, followed quickly and it was fine. Large plates of *botanas* included *guacamole* and freshly made corn *tortilla* chips, followed by *chalupas* (thicker *tortillas* with their edges pinched up, toasted, and then filled with shredded chicken in a *chipotle* sauce and shredded cheese) and then pickled vegetables mixed with *jalapeño* chiles. These are standard restaurant dishes, but were very well made. A salad with unusually flavored lettuce followed. When asked about it, Cuco responded that he washed the greens with a little io-dine to ensure that no nasty germs would upset our digestions. Since several of our group were already on bismuth tablets and other more potent remedies (one of the occasional unfortunate side effects of eating one s way through Mexico), we were all grateful. Chicken with ham and cheese, done *cordon bleu* style with cooked vegetables, was the entrée—another pleasant dish. For dessert there was vanilla ice cream with a strawberry Grand Marnier sauce. All in all, the meal was good, but it was not exactly authentic Mexican fare. So we asked our host about it.

Cuco, it happened, had worked for many years as the front man for a major hotel in Acapulco. There, he gained a wide reputation among its celebrated clientele and came to know North Americans well. He had even visited the exclusive northern suburbs of Chicago several year's ago at the invitation of one of the hotel's guests, and he recounted this and his other adventures with such people. After twenty-five years, he had returned to his native town to run this little restaurant and to let a few rooms for guests. The stories were not meant to inflate his reputation; to the contrary, he is quite level-headed. Instead he offered them to explain to us why, when he knew that a group of *yanquis* were coming, he prepared a meal that the regulars in Acapulco might eat—something familiar.

Then we told him why we had come: not for the silver shops, not as tourists in the normal sense of the word, but only as explorers into food-ways, food history, and customs and to make a documentary on the Easter rituals in Taxco. Immediately, Cuco's face lit up and he chirped, "Why didn't you tell me? My family has always been involved in the affair, and I am very much interested in our traditional foods of the season." In the course of conversation, we recounted our meeting with Dr. Juárez Castro the night before, telling Cuco about the various foods he had mentioned. Our new friend then asked if we had tried any of these yet. When we replied that we had not, he offered to make us at least two famous dishes and directed us to where we could get a third. The first, *huiltacoche* or *cuitlacoche*, is a specialty found in many parts of Mexico, though he claimed Guerrero' s cooks as the best interpreters of it. Second, he would make *huazontle* (amaranth) and one or two more specialties for us. The third, *jumiles*, we could find in the market place. Ever since we had arrived in Taxco, Dudley had been anxious to eat them: "You've got to try 'jumeeeles'," he would chant, as a kind of incantation. We would, eventually.

We agreed to return to Cuco's the next day so that he could prepare some of these specialties. "Come for breakfast tomorrow," he said, "or late in the morning for a brunch." First, he said, we should shoot tonight's procession. Afterward, when we were to meet again, Cuco promised to fill in the background about what had seen. Dave and Ralph quickly went to the hotel to gather up the video cameras. That night's procession was dedicated to souls in Purgatory. Headed by the image of San Nicolás de Tolentino, the procession was led by several of the fraternal organizations dedicated to the Easter celebrations, the *encruzados*, or cross-bearers, and their helpers. These were the first of many we would see close up. Bare-backed, barefooted, and hooded, these men walked with their arms outstretched and their hands gruesomely tied to bundles of thorns, as if crucified. A long chain of them stretched from the church of San Nicolás de Tolentino up to the small square we had passed, and then turned sharply into Guadalupe, the street leading to Santa Prisca. Fascinated as we were, we did not stay long because Thursday would be the climactic shoot. Ralph and Dave were getting a feel for what they would be doing. . . and later visiting their friends at "L'Esquina de la Abuela." Tomorrow would be another long day.

The Artists' Village of Ameyaltepec

Wednesday morning, after yet another dose of sticky-sweet *café de olla* and *bolillos*, we piled into the VW bus and set out for Ameyaltepec. For Dudley's sake, we rotated people into the space at back of the bus, although Dave continued to allude to the chef's cries of anguish the day before. Ameyaltepec was one of the key places on our itinerary because all of us were keenly interested in the artists who worked there, specifically our friend Nicolás de Jesús. Jan and I have many of his works, as do Dudley and Bill Goldman; in fact, this is one reason we all became friends and were on the trip.

We followed the same road south through Xalitla, Chilpancingo, and ultimately Acapulco, heading toward our destination. Well, almost. No one knew exactly how to get there. When we asked the day before, Pablo Nicolás had pointed to a mountain southeast of his village and said, simply, "It is there." Finding the road was another matter. The driver headed south and after a few kilometers spied a dirt road leading off to the left. The small sign said "San Agustín Oapán," which we knew was one of the villages in which *amate* artists worked. We drove along up and down small hills and arrived at the entrance to a valley: a crossroad with a small shrine to the Virgin in the middle. One dirt road ascended the mountain, the other went straight. A small, wooden hand-painted signpost said "Ameyaltepec." Thinking that it directed us straight ahead, we drove into the valley. Before us we saw a river, the Río Balsas, and after several kilometers a village along its banks.

This was not the topography of Ameyaltepec which we knew from Nicolás's pictures, and when we stopped the one lone pedestrian we could find near the village (the temperature was about 100 degrees again), he looked puzzled, wondering how we could have made such an error. Retracing our route to the crossroad, we turned up the hill and began to climb the roughest, most rutted, boulder-strewn road imaginable. Finally after almost half an hour, we arrived at the top of the mountain covered in yellow-brown dust. An iron gate stood before us and beyond that, down a winding path, lay the village we had come to visit. Looking down, we could see an immense vista of the valley with the Río Balsas lying flexed along it like a silver ribbon. Ranges of bone-dry mountain lay beyond and on all sides. Just below us, on the slopes, were desiccated corn fields, prostrate under the scorching sun. Such is the physical world of the artists of Ameyaltepec, which is very different from the worlds of their imaginations.

And yet, it was from this dirt-poor place that a school of artists was born. The story began in 1962 when folk-art dealer Max Kerlow asked an itinerant artist from Ameyaltepec, Pedro de Jesús, to paint some wooden figures he had in the store. Merchants had been traveling up to Mexico City since the 1930s to sell wares such as painted pottery and figurines made in the villages of the "Alto Balsas" region. The objects were carried over rough dirt roads on the backs of *burros* and there was plenty of breakage en route. Painting styles were colorful and decorative, featuring fantasy animal figures, some non-realistic humans, and plenty of floral and geometric designs. Perhaps there was something better. Pedro did well and the pay was good, so he asked his village neighbor, Cristino Flores Medina to come and help. Both worked in the back of Kerlow's store for a while. That is when *amate* came onto the scene. It is bark paper, and the technique for making it dates to pre-Columbian days. Once it had been used for *codices*, illustrated manuscripts of which a few still remain, but over the years the craft had been lost. . . save in one place. That was the village of San Pablito Pahuatlán in Puebla where the Otomí people still made it. *Amate* is made from the bark or either the mulberry or fig tree; the first producing white paper, the latter a dark one. Making *amate* is a laborious process that involves boiling the bark and pounding it with stones. Naturally, the fact that making *amate* is so laborious implies that it was made into cutouts that were used for ceremonial purposes, non-Christian ones at that. However, the modern Otomí did not paint on it, unlike their ancestors. Artist Felipe Ehrenberg knew about the paper and its history. He suggested that Pablo and Cristino might try using it as a medium for painting. It proved to be the better way.

The artists of Ameyaltepec now claim Ehrenberg as the stimulus for their school. He taught Pedro and Pablo de Jesús, Cristino, Francisco García, and others such as Roberto de la Cruz, whom we had met at Xalitla, how to paint on bark paper. It was an instant success, and today there are hundreds of artists turning out *amate* paintings. The demand for bark paper is so great that many trees in San Pablito have been stripped, leading to a serious shortage. Many of these paintings are not high quality, but the best artists produce stunning work. Paintings range from depictions of personal dreams, folk rituals stemming from mixtures of European and Indian ideas, pastoral themes, political protest, and milennarian visions. The styles of painting have changed over time. Originally, the paintings resembled pottery painting with floating figures. This was the seemingly crude style that Roberto de la Cruz showed us in Xalitla. By the mid- and late-1960s, styles had developed into the landscapes and village scenes that have become familiar. Soon the Ameyaltepec artists began teaching the craft to artists in surrounding villages, hence the many painters working today. Each village has evolved its own style, so that the work from San Augustín Oapán, Maxele, Xalitla, and Ameyaltepec is distinctive. All are extremely interesting and deeply evocative of the lives of these villagers.[2]

Our bus passed through the iron gates and entered the village's main square. We were preceded by a family, the Vargases as we later learned, riding *burros*. Not the swiftest transport, but the surest on such miserable roads. The village's main square was a paved area in front of the church, complete with basketball hoops. No one was playing because even energetic children would not exert themselves in such temperatures. The village itself stretched along the mountain edge on several levels. Spaces for houses, corncribs, small barns, and a small corral had been cut out of the rocky soil. The houses themselves were made from varieties of materials ranging from roughly hewn wood to adobe and the ever-present cinderblock. As we walked into the village, with Nicolás as our guide, Dudley quickly noticed that despite the rural quality and the dust, the village was well kept and well organized with some modern appurtenances. While there was only one telephone for the village, all the houses had electricity, and here and there we spotted a satellite dish. Still, Ameyaltepec's householders were farmers. A rooster crowed in the distance and pigs lay prostrate in farmyard pens. As we walked to Nicolás's house, a *burro* carrying several laughing children went by. . . cousins of our friend.

The de Jesús's family home was a two-story affair, with the living and cooking quarters on the second level. We had arrived about noon, just in time for Nicolás's mother to serve lunch. A handsome, sprightly woman, she did not look at all old enough to have adult children, much less be a grandmother. But she did share that marvelous talent of so many Mexican women: the art of cooking. She had been up since 4:00 A.M. preparing a meal for us. Its main components were *mole verde grasoso*, made with *pipián* (ground pumpkin seeds) and accompanied by *tamales al sinise*. The first was made with a whole chicken that had been cooked in pottery *cazuelas* for many hours on a wood-fired stove with appropriate seasonings. The *tamales* were something we would have again and again. They were made from plain *masa* mixed with wood ash—the ancient method of enhancing the nutritional qualities of corn and giving the final product a distinctive flavor—that had been wrapped in corn leaves and then steamed over a wood fire. The steamer was an old oil drum with a large sieve-like *tamale* pan set into it. Cameras at the ready, we followed Nicolás's mother into the tiny tiled kitchen where she ground sauces in her *metate* and then, literally, slapped together *tortillas*. In all, it was a completely delicious meal, partly due to the cook's skill and partly due to the fresh ingredients, and definitely due to the food's preparation in wood-burning cookers.

Then came a tour of the village. Each house was both a domestic unit and a workshop where several generations of artists worked. Félix Venansia sat at a wooden table drawing the outlines of a picture in black ink onto a large sheet of bark paper. Around him and at another table sat his daughters, filling in the drawing with colors. The process was an apprenticeship by which Félix's daughters, María, Elena, and Mariana, have learned the basic techniques of *amate* painting along with their father's particular style. The girls, all in their late teens, had been doing this for years and had been to school and earned diplomas for more formal training in art. Nevertheless, they were all committed to the village style, at least for the present, for reasons of income and tradition. As we talked with their father, he complained about lack of income. Had he the money, he said, the family might be able to build a better house. Once he used to travel to Acapulco to sell freely in the market there, but officials there placed restrictions on such freelance marketing. Now most of his sales were to stores in Mexico City, shops that paid the lowest prices they could. Dudley commented, in English, that perhaps some of the artists had more income than they let on because there were some nice things in the village, such as the satellite dishes. The artist as entrepreneur, we said to each other, is a hard fact of life in a region that is anything but wealthy.

Our camera crew focused on artist after artist, Lorenzo Venanzio Jiménez and his wife Clara, Francisco Lorenzo Santos, and others. In all cases, they and their families worked together. For North Americans who are inundated with tales of dissolving families, this seemed like something out of the past, that gave us hope for the future. Santos, a lean, wiry man with deeply creased cheeks and the leathery skin of someone who has spent much of his life outdoors, sat with sacks of white, yellow, and black corn surrounding him. We discussed farming in this dreary region, in part because his and his family's paintings showed green fields, colorful flowers, and birds. Like so many other artists, his work showed an Ameyaltepec of the mind and not of reality.

I asked him how many times a year he could harvest corn. "Only once," during the rainy season, he said. "There is no water otherwise." Nicolás had told us long ago that his village was virtually out of water. The single well that had supported the village for generations—the place is about 300 years old—was almost dry and drilling for a new one had proved fruitless. While we were visiting, a huge water tanker truck had pulled into the village square and was pumping water into tanks that had been set into the ground. It was something of an irony for a village whose name means "mountain of water." "Why," we asked, "did not the villagers simply leave for land in the valley, nearer the river?" "Simple," our artist friend said, "this is our home." Family and place mean more in Mexico than they do to us modern *norteamericanos*.

Nicolás had arranged a showing of the artists' work in his house, and that is where we finally met Cristino Flores Medina, the oldest living Ameyaltepec artist. He was one of the pioneers of the *amate* paper painting school and was someone we had looked forward to meeting. A man of indeterminate age, weather beaten and with large work-roughened hands, his paintings are minutely detailed impressions of the themes we had come to expect of the *amate* painters. He, too, had begun in the pottery-style painting of the early years, but now worked in larger panoramas. Some of his work was on dark *amate* paper. He and the others generally used simpler floral and avian designs on this medium, reserving the white paper for larger scenes. He spoke about how his painting had changed; of the early days with Pablo, Nicolás' father, and others who are deceased; and of how delighted he was that the whole village had artistic success in the wider world. It was surprising to us how many of these "rustic" folk had been to the United States to attend showings of their work and to sell it.

Looking through the works, we noticed that the image of St. George slaying a dragon, either as a single figure or within more complex pictures, appeared with some frequency. Was this the patron saint of the village or the region, we wondered. If so, was it popularized by Christian missionaries who meant the dragon to be the old pagan deities—the much-loved Quetzal-cóatl, for instance? That had been exactly what missionaries had done in the early Middle Ages in Europe. No, came the answer, he is the symbol of political action and of something even more profound, a millennialist impulse. A few years ago, the central government proposed building a huge dam for hydroelectric power and water control down river. If carried out, it would have flooded the whole valley and its villages, displacing some 40,000 people. A huge controversy broke out in which the affected peoples marshaled help from people inside and outside of Mexico. For indigenous peoples, the struggle came to symbolize their fight against centuries of mistreatment in many areas of Mexican life. Under the stress of losing their homes and with increasingly limited opportunities for these very entrepreneurial people, as Félix had said, they formed a quasi-religious movement that swept the villages: the old order will be swept away and the earth cleansed, just as St. George had slain the ravager-dragon. In some way, too, this kind of thinking—the suffering that comes out of worldly experiences, the reconstitution of society, and much more —lies beneath the rituals of Easter that we would observe in Taxco.

After several hours of shooting, we were ready to leave Ameyaltepec. As the bus was inching its way down the hill, our driver Edgardo asked if we might be interested in trying some iguana. Iguana? Why, we had been craving it ever since Acapulco; at least some of us, anyway. The driver said he knew of a good restaurant just down the road that always had it. It was very close, he said, only a quarter of an hour away. It was getting on to early evening and we were all getting hungry, so we said, "Drive on." He did, for about an hour. "It's only a little way now," the demon driver kept saying. We began to drowse as the hot air circulated through the bus windows. . . .

Preparing iguana

"We're almost there," went the refrain. Just as we were about to play St. George to the dragon busdriver, our guide pulled off into what looked like a roadside diner attached to a gas station on the outskirts of Chilpancingo. This was it and worth the trip, we were assured. At last, iguana!

The restaurant was the equivalent of a truck stop, but not part of a chain and not as efficient. Two pleasant women worked in the tiny kitchen set behind a small service counter. After the usual examination of the menu, most of us ordered iguana. It came in two forms: in a red *guajillo* sauce, or *al ajo* (with garlic). We got one or the other so we could share. Several of our party were more conservative in their food preferences and got dishes such as non-iguana *enchiladas*. After a good forty-five minutes, the platters arrived. Was it worth the wait? Jan told Dave to get out the camera and put it on Carol and me so that we could describe the experience for possible use in the documentary. Dudley stood by smirking, because he had tasted the dishes already. "Unusual," I said, and then described the sauce. Then came Carol's immortal line, a summary of how we Americans relate to taste: "It tastes like chicken!" she said. Well, it didn't. Carol had a stuffed-up nose and sore throat and could not taste anything. The iguana was awful: bony, virtually meatless, and rancid. The sauces? Not so great and with a worse after-effect. On the way back and for several days afterward, we still suffered from that iguana in sauce. Jan said that we should make a movie about it, "The Lizard's Revenge."

If iguana is a specialty of Guerrero and Michoacán, there must be a way to prepare it well. When we later told Cuco about this awful preparation, he clucked his tongue and told us that the real way that they're done is to put them live on hot coals in a small brazier and thus kill them. Once charred, the skins are easy to remove. . . of course they should be dead first! Actually, the charred iguana is soaked in water first, and then the skins are removed. They're cooked *Zochiace*, with alcohol. This brings up the natural flavor of the iguana and removes the "fishy" taste. In the end it tastes like chicken (the iguana we had was clearly not finished with alcohol!) The iguana is sautéed in oil with garlic and served in a sauce of *guajillo* and *ancho* chiles with garlic, of course; thus, *iguana con chile ajo*. Keeping that advice in mind, here is a recipe. You may substitute chicken for iguana under the assumption that "it tastes like chicken."

One of the great dishes made in Guerrero and in Michoacán is *pipián verde*. We mentioned that Nicolás's mother made something like a *chiliajo de pollo* for us. Actually, it was a *pipián grasoso* with chicken. The name comes from the oil that rises from the pumpkin seed to the top of the sauce. In the old days, Dudley says, cooks ground the seeds so heavily that the oil formed a gloss "like a mirror" in the *molcajete*. The version given here is one of Dudley's

Making pipian verde al grasoso

creations using venison. You could substitute chicken breast or boneless thighs, but venison is particularly good. *Pipiáns* are spectacular dishes, among Mexico's best treats.

Pipián Grasoso

1	lb.	venison tenderloin, cut into small chunks
1–2	T.	canola oil
1	C.	pumpkin seeds, toasted
10		sprigs cilantro
3		*serrano* chiles
6		*tomatillos*, peeled, washed, and cut in quarters
1		small onion, chopped
½		cinnamon stick
4	C.	chicken broth
		kosher salt and freshly ground pepper, to taste

Cut up the venison and set aside. Heat the canola oil in a deep, heavy skillet. Add the venison and saute gently for a few minutes, only until just done. Remove the meat and set aside. Meanwhile, heat a griddle or heavy skillet. Place the pumpkin seeds on it and toast, about 8–10 minutes or until partly browned. When done, place seeds, cilantro, *serrano* chiles, *tomatillos*, onion, and cinnamon in the bowl of a blender or a *molcajete* and grind well. Add 2 cups of chicken stock and mix well. Place this mixture in the skillet in which the venison was cooked. Bring to a simmer and cook for at least 15 minutes, slowly adding the rest of chicken broth. Stir in one direction only to prevent curdling. When the mixture has thickened, stir in the venison and reheat.   *Serves 4*

Iguana En Mole

If you ask someone from Michoacán or Guerrero about their really special dishes, iguana often comes up (no pun intended). Iguana is a specialty of the coast, where they are now raised commercially. They are quite boney and require cleaning to remove the "fishy" taste that sometimes appears. It is said that in Michoacán an interesting cleaning method exists. The freshly killed iguana is placed in a flowing stream and fastened in place with rocks. It is left overnight and when it is retrieved the next morning, it is perfect for final cooking. Fresh streams not being available, if you happen to get an iguana, parboil it and then begin the cooking process with fresh water. Here is the correct way to make iguana in the Michoacán style. In reality, the dish is a *mole*, therefore chicken may be substituted for iguana. Otherwise, get some fresh lizard and start cooking! This recipe, by the way, makes a large quantity, and you may want to halve it.

4		whole *guajillo* chiles, soaked, deveined, and seeded
4		whole *mulatto* chiles, soaked, deveined, and seeded
4		whole *pasilla* chiles soaked, deveined, and seeded
2		whole iguanas, about 2–3 lbs. each (or the equivalent amount of frying chicken), cleaned, parboiled, and drained
2	C.	*mirepoix* (chopped onion, celery, and carrot)
1		*bouquet garni* (bay leaves, thyme and peppercorn tied in a cheesecloth bag)
1	C.	lard or canola oil, plus 2 T.
3-⅓	lbs.	tomatoes
8-¾	lbs.	*tomatillos*

¹/₂		piece of bread, sautéed in small amount of oil
¹/₄	C.	shredded ginger
¹/₄	C.	cinnamon
¹/₄	C.	sesame seeds, toasted
¹/₄	C.	peanuts, toasted
¹/₂		plantain (cooking)
2		whole corn *tortillas*
2		whole cloves
5		cloves garlic
3		whole peppercorns
¹/₂		piece Mexican chocolate
		kosher salt, to taste
		sugar, to taste

Place the chiles in a large pan and cover with water. Use a weighted plate if necessary to keep them under water. Soak until soft, up to 2 hours if necessary. Devein and seed the chiles and set aside, reserving some of the water. Place the iguanas (or chicken) in a large stock pot or an *olla* (large clay pot) and cover with water. Add the *mirepoix* and *bouquet garni*. Bring to a boil, reduce the heat, and simmer for 1 hour, uncovered, or until the iguana (or chicken) is tender. Skim the impurities from the surface of the broth. While cooking the iguana (or chicken) prepare the *mole*. Heat 1 cup of lard or canola oil in a large sauce pan or *cazuela*. Add the chiles and fry lightly (do not burn). Set the chiles aside. In sequence, add the tomatoes to the pan, sauté until soft, remove, and set aside. Do the same with the *tomatillos*. Place the soaked chiles, tomatoes, *tomatillos*, and all of the rest of the ingredients (except for the iguana (or chicken), chocolate, salt, and sugar) in the bowl of a food processor or blender. Process until smooth. You will have to do this in several batches. Use some of the water from the chiles or the iguana (or chicken) broth for processing to make a fine consistency. Pass the *mole* mixture through a fine colander. Heat 2 tablespoons of lard or oil in a deep saucepan or *olla*. Add the *mole* mixture and season with salt and sugar, to taste. Bring to a simmer and cook for 10 minutes, stirring continuously to prevent burning. Add 4 cups of the iguana (or chicken) broth, bring to a boil, reduce the heat and simmer for 40 minutes. Add the iguana (or chicken), cut into small pieces, and the chocolate. Simmer for 20 minutes, adding more iguana (or chicken) broth as necessary to keep the sauce smooth.

Serves 8–10

Note: Serve with plenty of warm *tortillas* and good quality *mezcal*.

Taxco:
Processions, Cuco's, and the Market

Taxco

The next day we all prepared for the city's most spectacular night of processions celebrating Holy Week. After our usual sweet breakfast, we separated that morning to examine locations and to do a little shopping. The city has to be walked to be really appreciated, but if doing so, be sure to take a good pair of shoes. The elevation is enough to tax the wind of any flatlander, and the cobblestone streets are enough to tax anyone's feet. Ralph, in a fit of physical fitness, ran the city, declaring it, "Fantastic. . . for self-torture." Several hikes through the narrow streets and small squares lined with balconied houses and small shops are enough to show why the place has achieved its status as a national treasure.

Taxco is home to another treasure, one of the most renowned silverwork traditions in Mexico. Silver shops are virtually everywhere, and everywhere else there are plenty of private parties ready to sell their wares outside. (Dave and Ralph had met several young fellows, friends of friends, while at their favorite haunt. They later visited us at our hotel to sell some simple but good-quality silver jewelry at very reasonable prices.) Some good shops are to be found in the *Patio de las Artesanías*, at the edge of the main plaza. One is a cooperative formed by smiths from local villages. The most illustrious shop is Los Castillo in the Plazuela de Bernal, just at the end of the street on which our hotel was located. On the way, street vendors had set up elaborate displays of regional artisanal work: *amate* paintings, some jewelry, pottery masks from San Augustín de Oapán, wooden toys, and *sarapes*, among other things. The vendors were Nahuas from nearby villages, whole families trying to make a living in this high tourist season. Most of our group ended up buying some small items from them more out of sympathy than for the quality of the work. Were we being condescending foreigners? It is always difficult to decide what to do in such situations.

No such thoughts need worry the shopper at Los Castillo. The family of that name was one of the first to renew the art of silversmithing under the influence of William Spratling in the 1930s. So renowned did they become that the family has shops in other cities as well. What comes out of their workshops is often splendid, and it includes elaborate jewelry, vessels, and statues. The showroom glitters, and even more interesting is the workshop behind it. When visiting the store, I peeked behind a dutch door into the workshop and immediately turned to the manager and asked if we could take some footage of the artisans. He agreed at once and in short order I pulled Dave away from something important.

Once inside we saw several processes. One was hammering out silverware; another was casting small items of jewelry out of molten metal. We also saw an exceptional pitcher in the form of a swan being finished. As we were shooting, Dave became increasingly jumpy, twitching as he shot, but determined to hold his shots steady. Finally, having done just enough to get a sense of what silversmithing was about, he turned, sprinted toward the door, rushed out, and fled toward the hotel. I shouted after him, asking what was wrong. His fading reply was only this: "Iguana sauce. . . !" Such are the hazards of a cameraman in Mexico.

Loaded up with pink tablets and potent little white ones, Dave was ready to go out again later in the day. Meanwhile, several of us had explored the town later that morning. The cathedral of Santa Prisca (officially the *Parroquia de Santa Prisca y San Sebastián*) was one stop. It is always described as a masterpiece of colonial baroque architecture. Built between 1748 and 1758 with funds from the silver magnate José de la Borda, it is overly baroque in the style called *"churrigueresque."* The name is taken from a family of Spanish architects headed by José Benito Churriguera (1665–1725), whose lasting fame comes from designing the cathedral in Salamanca, Spain. To say that the style is ornate is to make that adjective an unreservedly modest modifier. Santa Prisca's facade is a tumult of decoration, flowers, and figures, and inside the high altarpiece is a mass of sculpted motifs covered in goldleaf. The decor conveys religious ideas that are formal and at the same time ecstatic, orthodox Catholic, yet bursting out of the constraints of space and (perhaps) liturgy. The Easter celebrations are just this way, while the conventional story appears on the altarpieces in the cathedral's nave—the Virgin, the Passion, and the souls in Purgatory. We had already seen the Virgin and a representation of Purgatory in several processions; the Passion would come that night and the next day.

Taxco has a fine small archaeological museum in Calle Profesor Porfirio A. Delgado, a small street behind the cathedral. Ralph, who is keenly interested in archaeology, and I went there soon thereafter. The museum's core display is the personal collection of William Spratling, whose name the institution bears. Two floors house some very fine work dating from the Olmec period in Guerrero up to items from the time of the Conquest. I had not realized how influential Olmecs had been in the region until seeing the material here: jade figurines, baby-faced were-jaguars, and jaguar-serpents, as well as small animals, frogs, and more. Vessels carved from jade and serpentine in the same style were common, but one carving was particularly splendid and suggestive: a relief of two men standing with knives and staffs over a recumbent jaguar. This is the theme of jaguar dances in villages today: the chasing away of bad spirits through the slaying of the ravening jaguar. The jaguar god was the equivalent of Tezcatlipoca, who in later mythology battled Quetzalcóatl. The carvings are part of a fantastical religious art tradition. No doubt the Olmec figures represent rituals and they wear the masks, particularly the jaguar masks, to represent myths about the jaguar god. They are found in archaeological sites all over Guerrero, and their meaning whispers down the ages to their descendants.

Not far from the Guillermo Spratling Museum, in the Calle Ruíz Alarcón and just down the street from Los Arcos, a new museum had opened—the Casa Humboldt. It is an old colonial house with a splendid geometrically decorated facade that was named for the great German naturalist and explorer, the Baron von Humboldt, who stayed there in the early nineteenth century. Today the building houses a collection of religious art, much of it discovered only recently in one of Santa Prisca's storerooms. Among these are paintings by Miguel Cabrera, the most famous Mexican artist of the eighteenth century, whose large-scale works can be seen in the cathedral. Casa Humboldt has been beautifully restored and is a model of what colonial houses of the well-to-do looked like during that era. What these upper-class types ate is another matter. It certainly was not the food of the common people, but something rather more Spanish in style with touches of local ingredients; this was, in the eighteenth century, a Spanish colonial society. Some of these differences would become apparent as we began to eat street food and restaurant fare.

Processions

"Taxco has been a pilgrimage site during Easter Week since 1598. All week long, villagers from some dozen surrounding villages march in processions bearing holy symbols. On the surface, the celebrations are Christian—Spanish. But beneath lies a deep layer of Indian religious ideas and rituals. It is hard to disentangle the two: colorful public ceremonies, dressing in costumes, and literally losing oneself in the ceremonies were common to both traditions. And didn't the Passion of Jesus remind Indians and *mestizos* alike of their own suffering?"—from the documentary "Hidden Mexico"

By around noon the first of many processions had assembled at a small square on one of the hilltops north of the city center. People from the nearby villages of Xochula, Tehuilotepec and Zacatecolotla were arriving, ready to march down one of the main streets to the church of Santa Veracruz south of the cathedral. They would, like the others, carry images of Christ before them as they walked accompanied by their bands. We watched from a viaduct above the Plaza Borda as they passed alongside it, the first of many processions to follow. What they were doing, what all the processions were about, was the annual recreation of the Easter story, the events surrounding the Passion and crucifixion of Jesus of Nazareth. The whole celebration, then, is a living testimonial to the most holy of all Christian holidays. The only difference is that this celebration is very Mexican.

The ceremonies begin on Palm Sunday, *el Domingo de Ramos*, the day Jesus arrived in Jerusalem, perhaps for Passover. On that day there is a procession from the church in the village of Tehuiotepec bearing a statue of Jesus mounted on a donkey. He is accompanied by images of the twelve apostles. Once this procession is finished, the benediction of the palms is given, followed by a solemn mass in the cathedral that gives special attention to children, who have their own small procession. We had seen preparations for this day in the old town center of Acapulco. There, basket weavers had made all kinds of religious objects from palm, ranging from crucifixes to birds with long tail feathers. These were said to be doves, symbols of the holy spirit, but they looked suspiciously like quetzal birds, holy symbols in the ancient Indian religions. These sorts of objects, real folk art creations, were to be found everywhere on Palm Sunday.

The next several days are given to more cavalcades that lead up to *Jueves Santo*, Maundy Thursday in English. That is the day that Jesus sat in the Garden of Gethsemane, which was the scene of his betrayal. Here he ate the Last Supper of unleavened bread (*tortillas* in this case) and Paschal lamb, washed his disciples feet, and was arrested by Roman soldiers who imprisoned him. *Jueves Santo* is the night of the most spectacular of all the processions and Taxco is completely packed with visitors that night. It appeared that everyone from both the city itself and the surrounding towns were there, as might be expected, since at least a dozen local villages and all the parish churches participate in the processions. There were surprisingly few *anglos* that we could see in the crowd, only a relative handful of the Germans, French, and Canadians who are a major component of the Mexican tourist business.

Another surprise was the television coverage given the event. We had supposed that we would be the only crew there, but when Jan, Dave, and Ralph met with the tourism board that morning to arrange camera positions, Jan met a BBC team as well as one from the major Spanish-language network, Telemundo. Entering the small Plaza San Juan late that afternoon, we found a monster tractor-trailer television truck complete with satellite uplinks. The thing literally took up one whole side of the plaza, and how they got it into that space or through the narrow streets in the first place was a puzzle to us. But we had already learned not to disparage the resourcefulness and daring of Mexican drivers.

Choosing camera positions consisted of finding any good place we could perch. Dave and Ralph had already found one. Their friends, the Cardona family who owned "El Rincón," had two houses on Benito Juárez, right along the main procession route. The house they let us use was multi-leveled, as all others, and had a balcony that opened on the street. It was perfect for panoramic shots of marchers as they passed down the narrow lane. Later that night Ralph was stationed there with the second camera for just that purpose. Dave started the evening at the Plaza San Juan and roamed up the main street to get close-up shots of people and events. Everyone retired for dinner first, splitting up among several restaurants. Jan, Carol, and I were sent to an undistinguished chain restaurant; others found themselves in a very nice place with the unlikely name "La Hamburguesía." Bob, Martha, and Dudley had a pleasant meal there and a little more. *Tequila* often comes at the end of meal, taken straight with lime and salt. After our colleagues finished their meal, Carol and the others eventually found them there making merry with some locals they had met. Soon all joined in, followed by even more diners. By the time I found them, everyone was very jolly, as were many other spectators. This was not disrespectful or even blasphemous, because many among the observers were busy eating the ever-present street food while the religious drama was being enacted.

By the time night had fallen, the processions were in full course. Crowds of spectators, ourselves included, lined the streets, and at times pressed up against the marchers, and at other times we moved away from the action like small waves on a lake. Street lights provided some illumination, but most came from candles held by the participants, making the scene look for all the world like a dramatically lit Mannerist painting. Our first glimpse of the proceedings was of a squad of men dressed as Roman soldiers, wearing gold-colored helmets and red cloaks and carrying spears. One leading the rest played a simple wooden flute. The tune was like nothing we had ever heard, sliding eerily from note to note. Surely the flute and perhaps the melody came from some distant time. Suddenly from out of the cluster of soldiers appeared a small man dressed in a white shift with long black knotted locks that hid much of his face. He carried a long bag filled with silver coins. This he rattled and clanked, rushing up to individuals in the crowd and shaking the bag. Children squealed and shrank back at this apparition. It was Judas with his thirty pieces of silver, but here he was not an odious, greedy betrayer, but the traditional trickster of folklore who is at once terrifying and amusing. Seeing this reminded me that commentators on such scenes have equated the Romans with the Spanish *conquistadores*, and if so, then Judas could be either those who cooperated with the Romans or a satire of them. He needed only a mask to be complete.

Close behind the soldiers and Judas came a group of marchers who carried a litter on their shoulders. On it was a statue of Jesus, blindfolded and manacled. He stood on a bed of purple cloth, the color that signifies royalty for Europeans and death in pre-Columbian ritual. The figure was surrounded by flowers: Easter lilies and one more of interest—the marigold. This flower meant life in the old religion and still figures prominently in the major Mexican holiday that memorializes the spirits of the dead. As always in Mexico, beneath the surface lies something more profound.

Then came the most spectacular and gruesome spectacle of all, the penitents. Rows of male penitents walked slowly or stood waiting for the long procession to move again. They were dressed in black, but only from the waist down. They were barefooted and wore black hoods over their heads. On their backs they carried bundles of 144 thorny blackberry stalks weighing fifty or sixty pounds. Their arms were stretched wide and tied tightly to the bundles with coarse ropes. Lighted candles were set into their hands, often with hot wax dripping onto their hands. Hidden under the penitents' hoods, twisted ropes passed through their mouths like horse bits to stabilize the bundles. Coarse horsehair belts cut into their bare waists. Each night the penitents walked some ten miles carrying their burdens. . . barefooted on cobblestone streets. These penitents, the *encruzados*, had helpers, a brotherhood of encouragers who might be asked to give them some water, to adjust their loads, or to encourage the penitent to bear his suffering. By the time we saw the *encruzados*, the thorns had begun to bite deeply into their bare shoulders so that blood ran down their naked backs in small rivulets. If the thorns are borne in imitation of Jesus's scourging and crucifiction, then the wounds at least are authentic.

Seeing these men straining under their loads caused a hush to descend upon the crowd. We could not see their faces, but their eyes shone out in. . . who can tell—ecstasy, pain? What followed was even grimmer. Interspersed between groups of *encruzados* were individual flagellants. Dressed in the same black costumes as their fellow sufferers, these men carried knouts. As they walked, they flung their arms backward over their shoulder and smash the knotted straps onto their backs. Sometimes they stopped, kneeled, and scourged themselves more thoroughly. Most of the damage is done to the lower back, which on some men was deeply reddened at best, and on others was bloody with open wounds at the worst. We saw one very slight man, his back mutilated with beating, stagger and almost collapse. Helpers went to his aid and propped him up, and he went on in the parade. All of this was the most extraordinary sight, and it gave an immediate impression of how deep the religious ascetic impulse can run in believers.

We moved up Benito Juárez toward our balcony location in time to see women penitents walking in long lines. They were completely covered in black, including hoods, and around their bare legs were chains that shackled each to the other. The women walked stooped over, dragging their chains in total silence. We learned later that these penitents wore coarse ropes around their waists. Between groups of chained penitents walked more flagellants. It was as if the famous scene of a procession of religious flagellants in Ingmar Bergman's movie "The Seventh Seal" had come to life. All of this suffering in silence, awful as it was to witness, was moving to all who saw it, even to those who continued to eat *tacos* and ice cream bars as they watched.[3]

Fortunately, not all of the ceremonies were so somber. From far up the Calle La Garita, masses of people moved slowly down toward the city center. The actual marchers were clusters of people surrounding images, floats mostly, or statues carried on men's shoulders. Each image or statue came from one of the local villages or parishes and bore the name of its origin surrounded by flowers. As they approached, we heard the small bands that accompanied them. "Band" is too grand a word, since there were usually only a handful of players: drums, a trumpet or two, and a violin. The music was rough versions of popular devotional songs, and the rhythms were purely Mexican (not modern mariachi with its blaring trumpets). It was a delight to see and hear them: group upon group walking slowly along the assigned route. The whole event lasted well into the night, and now on our balcony perch, we stayed up to watch, to chat, and to share snacks with the amiable owners of the house. In all, it was an unforgettable event.

What was it all about, this kind of mystical rapture that drives people to mortify their flesh? We talked with José Alvarez Quinto, our friend Cuco, who told us how the religious fraternities operated. His knowledge came from direct experience, perhaps even participation, though he would never say so. Each church has its own organization of penitents that gives permission to would-be participants. All are part of an overarching association; the *Comité de Procesiones* is the major one. They arrange the order of the processions, place the people in them, and hear applications to become a penitent. This is an anonymous organization with a self-selected president. They also arrange the teams who "encourage" the penitents. Only through the organization can one participate in the events of the season. The organization can even arrange for outsiders to be brought in. Cuco thought that he once saw a North American penitent, but he wasn't sure. Normally, permission to be a penitent runs in families. When a father who has been a penitent is on his deathbed, he will ask his son(s) to follow in this: "Do not forget, son, I am a penitent. Will you promise to keep the faith?" And more often than not, the son follows. However, the penitents are transgressors, or so they say, who make a solemn promise to God in order to relieve themselves of sin. The acts are penances and supposedly not symbolic. This may or may not be true, since there is a folklore attached to these actions. They represent individual sufferers taking upon themselves the sins of humanity, just as Jesus did. They also do it to ensure that no adversity will befall them or their families. In this way they cleanse their souls for themselves and their families. Onlookers, too, must participate in this idea: to suffer vicariously or at least to be solemn in the face of such extreme acts as these.

We had to ask whether Cuco or his son had ever been penitents. He said not, but that his family has been engaged in the details of the ceremonies in another interesting way. His family holds the skeleton of "Santa Ursula" in their house. The skeleton has been in the family for 120 years. His father's grandmother had found it—it had been tossed out of the house of a local grandee—and taken it home. She knew it was Santa Ursula because the saint spoke to her. Today it resides in the family house with a silver crown upon its head. When the time to prepare for the ceremonies arrives, the *comité* comes to Cuco and asks whether Santa Ursula will consent to appear (but only on Holy Thursday), and he tells them what her wishes are. This year she had declined and that is why we could not see her. How does Cuco's family know the saint's will? They just know—the believers, that is. Cuco's son told us that now he heard the saint's' voice speaking to him in his head. There was no rational explanation for it, only that the divine does work in the mundane sphere of existence.

There are other reasons and explanations for the Easter events in Taxco. One is the linkage of Mexico to medieval Spain; the other is the celebration's connections with the religious ideas and rituals of the indigenous peoples. Luis Weckmann discusses "blood processions" as a kind of collective self-sacrifice that was given to the *indigenas* by missionary friars in the sixteenth century and was also practiced by the Spanish. From the beginning, the earliest written evidence is in one of Cortés's letters in 1529; the ceremonies were held during Holy Week or at times of some natural disaster. Mass public demonstrations of flagellation came from Europe and date back to the era of the Crusades (when millennialist movements abounded) and increased during the time of the Black Death (beginning in 1347, the era depicted in the great movie, "The Seventh Seal"). To the Europeans, bubonic and pneumonic plagues seemed to be the scourge of God and required the most extreme penance to save oneself and the community. The same thing happened in Mexico City in 1575 during an epidemic when the Virgin of Three Remedies was "offered" several "bloody processions." During Holy Week that year, the Spaniards did the same, saying that they were imitating the practices of Sevilla. Flagellants were condemned by the church and royal authorities, but nothing mitigated the participants' beliefs. In the sixteenth century Spain was home to fraternities of bloodied penitents that were established for the Holy Week celebrations. Toledo and Sevilla were strongholds for the rituals, and it was there that penitents began to wear masks or hoods so that the clergy would not recognize them. If, the logic ran, the individuals were suffering for the entire community, they should be anonymous. Besides, who wants the public at large to know that one has committed great sins that justify bloody penance?

Native rituals cannot be ruled out as an underlying reason for this outpouring of devotion and blood. Certainly, some of the symbols surrounding the devotions are pre-Columbian. Weckmann thinks that the ceremonies are purely medieval Spanish, but many others see deeper roots. We know that ancient rulers, among the Maya in particular, mutilated themselves during important religious ceremonies. Their royal, perhaps holy, blood was offered to gods as insurance against disasters, ensuring that rains would come and that the sun would shine, along with doubtless many other desirable results. The ancient rituals may have been held in private, but just as likely they were done publicly, at the top of the temple pyramids that marked every city. The ritual of human sacrifice would seem to hold similar ideas within it. That somehow these two traditions mixed together in Mexico may be the reason why when this "frenzied asceticism" spread to the Philippines, it was noted as showing "marked Mexican influence." It should also be observed that Easter coincides with the ancient the great spring festival, the resurrection of the year. That was the time the peoples of the hot lands looked forward to the coming rains, when all the world would become green again. In both traditions, then, there is an idea, and not necessarily a Christian one, that through shedding blood and suffering comes hope.

The Return to Cuco's

It was quite a night. The next day, we finally got back to food between some shooting of the continuing religious drama. We took Cuco up on his offer to serve us some special Easter dishes and went to his place for a breakfast-time shoot. Cuco explained that typical Easter dishes (*platos de Cuaresma*) include *huazontles* (amaranth), *tortas de papas* (potato cakes), *tortas de camarones* (shrimp cakes), *romeritos* (greens) with *mole* sauce (greens), *quelites* (another type of greens), *habas* soup (the delicious lima bean soup we ate at Los Balcones), *torrejas* (a Mexican version of French toast, soaked in a *piloncillo* sauce), and, this being Guerrero, *pozole* made not with pork but most often with sardines (canned with tomato sauce) and usually with an egg on it. Bill Goldman asked if there were any traditional breads served with these. Cuco replied not really, except for Mexican-style sweet breads with raisins and other dried fruits. He then proceeded to make several dishes for us while explaining something about them.

Huazontle, or fresh green amaranth, grows in the *calmiles*, or wasteland areas. It is, really, a wild plant that grows everywhere. As such, one of its virtues is that it is one of the first greens of the year. No wonder it was always associated with the vegetative gods of old. The plant has several uses. Its seed is highly nutritious and has a higher protein content than rice. That is one reason why amaranth has been making a comeback lately, especially in health-food stores where its indicated use is as a cereal. The seeds can be ground into flour, but in Mexico they are the major component of a candy called "alegría," made with honey or *piloncillo*. It looks like Middle Eastern sesame-seed candies and so is surely an adaptation by Spanish confectioners of a sweet that had been introduced through Moorish Spain. However, fresh green amaranth is something different and has always been highly important during spring festivals. To prepare it, Cuco blanched the long stalks with their seed bearing tips. He then made an egg-milk batter and set out a plate of flour, along with some "belt cheese" (a special string cheese). To assemble the dish, he rolled up a bundle of stalks and placed a square of cheese in the middle. The bundle was tightly squeezed together, battered, and floured, then fried in hot oil until lightly browned and served with a *guajillo* sauce. To eat it, the bundle is broken open and each stalk is removed, placed into the mouth, and then pulled out between the teeth so that the seed part remains. The flavor is like broccoli and is quite delicious. Since returning, Dudley and I have made *huazontles* on several public occasions, always to some acclamation.

Preparing huazontles (*amaranth*)

Fish is always significant during Lent. For the *tortas de camarones*, Cuco ground some dried shrimp, mixed them with an egg-breadcrumb batter, formed croquettes, and then deep-fried them. The final coating is a *mole*, not *poblano*, the famous preparation of which Dudley is the past master, but one of the many versions from Guerrero. The *torta* itself was fairly ordinary, and the *mole*, not being spicy, was subtle and altogether savory.

Then came a dessert, the *torrejas*. Good Mexican white bread was soaked in milk, then two slices were layered with cheese, battered, and fried. The final dish was served in a *piloncillo* sauce. It was interesting, but the more indigenous Mexican dishes are always better. What makes these dishes of interest is the mixture of techniques and ingredients that compose much of Mexican cookery. Battering and deep frying are medieval European (mariners brought the same technique to Japan where it became tempura), as are cheese, bread, and sugar and sugar syrups. Amaranth, greens, and chile sauces are indigenous. The two blend together into something new, recognizably European, yet with different flavor principles and textures, and certainly with different color schemes. We would see much more of this as we continued our journey.

We said farewell to Cuco with promises to see him again. (We did when he came to Chicago for a visit.) This was Good Friday, and there were yet more processions that we wanted to get on videotape. The main events were reenactments of the beating of Jesus, as he bore the cross to Calvary, his three falls, the Crucifixion, and his descent from the Cross. That day, ever-more wounded *encruzados* and flagellants continued their progress through the city. We shot many more scenes of them and of the activities in the main square. School had been let out, and the place was filled with children, vendors of all kinds of goods (including foods), parents, grandparents, and dogs—a real cross-section of the city. Seeing people munching on frozen ices, we had to have some, too. The flavors were wonderful, from mango to berry and *cherimoya*, along with all kinds of other tropical fruits. At the top of the square I had spied a vendor of my all-time favorite street food: hot dogs. Mounted on a handcart was a glassed-in rotisserie grill on which bacon-wrapped hot dogs were cooking. I had to have one—on camera, of course. It was served on a normal bun with a choice of condiments; my choice was a green sauce. The sausage itself was the garden-variety imitation Oscar Mayer, but the sauce was sensational. I gobbled the whole thing before Carol or Dudley or anyone else could get their teeth into it. If I were to have a hot-dog stand in that paradise of all hot doggeries, Chicago, that spicy green *tomatillo* sauce would grace every hot dog I served.

Just off the Plaza Borda alongside the cathedral, several larger stands had been set up in expectation of the celebratory crowds that were beginning to collect. We stopped at two stands to expand our knowledge of the local street fare. The first billed itself as serving a specialty of Puebla: fried plantains. Dudley, the patriotic native of Puebla, declared this a counterfeit since these large unsweet bananas grow only in jungle regions of his state. We tried one anyway and it was awful. The plantain was skewered with a stick then deep-fried. The purchaser then had a choice of toppings, each some kind of sweet goopy sauce, followed by condensed milk, fruit jams, and coconut. . . and this was the least sweet version they had. Even Dudley could not eat these, despite their supposed Puebla provenance. Ever after we teased him about this, declaring that if we ever had to eat "bananas Puebla style," we would all "beeee seeeck." Good thing Dudley has a wonderful sense of humor—he has to!

The next stand was much better. You can't go to Mexico and not eat *tacos*. Incidentally, the word is slang for a wad of bills or a plug, because the *tortilla* is so packed with fillings. The *taco* stand was a long counter holding trays filled with ingredients and sauces of choice. The energetic cook-server, dressed in an immaculately clean apron and low chef's toque, asked what we would like to try. Everything, we said, so he quickly cooked or heated various ingredients on the griddle close at hand and served them forth. *Taco* shells in

Taco *makers*

"Where did the atole (atohli in Nahuatl) go?"

this region are soft and very thin. For about $1.50 we got a large variety of fillings, ranging from pork to sausage, beef steak, *chorizo*, diced potatoes (Carol gulped that one down), and cactus. Condiments included *salsa picante*, *guacamole*, and *salsa verde*. We tried them all and were delighted with the quality and flavor. Ah, we all said, this was street food as it was meant to be, humble dishes that are among Mexico's culinary glories.

After more shooting we retired for dinner. Several of us dined at El Palazzio, a pleasant restaurant with a balcony view of the street. The *Guacamole*, as is almost always the case in Mexico, was fine, and a couple of the entrées were simple but good. One was beef Guerrero style, a grilled fillet of beef covered in onions, green chiles, and melted cheese. As it also often happens in Mexico, the beef was tough but full of flavor. Chicken Guerrero style had similar ingredients but had been baked in foil, so the meat was steamed and quite tender. A few more *bertas* and anything tasted good! Afterward, now stuffed, we again worked filming processions and then retired early. We had a long day ahead of us: morning in the market where we would finally get to try *jumiles* followed by a long bus ride to Michoacán for the second part of our program.

The Market

As always in Mexico, the best place to start the hunt for food is an early-morning tour of the local market. Taxco's market is especially interesting because, like the town, it is built in several levels up a hillside, upon the crown of which stands the cathedral. The market is larger than it first appears because of its many levels. When you talk about labyrinthine, this is it. Dudley and I had been through it several times scouting out locations and asking vendors if we might videotape them. We began at the top level in the meat section, where Dave got good shots of freshly butchered meat and meat cutters. Seeing intestines hanging on hooks and handling whole pig heads may not be very appetizing, nevertheless, it is the way authentic markets really are. Custom dictates that buyers know that the food is fresh, something like our own farmers' markets. Passing through the usual stacks of vegetables, fruit, and prepared *moles*, we made our way down to the *fonda* section located at the bottom end of the market complex. Along the way we passed many wonderful-looking elderly women perched on the market steps and in small interstices selling small amounts of vegetables, herbs, fruits, and some handwork. Without their own stands, these people were at the bottom of the economic ladder in Taxco, as they have often been in Mexico.

We came to the *fonda* of Señora Nicolasa Romero, where we were told we could find what we had long sought. Like her neighbors', Romero's *fonda* was a simply tiled counter with a preparation area just beneath it. To one side was a gas cooktop with a large pottery *cazuela* resting on top. In it was an ancient stew, no doubt the starter for the day's production. Sra. Romero had been operating her little stand for many years, and when we asked if she would make *jumiles* for us, her face crinkled into even more folds as she broke into a what might have been a smile had she had more teeth. Yes, indeed, she would be happy to show us how it is really done, she said just bring the ingredients. Dudley and I went off to find a seller. There were only two in the market that day because the season for *jumiles* had passed. One woman sitting at a little stairway landing had some in a big pot. We looked in and saw. . . small, green triangular-shaped insects crawling on a mass of leaves. The seller reached in, grabbed a handful, and stuffed them into a small plastic bag. As she did, one or two crawled to the jar's lip, ready to fly away. She snatched them in one deft movement and in another popped them into her mouth. Just a little snack, she grinned.

We returned to Nicolasa's *fonda* with our prize. In the meantime she had boiled up a tomato and a *serrano* chile. When it was ready, she took a good bunch of *jumiles* and set them in her *molcajete*. Taking her *tejolote* or mortar, she smashed them, their exoskeletons making crunching noises. Quickly throwing in the *serrano*, a little onion, and a pinch of coarse salt, she continued to grind. When this sauce was ready, the cook threw in the parboiled, peeled tomato, ground the whole lot to her satisfaction, and then declared it was ready. Taking a fresh *tortilla* in hand, she spooned a strip of *jumile* sauce down the center, folded it, and gave it to us. Crushed *jumiles* have a pungent odor and the taste is even more so, something like a cross between iodine and cinnamon. Dudley wolfed down a whole *jumile*-filled *tortilla*, rolling his eyes and muttering his characteristic "Mmm. . . mmm. . . mmm. . . !" The rest of us ate some and reckoned that one could get used to the dish, but that it was an acquired taste.

So, what was the big deal about *jumiles*? It has to do with tradition, once again. *Jumiles*—the name means mountain lice—are beetles that live on *encina*, or Spanish oak trees. There are two types of *jumiles* in Guerrero: the black *jumil* which is mostly found in Chilapa in the Costa Chica area and the brown variety found in Taxco. Insects were an important part of the pre-Columbian diet because they are highly nutritious. Biologists have studied the humble *jumil* and found it to be a good source of animo acids, proteins, and iodine. But beyond their nutritional value, there are social aspects to the little bug. *Jumiles* migrate and arrive in Taxco in the autumn. There they breed and remain through the winter. Their special place is Mt. Huixteco, the mountain that stands above the city. Every year in November, after the Day of the Dead, there is a great festival in which everyone in Taxco goes up the mountain to gather *jumiles*. It is a huge party, a great picnic, and an occasion for community solidarity while, at the same time, people say that the *jumiles* renew the city and its citizens' lives for the coming year. Why should that be? Because Mt. Huixteco is the ancient sacred mountain. Dr. Juárez Castro told us that the mountain, one of seven on which the city is built, was called the "father of waters." It is the heart of the city and *jumiles* are its edible symbol. That is why the people of Taxco have a famous saying: "Once you've eaten *jumiles*, you'll never leave Taxco." Unfortunately, we did have to leave—for Michoacán. But all of us vowed to return, even if we would have to eat *jumiles*.

The following recipe is for the *huazontles* dish that Cuco made for us that morning in his restaurant. It is a more or less standard recipe that can be adjusted for size. Everything depends upon getting fresh amaranth. The grain does grow wild all over the United States, so you need only look for it, or, if unsure, get a guide to wild edible plants such as one of the volumes in the *Peterson Field Guide* series. Since Mexicans eat many wild plants, this is a good volume to have if you are interested in authentic Mexican fare. One more note, on cheese: we call for *panela*, a common cheese that is something like the semi-soft melty Chihuahua style cheese. If you can find authentic Guerrero or Oaxaca string cheese, then use it.

Huazontles Rellenos de Queso

(fresh amaranth filled with panela cheese in guajillo sauce)

10	stalks fresh amaranth
¹/₂ lb.	*panela* cheese, cut into cubes
10	sprigs of *epazote*
5	eggs, separated
	flour

Guajillo Sauce:

5	tomatoes, toasted
¹/₄	medium onion
2	cloves garlic
2	*guajillo* chiles, soaked and seeded
	salt and freshly ground pepper, to taste

Have a large pan of boiling water ready. Place fresh amaranth in it and blanch for about 5 minutes. Remove from pan, place under cold running water, and drain. Place egg whites in a bowl and whip until quite foamy. While beating, gradually add each egg yolk along with salt and freshly ground pepper. Make bundles of amaranth and place cubes of cheese in the center of each along with 1 sprig of *epazote*. Have ready a deep fryer with oil heated to about 350°. Spread flour on a plate and, holding the amaranth bundles together very tightly, roll each bundle in flour and dip in egg mixture. Set battered amaranth bundle in the fryer and cook until exterior is well browned. Remove from the fryer and drain.

Guajillo Sauce:

Toast the tomatoes on a griddle until the skin blisters and begins to blacken. Remove them from the griddle and remove the skin. Place tomatoes, onion, garlic, and soaked seeded chiles in the bowl of a blender or food processor (better still, use a *molcajete*). Process until a smooth sauce is formed. Heat if you wish. Serve with *huazontles*.

Serves 4

Salsa de Jumiles

(Sra. Nicolasa Romero)

Want to try *jumiles*? Here is the recipe. First, catch some *jumiles*. Seriously, you can get them in North America frozen or dried, although likely only through Mexican markets.

2	C.	water
3		whole tomatoes
3		whole *serrano* chiles
1		clove fresh garlic
1/4		medium onion
1/2	t.	coarse salt
1/4	C.	*jumiles*

Bring the water to boil in a small pan. Add the tomatoes, *serrano* chiles, garlic, and onion. Simmer for 10 minutes. While these are cooking, place the *jumiles* in a *molcajete* and crush them. Remove the vegetables from the pan, add them to the *molcajete*, and crush them into a sauce. Add salt to taste while grinding. If needed, add some of the water in which the vegetables have boiled to thin. Serve in the *molcajete*.

Serves 4

4

MICHOACÁN

Michoacán I

The Journey to Morelia

After breakfasting on insects, we set out by bus for the state of Michoacán. Not the old VW bus that had rattled our bones, but a spiffy new, large, well-sprung, air-conditioned bus. First we saw Bob and Marta off. They were returning to Chicago on the same flight, back to real work. Then we drove northward out of Taxco, stopping at a mountain top to photograph panoramic scenes of that little jewel of a city. Like all the roads (mostly two-lane) on which we traveled in these mountainous zones of Mexico, this one was as long vertically as it was horizontally. We went through town after town, climbing up and down mountains, following trucks, passing trucks, and getting passed by the skin of our bus by other vehicles—in short, driving in Mexico. We chatted and planned in greater detail the next stages of the trip. We relied heavily on Bill Goldman's advice, since he is the great authority on Michoacán, especially its arts and crafts. As we drove, Bill again mentioned a place where we should stop en route. Dudley had suggested we stop in Toluca because it is where Mexico's best *chorizo* is made. I wanted to visit the anthropological museum nearby. Since we had little time, we ended up shopping for pottery.

After the bus climbed one last mountain, the road suddenly dropped down into a broad plain that was an extension of the Valley of Mexico. As we entered it, our driver suggested that we look to the right. There on a high bluff was an archaeological site called Teotenango. It is a city-ceremonial complex dating back to the Classic Period, the age of Toltecs and later, that obviously controlled the trade routes running up from the valley into the mountain communities with their valuable minerals. It was too bad we could not trek up the mountain, since its view of all the low-lying lands beneath must be spectacular. But we still had a long way to go, in all, a more than six-hour drive to Morelia, our first destination.

When we stopped by roadsides to shoot scenery from time to time, we sometimes noticed small crosses set up bearing small wooden plaques with names on them. Asked whether these were perhaps prayers put out for travelers, one of our guides told us that they were prayers for travelers—voyagers to the next life. The crosses were memorials for people who had been killed in traffic accidents. Considering the road's mountainous terrain with its many sharp curves, that revelation was not the surprise one might suppose.

After leaving Taxco, we drove up through towns such as Acuitlapán and Cacahuamilpa—all Nahuatl names—and then to Ixtapán de la Sal in the State of Mexico (the state, not the capital). Paco, our guide from the tourism secretariat, thought that we ought to see this last town, which is famous for its mineral baths. The town sits on natural sulfur springs and has become a small resort in the mountain country complete with pleasant hotels and, we were told, good restaurants. Looking at his gastronomic guide, Dudley read off these special dishes of the state: *patas de puerco* (pigs' feet), *obispo* (fried chitterlings served with *tortillas* and very hot *salsa verde*), and *arroz verde con plátanos fritos* (green rice made with fried bananas), among many others. Those among us who were not somewhat carsick began to salivate. Our bug breakfast had not filled us up. Dudley continued before anyone could stop him, telling us that certain drinks were also famous, including *mosquitos*, grain alcohol mixed with orange juice, and *chiloctli*, *pulque* (*maguey* juice) fermented with *ancho* chile and *epazote*! Although we ate and drank none of these, we did have something better later the next day.

We parked not far from the town's lovely little church, walked across the small grassy town square, and headed for the market. The central area was as neat as a pin with signs set around it reading "Do not litter," and "Keep off the grass." They were an unusual and welcome sight in Mexico. Not far from the market we spied, or smelled, more like it, a bakery at work. Dudley and I walked over there while everyone else ambled toward the place where we had arranged to meet shortly. We thought that we might find some special sweet breads made during the Easter season. The bakery was another spotlessly clean place and had the usual metal racks loaded with sweets, rolls, and breads. Dudley immediately struck up a conversation with the owners, who quickly allowed us into the back room. There, alongside banks of bricked ovens, stood a group of bakers before a long table, pulling hunks of dough from a huge pile in the middle. They deftly rolled the pieces between their hands, making them fat in the middle and tapered at the ends. They were making *bolillos*, my favorite Mexican roll. We could not resist getting some from a batch taken straight from the oven. Is there anything better, we mumbled to one another, mouths stuffed, than fresh hot bread?

Munching as we went, the chef and I made our way to a long, low-slung building. The street alongside it was covered in nylon tenting for the many street vendors who were selling everything from t-shirts and jeans to cheap kitchenware. There was not much artisan work in this resort town. The market was set on two levels and had more open space than others we had seen. We browsed for a bit, then descended to the lower level, which was the lair of the butchers. There we found a real treasure: not art, but food. In one corner we spied a small *fonda* with the sign *"cabrito barbacoa"* over it. Dudley knew exactly what this was. We bellied up to the counter where two young women were preparing food. They were utterly charming, all giggles and smiles, and delighted in our monster appetites. After one taste of what they served, our appetites grew even greater. The barbecue was made with whole young goat. Before cooking, it is marinated in a *guajillo* chile *adobo* laced with *mezcal* and seasoned with *hojas de olor*, a mixture of herbs such as oregano, thyme, marjoram, and avocado leaf. A pit is dug into the ground and stones heated to red hot are placed in it. The marinated kid is set on a rack and placed in the pit. Then water is poured into the stones to create steam. The whole thing is covered over and the meat is allowed to cook for at least four hours. Splendidly flavored tender meat, that literally flakes off the bone is the final result.

The cooks fed us plate after plate of the stuff, along with *tortillas* that they made on the spot, a freshly ground *molcajete* sauce, and a condiment or appetizer of *pico de gallo*. What a great lunch that was! We still talk about it.

After our visit to Ixtapán de la Sal, we drove on toward the city of Toluca under newly overcast skies partly created by a changed climatic pattern and partly caused by the ever-present pollution in Mexico's heavily populated and industrial areas. On either side of us were wide agricultural fields watered by large sprinklers. This was one of those industrial farming areas that produce so much food for regional, and perhaps national, markets. The region's high productivity may be the reason the Toluca wholesale markets are among the largest in the country. Had time permitted, we would have loved to videotape the action as comparison with the antique farming practices we had seen, and would see again. But we had no time. Toluca has an interesting history and there is considerable archaeological work going on in the vicinity. From at least the Formative Period, the region was a trade center for peoples from all over Mexico. After the Conquest, the Spanish Crown gave Cortés Toluca and the surrounding country because of its wealth. All that history can be seen in the city's churches and especially in the nearby *Centro Cultural Mexiquense*. It is a complex of museums about ten kilometers from the city and includes a museum of modern art, a museum of popular culture, and an archaeological and historical museum. I was interested in seeing the material from regional sites such as Malinalco, Calixtlahuaca, and Teotenango. Would that we could have visited the sites themselves! Next time, we said to one another, we'd come back and definitely sample the local food specialties.

Metepec is just outside of Toluca. The main route, mercifully something of a ring road, is a multi-lane commercial highway from Ixtapán de la Sal. Just along the highway is the Alfarería Soteno, headed by one of Bill's many friends in the world of artisans, Oscar Soteno Elias. It is really a small compound of workshops, showrooms, and living quarters grouped together. We pulled into the front area, descended, and were greeted warmly by the potter-merchant family. They had lots to sell. Metepec, it turns out, has long been famous for its potteries and has a distinctive local style. The Sotenos have their own style: particularly beautifully colored sunburst plaques with human features on their faces. Their vaguely pre-Columbian work is irresistible. All of us bought plenty of plaques (a row of them decorates one wall of my kitchen), along with some masks from Guerrero that the shop stocked. Among the folk art were trees of life and trees of death. The latter were used in celebrations of the Day of the Dead in November and are the most celebrated products of the Soteno's workshop. Anyone who has visited Mexican artisan shops will have seen versions of these pottery trees covered with all sorts of symbolic items. Those from this *alfarería* are among the best in Mexico.

After that came the real buying. Dave was taken by some really hand-some large pots, the kind that stand outside, and some wall sconces for plants. Dave is a mad gardener, as is Jan, and he had to have them and did. How we would get a half-dozen big heavy pots back to Chicago, much less manage to drag them around Michoacán with us, was another matter. Oscar said that he could send them, but at some cost. After some mulling, Bill suggested that we bring our pottery to Morelia and leave it with his friends at the *Casa de Artesaniás*; where they routinely packed and shipped such goods to the United States. That is what we did. Whether that turned out to be cost effective is arguable, but we could not easily find this unique, beautiful pottery at home. As we visited more and more artists and artisan shops, this became a greater and greater problem because all of us wanted some of everything we saw. Bill and Dudley's shopping mania had gotten into us . . . and Mexico is the place to do it.

It was a good thing we had a large vehicle. After loading our new acquisitions, we set off again for Morelia. The route rose again into high country. We entered some of Michoacán' s renowned mountainous forest areas in the national parks near Zitacurao and later near Zinapecuaro. Dense stands of evergreens and some mixed deciduous forest gave us a small sense of what much of the state must have been like when the Spanish first arrived, or, indeed, what it must have been like even early in this century.

Some of Michoacán's original environments remain, for this has always been one of Mexico's most beautiful states. Its geography is even more greatly varied than most other parts of the country. Guerrero, for instance, has three main environmental regions, and Michoacán has nine, each distinct from one another. Much of the state is mountains and hills interspersed with valleys and depresssions. The larger Balsas and Lerma rivers water the state as do smaller rivers such as the Cupatitzio. There are also some good-sized lakes. The southern half of Michoacán is taken up by the Sierra Madre del Sur and a thin strip of flat coast. Even in these two regions the climate and vegetation varies. The mountains have two zones: hotter, with more rain in the lower elevations toward the coast, and drier in the high country with thornbush and pine vegetation. The southern hillsides have tropical forests where *zapote*, *chirimoya*, banana, *guajes*, tamarind, and *mango* grow. Here, too, are still to be found wild jaguars (the largest and fiercest cat in the Americas), *ocelotes*, *tigrillos* (another night hunter not much larger than a domestic cat), pumas, wild boar (these are descended from pigs brought by the Spanish), otters, and even *coypu* (the rodent from which the fur nutria comes). These slopes and the coast are zones rich in natural life. Although they have been threatened by the chainsaw, there are strong environmental organizations fighting to preserve this marvelous native habitat.

A zone stretching 200 kilometers long and thirty wide lies to the north of the Sierre Madre del Sur's peaks. Cut off from Pacific winds, it is hot and dry, so much so that it is called the *tierra caliente*, the hot lands. Here is a land only lightly touched by European plants and animals. It is home to cactus, thorn, tumbleweed, scorpions, tarantulas, and desert reptiles. More salubrious is the adjacent region known as the *ladera sur*, or southern slopes. Scenic mountains, plains, waterfalls, and volcanoes give this area its allure. The southern and western part of the area is dominated by the Tancitaro volcanic range. The land here is deeply folded, and the altitudes range from 600–4000 meters so that there are mountains, plateaus, and plains. The climate here is temperate, 70° to 85° F year round. It is more like southern California than anywhere else, but there is more rain in the summer months. The Cupatitzio River rises up through the region, with the waterfall at Tzoríracua its most spectacular site. The river and the beautiful landscapes—mountain ranges covered with leafy trees and fertile soils—make the place, especially around Uruapán, one of Mexico's garden spots. It was one of the best places we visited.

North of this garden belt are the Montañas Occidentales. In the southern part of this range is Paracutín, an active volcano from 1943 to 1952. These mountains also have varied landscapes—some are wooded, others are bare red earth and stone—but the hills that roll down to the lakes, the famous Pátzcuaro and the scenic Zirahuén, are good farm and grazing lands. Pátzcuaro is home to some of Mexico's real food treasures: *pescado blanco* and *charales*. The foothills of the eastern mountains contain two regions, one in the north, the other in the northeast. The Valley of Zamora is particularly interesting because it shows the powerful role elevation plays in climate. It is a region of old volcanic mountains interspersed with low lands with lakes, marsh, and miasmal swamps complete with mosquitos. This is a land of heavy agricultural production, in particular the sugar cane that was once the leading export from the area and that necessitated settlements of Africans to work the fields. Agreeable in climate, agriculture, and landscape, the central region has always attracted a larger population. It has pine and fir forests, rolling hills, and some mountains, lakes, and rivers as well as the state capital, Morelia, with about one million inhabitants at present. Our tour took us through several of these regions, and as we traveled we were constantly amazed by the varieties of landscapes juxtaposed against one another.

At the end of the three- to four-hour drive eastward from Morelia into the mountains near Zitacuaro and the old mining town of Angangeo, there is one of Mexico's greatest natural wonders. It is not waterfalls or spectacular mountain scenery that one travels to see, but a special biosphere reserve for insects. Here stands the famous *Sanctuario de las mariposas monarchias*. It is a forest of fir trees where every November swarms of monarch butterflies migrate from North America. Here they winter, breed, and feed before journeying back north in March. It is hard to imagine these fragile creatures flying thousands of miles, and we were desperate to see this phenomenon. Bill told us that he had been there when the woods were filled with clouds of brilliantly colored butterflies, and the ponds were literally alive with them when they lighted to drink. We never did see them because we were too late in the year; they had already flown the forest. "Next time," we said, as we did for the many other things we hadn't the time to see in Michoacán.

Morelia I

After a long drive, we finally approached Morelia at dusk. The route, Calz. Francisco Madero, took us past the Plaza Villalongín where the Fountain of Tarascan Women stands. A sculptured group of romanticized indigenous women, it symbolizes a state with a large population of various native peoples. The fountain had just been lit as we drove by; an impressive, if slightly kitschy, sight. Francisco Madero turns out to be the Morelia's main street, and it contains the cathedral, *zócalo*, and government buildings. As we approached the center city, we saw before us a crowd of people in the street with white-helmeted police standing by.

Now we were worried. Just before we left for Mexico, the country had suffered some serious political upheavals. The ruling party's candidate for president had just been assassinated (signs and posters painted on almost every mountainside and every other available public space still proclaimed his name). Peasants in Chiapas, naming themselves for the great revolutionary leader Emiliano Zapata, had risen in protest against their poverty and ill treatment. Peasants in other states such as Michoacán threatened to follow their example. Protest marches had also been held in Mexico City. Morelia is a university city and many of its students sympathized with the lower orders of society. Everyone we spoke with in Mexico seemed uncertain about the direction of the country and the economy and the effects they would have on their lives. So, when we saw a large mass of what seemed to be protestors in the street, some waving yellow-and-red-striped banners, others shouting, dancing, and throwing firecrackers, what were we to make of the scene? Would we be able to continue the shoot or had the Revolution begun? A traffic jam had resulted, and all vehicles were now diverted to side streets by the police. As we neared the intersection where we were to detour, our guide leaned out of his window and asked the policeman what was happening. "Oh," he grinned with glee, "our football team has just won the semi-finals over (the much hated) Guadalajara, and we are going to the championship. . . first time in a generation!" Sports, not politics, had brought out all this public emotion. Sounded just like our country!

Our hotel was excellent, the Posada de la Soledad (in Ignacio Zaragoza, just off Francisco Madero in the city center). The place looked like a large old *hacienda*, which, in fact, was what it was modeled upon. Built in 1719, it was originally a convent and then the house of a grandee. It had other uses before finally being turned into an elegant hotel. The large, open courtyard is surrounded by stone arches behind which lie guests' rooms, a lounge, bar, and restaurant dining room. A broad central staircase leads up to rooms on the second floor, all of which surround the central open patio. Plenty of vines and plants decorate the building—it has a country atmosphere in the middle of the city. Incidentally, Morelia's atmosphere was something like Mexico City's. Ralph, who runs several miles each morning, had to return early because he had problems breathing. Nevertheless, we liked the hotel very much, and enjoyed its rooms, its service, and immediately upon settling in, the good, strong margaritas we slurped down after gathering in the lounge.

That night we were to meet with our guide, Servando Chávez, and an old friend of Bill's, Martín Aguilar Chavas, a government official who would help us in our travels around the state. They collected us late that evening for a meal of mainly *antojitos* (snacks or appetizers), *horchata* (a rice-based non-alcoholic drink), good Mexican beer, and more margaritas at a pleasant restaurant. The *antojitos* were as expected, but one was made with fresh sour cream, and we had a cream-finished *salsa* that was very good. We soon learned that many dishes in the state use fresh dairy products because Michoacán is now very much cow country. In the course of the conversation we asked about what we should see in Morelia. Martín began to tell us about the city; later Servando would take us on the tour.

Morelia was originally a Franciscan monastery with a settlement that grew up around it by 1541. It officially became a city in 1546 and was named Valladolid after the city north-northwest of Madrid that was once the residence of the Castillian royal house and where Ferdinand of Aragón and Isabella of Castilla were married. Several noble Spanish families settled in what was to become Morelia and created a Spanish colonial city. Morelia retains that graceful quality, as a quick perambulation of the central area shows. It is all eighteenth-century facades and arcaded streets. To keep it so, the city has mandated that all new construction must be done in the colonial style. The current name of the city dates back to 1828 and honors a hero of the Mexican independence movement, José María Morelos y Pavón.

Like the names of so many other places, this city's name celebrates Mexican nationalism.

Our hosts then said, between mouthfuls of the ubiquitous *guacamole*, that we would have to see the cathedral, both up close and from a distance. We decided to do that the next day. I am not a big fan of baroque churches, but this one is quite simple in design and decor because in the nineteenth century it was redone along classical lines. The exterior remains as it was when finished in 1744, with double towers reaching up to more than 200 feet in height. One older element is a statue made from dried corn that bears a gold crown; evidently it was presented to the church by King Felipe II of Spain.

Almost opposite this monumental structure are government offices that occupy an old eighteenth-century seminary. Buildings of a similar date line the whole street, and their facades are a mixture of styles, including a little orientalism. The Museum of Michoacán is housed in one of these. It has a good collection of objects ranging in time from prehistoric periods up to the modern era, as well as a very good display overview of the state's highly varied ecological zones. Most spectacular, though, are the murals by one of Morelia's best artists, Alfredo Zalce. He has several in Morelia, including one on the staircase in the government building that shows the heroes and villains of Mexican history. Speaking of Zalce, as we were driving through the city at Santa María near the fine little zoo, we came across a group of splendid statues done by him and depicting—what else?—Mexican history. Bill, a friend of the artist, told us that at age eighty-seven Zalce is as vigorous as ever and is still painting, sculpting, making prints. He is, in himself, something of a monument, and a link to the great age of muralists such as Rivera, Siqueiros, and Orozco, and the late Tamayo. Public art has a long and glorious history in Mexico among a people to whom artistic creation is an important facet of life. . . and that includes food.

We were ready to do the town the next morning, Easter Sunday. We began at the east end of the city center at the aqueduct and the Chuauhtémoc woods along which it stands. But first, we had breakfast at the hotel. On Sunday tables are set out for breakfast and lunch in the areas beneath the second-floor balcony, behind and underneath the supporting arches. A buffet had been set up, and laden with various egg preparations, sausages, ham, bacon, *enchiladas*, beans, breads of all sorts including *bolillos* and sweet breads, fresh juices, plenty of fruit, and good Mexican coffee. It was a fine spread and the gluttons among us dove into it with gusto. The more abstemious of us usually ate continental breakfasts, not only because the thought of a large breakfast was too much to bear at so early an hour, but also because we knew we would be eating the whole rest of the day. In addi-

Preparing *enchiladas*

tion, Kim, cameraman Dave's wife, had flown down to accompany us (really, to keep an eye on him) and to act as crew counselor. In addition to being a professional psychologist she is major Foodie, but a guilty one who is always worried about fat in her diet. At breakfast she strengthened the resolve of some us to refrain from gorging on delightfully oily food. Later, when Dudley told her how healthy most real Mexican food is—vegetables and benign carbohydrates—she fell to, sampling everything, like the rest of us. Good food is remarkably addicting.

It is only a short drive to the aqueduct from the hotel. Just north of the aqueduct is a small, well-kept park with flowered borders and park benches where some of the city's senior strollers rested. In the park's center is a huge equestrian statue of the man for whom the city is named: Morelos. At the north end of the park, across the street on the Avenida Tata Vasco, stands the San Diego church. Running between it and the Plaza Villalongín, back east toward the city, is a broad avenue with a tree-shaded midway down the center, the Calz. Fray Antonio de San Miguel. The street is more a wide walkway than a street for vehicular traffic, and it is filled with bookstores, cafés, and other small shops. Dudley and I later toured the bookstores to see what used treasures we could find, such as old cookbooks or tracts about old food ways and customs. But first we had to examine the aqueduct.

The aqueduct is the symbol of a city that had once been the capital of Spanish Mexico and is still proud of the structure. Today arches adorn taxicab doors and other commercial ventures. The aqueduct is built of stone and has more than 250 arches supporting a water channel into the city. Aqueducts always put one in mind of ancient Roman engineering, the ruins of which are still to be found in southern France and Spain. Morelia's aqueduct is not quite that old, dating to the 1780s, but doubtless its architects had in mind the old Roman models that they saw in their homeland. In this small corner of Morelia, evidence of continuity between past and the present abound, and, at the same time, the theme of change is everywhere.

The San Diego church reflects these kinds of changes. This eighteenth-century building, is not big or particularly prepossessing from the outside. Our guide suggested that we simply step inside, since it was Easter Sunday. The early services were over and there were few worshippers in the church, which was just as well, since that allowed us a better view of the interior. As simple as the exterior was, the interior was exactly the reverse. . . overwhelming in fact. The central dome and side chapels were covered in geometrically arranged rows of plaster flowers, each brilliantly colored. Where there were not plants, the designs were geometric, many of them in gold. All of us were stunned at the sight; it was like entering a world in which the heavens flowered. It was baroque, of course, but nothing like the grotesque writhing forms of the ripe churrigueresque style. This was one of the most beautifully decorated churches any of us had ever visited, a jewel that must be seen. Talking about it with Bill and Dudley, they mentioned that there were a few others like it in Mexico. (Tlalpujahua near Toluca is one.) Were the motifs Spanish? The impression given by the flowers and geometric designs was of an oriental carpet, so perhaps it was another thread in the weave of Moorish and Christian influences that was Spain. Maybe, but more likely it is purely indigenous in inspiration. The row upon row of multiple flowers in dazzling colors and the geometric patterns in triangles seemed so like the icon-topped litters carried in the Easter processions with all of their ancient symbolism. We had seen geometric designs on pottery and would see many more in other indigenous crafts such as embroidery. What this splendid little church spoke of was how Christianity took on native hues when it came to a new land. Later we were to see some of the sites where that great cultural mixing began, but no matter what I saw after that, San Diego is, to date, my favorite church in Mexico.

Opposite the San Diego church, at the northeast corner of the Calz. Fray Antonio de San Miguel and Avenida Tata Vasco, is another park, a tiny one, with several small stone monuments at one end. We were standing among them while Dave finished shooting San Diego's interior. We soon noticed that some of the monuments were topped by sculptures of temple pyramids, while others were inscribed with various symbols of other pre-Columbian peoples. When we asked about them, we were told that they were relatively new and represented the native peoples of Michoacán, both ancient and modern. Anyone who visits Mexico will see many representations of the former native civilizations in public places, from names of peoples to rulers. Cuauhtémoc, the son of Moctezuma who resisted the Spanish invaders and was cruelly executed by them, has become a national hero. One of Mexico's most revered presidents, Lázaro Cárdenas, named his son, also a political leader, for this ancient king. Why these monuments to, or celebrations really, of the pre-Columbian past? Why so much emphasis on long-dead native kingdoms when modern *indigenas* peoples are still at the bottom of the social hierarchy?

Looking across the way, we could see the giant statue of Morelos. At the end of the avenue was the Plaza Villalongín. They are both memorials to leaders of Mexican independence. Seeing these monuments together and recalling the references of my "Uncle Pepe," the answer to my question was obvious. To quote our documentary, "It has to do with nationalism. The city of Morelia, named for the great hero of Mexican independence, José María Morelos y Pavón, was a cradle of Mexican nationalism. Almost 200 years ago, Mexican revolutionaries deliberately created a new national consciousness. Morelos, himself a mixture of Indian, Spanish and African heritage, spoke of a single nation without reference to color or class. It is this pride of nationhood that permits Mexicans to reclaim their whole past, from pre-Columbian times onward, as their own national history."

Mexican nationalism, though, is an interesting thing; it is a deliberately created myth and a fairly recent one at that. Every year on September 16th, Mexicans celebrate an official holiday, "El Grito de Dolores." On the morning of that day in 1810, Miguel Hidalgo y Costilla, a parish priest in Dolores in

Guanajuato, issued a "cry" for independence from Spain. (It was actually part of a plot to be carried out later that year.) In it he asked if his people would make the effort to regain the land taken from them by the Spaniards 300 years before. In the name of the Lady of Guadalupe he cried, "¡Viva México!" Independence did not come for more than a decade, but it was the beginning—a small beginning, if we think of the nation state as having the allegiance of all of its inhabitants. The fact is, except for a few leaders such as Morelos, the Mexican independence movement was created by and for a small part of Mexico's population. Mexican society was, and in many ways still is, stratified by class, ethnicity, and skin color, (or as they used to say, "purity of blood").

In the late eighteenth and early nineteenth centuries Mexico was still a Spanish colony. Spaniards from Spain stood at the top of the social and economic heap. Called *peninsulares*, they held the major government posts, ran the military, and were the highest ranking churchmen. Beneath them were a layer of *criollos*, also native-born Spaniards who were mainly educated, upwardly mobile, but kept in their place by their arrogant Spanish "betters." *Criollos*, who were really the middle class, owned most of the *haciendas* and mining industries and wanted more. Beneath them were the *mestizos*, or those of mixed ancestry, and at the very bottom came the *mulattoes*, indigenes, and a small group of Africans. In truth, many *criollos* were *mestizos* or were related to *mestizos*, but they were "whiter" or richer than those beneath them and could claim some direct Spanish ancestry. The *mestizos* at the bottom labored on *haciendas* and mines and were considered peons, while many native people retreated to their villages where they preserved at least some, and sometimes many, of their ancient customs and languages. The distribution of wealth was grossly uneven; the few very, very rich had grand houses and every luxury Europe could provide. The poor were just as we would imagine the poor in a preindustrial age or in a lesser-developed country. Some farmers just scratched out a meager living, but many could not and poured into the cities where they lived as miserable beggars on the streets. Independence did not arise among these downtrodden groups. It came from the expectant *criollos*.

Hidalgo was a *criollo*, yet he called for "Mexicans" to reclaim their patrimony from the Spanish invaders. Hidalgo was a plain man from a poor family who worked his way up through the clerical ranks, and he seems to have wanted social and economic justice for all Mexicans regardless of rank and skin color. Hidalgo was captured by loyalist forces soon after his call and executed. His place was taken by Morelos, the greatest general of the early independence movement and the man partly responsible for the declaration of independence announced in Chilpancingo. Morelos, unfortunately, was also captured and executed in 1815 by Loyalist and Spanish forces. Two men and two themes emerge from the era. One is the concept of "Mexico for Mexicans," the idea of a fatherland without reference to social and economic issues. In that sense, Aztec emperors were coopted into the service of the great national myth. The other, evidently Morelos' sentiments, was that the nation must be of and for all the people, all of whom must participate in it: if there were popular sovereignty, then perhaps even the lowest of the low might rise to social and economic respectability. These twin themes were played out, in one form or another, over the next two centuries.

Mexico remained a class-bound society that has had any number of reform movements and revolutionary activity. Out of these a more modern nationalism was created. For example, Benito Juárez, the only full-blooded Indian ever elected president (1856–1872), presided over the confiscation of church property, the redistribution of land, and a new educational system. Then, in the violent Mexican Revolution that began in 1910, one leader, Emiliano Zapata, insisted on land for the peasantry, as well as their access to education and greater opportunities. Eventually, Lázaro Cárdenas, the former governor of Michoacán who was elected president in 1934, carried out more social reforms: land distribution, the construction of rural schools, public works, and the expropriation of Mexico's oil resources. The last saw the creation of Pemex, the government oil monopoly, that is a source of considerable national pride. Cárdenas and others, clearly playing on anti-U.S. sentiments to effect internal reform, forged modern nationalism. The great muralists who created art for the masses often portray just these themes. Whether all Mexicans actually believe that this ideal has been carried out is another matter. Most are cynical about politics, although they love to argue the subject. Dudley refers to his father's term for revolutionary leaders: "robolutionaries," a combination of robbers and revolutionaries, excepting only Morelos and possibly Zapata. (Images of Marlon Brando playing him in that wonderful movie always come to mind when I hear the name.)

What does all this discussion about social history and nationalism have to do with food? Just this: the *peninsulares* who ruled Mexico before independence tried to be as European as possible. In the eighteenth and nineteenth centuries that meant French cuisine. When they came to New Spain, these grandees brought their French cooks with them, and they influenced the course of Mexican fine dining. Later, after independence, the new elites—rich former *criollos*—followed these same patterns as best they could. When the politically reactionary among them succeeded in having France invade Mexico and place Austrian Prince Maximillian in power (1864–1867), they gained a new model of elegance, and the emphasis on a French culture and cuisine was renewed. If, then, society was stratified, so was its food. Street food or village food was not reflected in the meals of the great cooks and diners. Today, although elements of French cookery have trickled down into ordinary fare—usually through restaurants and cookbooks for the middle classes—differences remain. That is why the recipes in "elegant" or "beautiful" Mexican cookbooks bear only some resemblance to the dishes of "real" Mexico. They are mostly the creations of professional chefs and cookbook writers. Good and interesting as their dishes may be, if we look at food as an historic artifact, then we should see these upscale books as belonging to a class-bound system reinforced by French (and Central European) influences.

This discussion made everyone anxious to move on, so we climbed into our van, headed south from the city, and drove up to the beautiful residential Santa María area high atop a hill. From there we could see all of Morelia below us with the dark twin cathedral towers standing as the center from which the rest of the city extended. Just as we were shooting some panoramic shots (they are called "B-roll" in technical lingo), Servando received a call on his portable telephone. There was a *fiesta* going on in a small town north of the city. Did we want to see it, he asked? There was also a wonderful place for lunch not far away, he said. Without a moment's hesitation, we jumped back into the van and took off at breakneck speed down the winding road from Santa María, heading back through the edge of the city and out toward the airport that lies twenty-five kilometers to the north. Our new driver, José, was swift but excellent—no one closed their eyes out of the fear of seeing their imminent demise when he passed other vehicles on the narrow two-lane highway. At least this time, if fortune had failed us en route it would have been among more pleasant surroundings. Compared to the barren landscape of Guerrero, this region of Michoacán was rich—not lush, but greener—and there were rolling hills with stands of trees and ponds in the hollows; in short, signs of life were everywhere, even in this dry season.

Tarímbato lay just off the main route. We entered a street that ran into the town and drove along it between rows of houses. Every household and family seemed to be standing in their doorways, filling the street, or walking toward the town center. José inched the van through the crowd until he could go no further and then pulled to the side. We leapt out with our cameras at the ready because we had heard the music by then. Our escorts cleared a path for Dave and Ralph into the center of the crowd. There was the front end of a parade with a big bull head dancing and prancing; arching high above the head was a framework filled with *papier mâche*—like the bull—and painted and spangled with representations of the church and its surrounding countryside, with the legend "Tarímbato, Mich." One single man was the support and motive power of the whole contraption, but his helpers surrounded him and held up the superstructure with long poles. Still other helpers walked before him with longer poles that were used to hold up the power lines that drooped across the street between electrical poles and houses. We had seen the same thing done during the Taxco processions. The street was aswarm with people around this figure. . . all of them dancing, shaking, and vigorously jumping up and down to music. The town brass band followed the frolicking bull and played a bouncy tune, over and over again. How different was the mood between this and Taxco. Of course this was Easter Sunday, so the people were celebrating the Resurrection and many had been partying and drinking since midnight. Some of the town's officials were in the crowd. When we tried to talk with them, we were answered with hugs, big bleary smiles, and offers of beer, *tequila*, and who knows what else. What a party!

No *fiesta* among Mexicans is ever complete without food. The small town square was already filling with vendors serving the usual roasted corn, *tacos*, *tamales*, cotton candy, *buñuelos*, and more. Everyone was pouring hot red sauces on everything except the sweets, hoping that the chiles would serve as an antidote for the excesses of the previous night. At one end of the square a stand held colored Easter eggs, only these were not typical eggs. Each was filled with flour, to be used this way: someone who does has an egg in his or her hand walks nonchalantly up to a friend, who does not know or feigns ignorance of what is to happen, and in one swift movement cracks

"Full stomach, contented heart."

on the victim's head. Eggs symbolize rebirth, but perhaps not when broken on people's heads! Actually, it seemed to be a children's game. Every young person we saw had white-powdered hair, and all were very cheerful about it.

All that activity made us—what else?—hungry. First we needed a refreshing drink. We took the other route out of Tarímbato, a side road where our guide knew just the spot. We had been anticipating *pulque* for the whole trip, and now we were going to try it. Before we left for Mexico and while we were there, almost everyone to whom we mentioned our quest told us not to drink the "stuff" because it was unhygienic. Along the roadside was a tin-roofed stand with two long wooden picnic tables for diners. Some small cooking utensils were set off to the side, including a steamer for a kind of *tamale* made in Michoacán, and next to them sat several large plastic drink coolers. Right across the road was a field planted with *maguey*, from which *pulque* is made. Carol and I sat for the camera and were brought pottery mugs filled with several varieties of this drink. They were in different flavors: pineapple, chocolate, strawberry, and natural. The natural one was gray, somewhat milky colored, and slightly thick; it was something like *horchata*, the rice drink, and had a sweet, slightly tangy flavor, not unlike the beer to which it is related and also similar to the *tuba* we had tried in Acapulco. After shooting the sequence, we all sampled the various *pulques*. They were quite good, and tasted something like fruit juices with a kick. Ralph tasted the natural one and instantly declared that it tasted like *chicha*, a mildly alcoholic beverage he had tasted in a village he visited in the Amazon River region of Perú. *Chicha* is fermented with human spittle as the starter and Ralph insisted that *pulque* was as well. "Oh no," Dudley declared, "the juice is merely sucked out of the *maguey* plant with a straw and allowed to ferment naturally." We have discussed this ever since and still have not resolved the question of whether human saliva has anything to do with the creation of *pulque*. This is probably the reason why so many people expressed disgust with the beverage. It may also have had to do with something else—social class.

Pulque is a key element in the history of food in Mexico (see Chapter 2) . It comes from the *maguey*, or century plant that is found in the hot regions of central Mexico. Next to corn, it was the most valuable plant in the native peoples' inventory, providing everything from fiber for weaving to paper, needles, thread, and food. Not only does liquid come from the *maguey*, but it shelters prized insects such as maggots or *agave* worms (delicious when fried) and ant eggs that are put into a stew called *escamole*. The liquid, though, is what the plant gives in greatest abundance. When the season is right, the *maguey* produces large quantities of sap. It is collected by a *tlachiquero* who cuts a hole in the plant and inserts a long gourd into it. To begin the siphoning process, he sucks on a hole in the cube part of the gourd, and when the juices begin to run, he covers the hole up. The liquid is called *aguamiel*, literally "honey water," due to its high sugar content. Once collected, the *aguamiel* is brought to the site of fermentation, placed in a wooden container, and allowed to stand. Dudley says that at one time tappers used to store the juice in goat or lamb stomachs and used to sell it just like that. Natural enzymes get into it (in the same way that beer was once produced) and when it reaches the desired strength (it can be potent), the *pulque* vat is tapped. *Pulque* can be fermented with fruits or nuts to give it different flavors. Why the disdain for *pulque*? (The word *pulquería* implies a low-class drinking place. It was and still is the drink of Indian and *mestizos*. Before the rise of major-beer brewing industries in the mid-nineteenth century, the rural poor could not afford such luxury beverages as wine. They stuck with their ancient and once sacred drink, *pulque*. The marks of these ancient social distinctions are still to be seen, felt. . . and consumed.

We did not stop to eat at the *pulquería* because Servando said that we could not miss one of the best *carnitas* restaurants in the region. We drove to it along the road to the airport. Alongside that road we found the "El Dorado." The Vargas family has operated the restaurant for some five generations. Like many other roadside places, this restaurant is a group of small buildings, some residential, others dedicated to the preparation and serving of food. There is a take-out/office area and next to it a dining room. In front of the buildings a heated glass case holds piles of shredded meat, sauces, and the inevitable *comal* on which the server toasts her handmade *tortillas*. Alongside the complex is a garage-like structure where meat cutting and other preparations are carried out. Between this building and the dining rooms is a lean-to covering the main cooker. The cooker is a concrete-lined hollow with a firepit in front of and connected to it. A wood fire is lit and a large copper tub of well-used oil is placed onto the heated cooking hollow. The oil is heated to boiling and the cooking begins.

Carnitas, or "little meats," done in Michoacán style are whole joints of pork and organs that are marinated in a secret recipe containing oranges and many herbs, thrown into the oil, and literally simmered for some two hours or more. The meat is freshly butchered on the spot but the cutting done in a very rough way. The meat is not trimmed of fat, or, if so, very little is trimmed so as to add flavor and oil to the cooking medium. The result is meat that is tender on the inside with a crispy exterior and plenty of fried fat, or the *chicharrón* that Mexicans love. *Carnitas* can be served in several ways, either shredded or in larger chunks. Shredded *carnitas* may be a leaner dish, since the chuck method almost demands that the fat be left on the pork and that whole pieces of *chicharrón* be put on the plate. We ate some of both and dosed the meat with spicy red and green table sauces, chopped onions, and chiles. *Carnitas* are eaten folded in fresh, hot *tortillas* and that is what we did, gorging upon them and washing down the lot with Mexican beer. It was just the thing for a hot day.

Some of the differences between Mexican cuisine and North American food became apparent to us while eating these *carnitas*. Mexicans love different textures in their foods and often balance several on one plate. The soft, gelatinous fat will be matched by the chewier meat, its blandness enhanced by sauces that are bold but at the same time complex. The fresh *tortillas* with which almost everything is eaten add a rougher edge to the texture profile as well as a characteristic flavor. If there is a parallel between Mexican and another world-class cuisine in respect to texture and flavors, it is China. In that country's traditions, some of the same ideas about medicine and food are to be found. Compared to Mexican and Chinese culinary tastes, ours in North America seem primitive. Almost any of our fast foods are testimony (not Chicago hot dogs, however) to that proposition. Our overriding food texture is lightly crisp on the outside (fried) and soft or not-too-chewy on the inside. Beef, our traditional national dish, must be tender, as if the heavens themselves had decreed that no one should be troubled by chewing too much. Our flavors have always tended to be bland, although there is some increasing sophistication in that area, due partly to the influence of southwestern, southern, and Mexican traditions on the national palate. As for things gelatinous, we tend to eat them only if they are sweet. Even when our foods cross the border the other way—pizza, hamburgers, hot dogs, and french fries among them—in Mexico they tend to take on a native cast. That is why the hot dogs in Taxco, ordinary to begin with, turned out to be so good.

The *carnitas* were sensational and we headed back to Morelia late in the day, hoping to rest up for the next day's hectic production work. By that night, however, all of us were hungry. Walking up the street from our hotel into the Avenida Francisco Madero, we saw that the small central park was alive with people and music. An elevated bandshell stood in the center and on it a white-jacketed brass band played marches and light classical tunes. They were not quite as colorful as the band in Tarímbato, but they were much better musicians. Around them were street vendors selling the usual t-shirts, jeans, souvenirs, and food. Hamburgers, fries, hot dogs, raw sugar cane, *buñuelos*, *licuados* (fresh fruit drinks), and candies were for sale. Morelia is a candy-making center and we saw plenty of *dulces* of all sorts. Dudley then told us that the best street food was to be found at the "Cenaduría La Imaculada." In a square next to one of the churches in the city's central area were famous stands and cooks. Here Esther Gallegos produces *pollo placero* (more on this later) that is made with *guajillo* and *pasilla* chiles. She also has *gorditas* filled with potatoes, pork, *pasilla* chiles and black beans. *Uchepos* (a sort of fresh corn *tamale*) is a Michoacán specialty, and Señora Maríe Guadalupe Tinoco has the most celebrated in the market. For sweets, what could be better than Concepción Aguilar's *buñuelos*, renowned throughout the city? They are called "stretched" because she pulls the dough out by hand, deep fries it, and then dips the savory cooked dough in hot *piloncillo*. There are also *churros* which are increasingly sold in North America, although the versions here are nothing like these fresh, handmade delights. Freshly made products, often created by women using their own family recipes, characterize much of Mexican street food, and that is why it is so glorious.

Pollo en Cuñete

This chicken dish that Dudley found in Michoacán is well known in that state. Its ingredients are the now-familiar mixture of European and Mexican, although they are now more Spanish than otherwise. The bell peppers give the dish a Basque-country complexion, and the vinegar makes the dish an *adobo*. The final flavor is sour-sweet, all the more so since it should sit overnight to meld the flavors: The name of the dish, "Chicken in a Ditch," implies long marination, like sitting in a damp ditch overnight. No doubt, the *criollo* revolutionaries ate something like this when in Chilpancingo—they are said to have eaten the town completely out of food!

6		whole red or yellow peppers, roasted, peeled, and sliced
1		large chicken, cut into 6–8 pieces
½	C.	canola or olive oil
2		large Spanish onions, sliced
½	C.	white vinegar
2	C.	chicken broth
3		bay leaves
1		sprig fresh thyme, chopped
1		sprig fresh marjoram, chopped
10		whole black peppercorns
		kosher salt, to taste

Prepare the peppers as described in the Techniques section (p. 242) and set aside. Disjoint the chicken and set aside. Heat the oil in a deep, heavy pan. Add the onions and saute until transparent. Remove the onions from the pan and reserve. Place the chicken in the pan (adding more oil as necessary) and saute until all the pieces are lightly browned. Remove the chicken from the pan and pour in vinegar.

Scrape the bottom of the pan quickly, until all the crust has been removed. Quickly return the chicken, onions, herbs, peppercorns, red and yellow peppers to the pan. Cover with chicken stock, bring to boil, reduce heat to a simmer, and cook for about 35 minutes. Taste and adjust salt. Remove from heat and allow the whole dish to cool. It can be eaten this way, but is much better if allowed to stand in the refrigerator overnight.   *Serves* 4

Churros

Churros are purely an Old World dish. Fried-dough preparations range from Roman and medieval Western Europe across Central Asia to China. In North America they appear as funnel cakes and doughnuts, as well as in many other forms. The long sticks, *churros*, are found almost everywhere—from Mexican food stores to shopping malls. The fresh variety is always better. They are easy to make provided you have a pastry bag with a star-shaped tip. Or, you could get a special *churro*-maker from a Latin American store and go into business!

2 C.	flour
1-½ C.	water
1	egg
	enough cooking oil to fill a pan 2–3-inches in depth
	granulated sugar

Beat together the flour, water, and egg to form a thick, smooth paste. Heat the oil to 375°–400°. Spoon the paste into a pastry bag. Squeeze the paste out in long strips directly into the hot oil. Deep fry for 5 minutes or until golden brown. Remove the strips from the oil, drain, and cut into 3-inch pieces. Spread some granulated sugar on a plate and roll the hot churros in it.   *Makes about* 12

Tzintzuntzan and Pátzcuaro

The next morning the crew was at work again shooting in the city. We were preparing to leave for our next destination, Pátzcuaro, which was to be our headquarters for the next few days. It is only a forty-five minute to an hour drive from Morelia, so we took time to visit the *Casa de la Artesanías* in Morelia. Bill's old friend Arturo Olivares works there, as does another friend,

Kisella Sotomayor, the manager of the museum and shop. Dudley, Bill, and I had spoken with Arturo long before to arrange a trip to a Purépechan village. In his capacity as a curator and collector for the shop, he knows virtually every native village in the state, speaks their languages, and certainly knows their art work. When the president of Mexico's wife came for a visit, Arturo was the expert whom she asked to accompany her. Kisella also knows a great deal about the peoples of Michoacán, and she is an expert on food—knowledge she got from her mother, of course. Moreover, and vital to the collectors among us, Arturo and Kisella had agreed to take our growing collection of purchases, pack them, and keep them for us while we were working on location. They were good friends to have.

The *Casa* is only three blocks from the cathedral, in the handsome old convent of San Francisco. Outside in the small plaza you will always find vendors of handicrafts, some of them quite good. Inside, however, visitors will see some of the best artisanry that the state has to offer. Once one passes through the building's large wooden doors, the large open room on the left has glass cases filled with displays of crafts from the different regions of Michoacán. Around the arcaded inner courtyard run similar cases showing arts and crafts from other states. Along one side of the building is the large shop where collectors of fine arts and crafts can browse to great effect. Lacquerware, pottery, sculpture, painting, woodwork—including masks of many designs and lacquered boxes—metalwork, jewelry, and textiles are all for sale. Everything comes from the artisans and artists of the villages, and if the visitor is not going to the locations where a certain kind of work is being done, then the *Casa* is the place to acquire treasures from that region. The prices are not unreasonable. For us, the displays in both the museum and shop of the *Casa* were valuable because they gave a good overview of work from the regions we were going to visit. What we saw also put the work from those regions in the larger perspective of the entire country's folk art. And, seeing the best from the various artists, since the staff knows what is good and what is not, we refined our shopping skills. Kisella, an enthusiastic young woman, and her staff were as pleasant as could be, and we agreed to come back for some last-minute buying when we returned to Morelia. Arturo said that he would meet us in Pátzcuaro later for our journey into the back country.

We loaded our van once more and set out for Pátzcuaro. It is only a short distance from Morelia, but we stopped often to shoot scenes that interested us. We were going to the potters' village of Capula. (The potmakers were closed down that day.) As we were driving along Highway 57, Bill suddenly remembered a village Arturo had mentioned as being of interest to our project, a place well known for its cheese. What is Mexican food without cheese?

Without another word, we turned down a small side road leading to Itz-icuaro. Scenically speaking, it is not much of a village, just a cluster of houses with a semi-paved main street running through it. At the entrance to the village was a wide space with several small buildings. In front of the buildings stood a small square structure with a door in front and a service window on one side. A *vaquero* (cowboy) sat on a horse next to the window. As we watched, a hand holding a bottle of beer appeared from inside and handed it to the rider. He, dusty from work, took a long pull from the bottle, smiled at us, turned, and rode off. Two more *vaqueros* rode up to the window soon afterward, a man and a boy. We had to get a shot of this, so Dave rushed inside. Under the window was a cooler filled with beer and soft drinks and an attendant ready to pass bottles out to customers. When asked about his business, the earnest proprietor said that herding all the cattle around there was hot work, so he got the idea for his business from seeing fast-food places in the city. Here it was, in this small village: perhaps the world's only ride-in bar.

Around the back in a large once-whitewashed building was the cheese-making plant. Jan approached it with some trepidation. We had visited a number of cheese plants in Europe and the United States, but once had been to a small plant in Wisconsin at a point in the process when the entire factory smelled like, well. . . vomit. This plant was fine, although it would never pass U.S. health-inspection standards. We watched as the whole process took place before our cameras' lenses. Perhaps half a dozen workers did everything, chief among them several older women who had years of experience. They poured fresh milk from large cans into what looked like old-fashioned washtubs. They set the cans over a wood fire and heated the milk to scalding point while stirring. The milk was then set aside to cool and was finally poured into other pans where it was mixed with a bacterial culture, gently heated again, and then allowed to stand. After a time, the workers separated the curds from the whey and put them into cloth-lined forms to drain and age in a large cooler. These would be *queso fresco*, fresh cheese. When each cheese was ready it was weighed by hand on an old-fashioned balance scale, wrapped in plastic or paper, and sold over the counter. The workers used almost the same process to make *requesón*, something very much like ricotta cheese. We tasted both—gobbled, more like it, because the cheeses were so good. Maybe it was the atmosphere of the place, or perhaps it was the freshness of the hand-made cheese or its flavor from the wood fires, but these were about the best cheeses any of us had eaten anywhere. We bought several packages to eat on the road with *bolillos* and some *cecina* (beef jerky) that we had picked up in the Morelia market. That is the way to travel, snacking en route.

Mexican cheese is as varied and can be as good as any country's. Since the Spanish introduced cheese to Mexico in the sixteenth century, it has been an integral part of Mexican cuisine. Some people (Jan one of them) even think that all Mexican dishes have to be covered in cheese, preferably melted. That is not the case, nor should it be if we think about the pre-Columbian diet. That cheese was taken into the diet so rapidly must be due to the introduction and proliferation of the cattle who were looked after by the now servile indigenous population. Secondly, cheese would have re-placed something analogous in the native diet. Since cheese is a "rotted" food of a certain consistency, the item it replaced might have been *tecuilatl* or spirulina, a slime that Spanish sources say was collected and eaten by the Aztecs. Once collected, this green or black substance was shaped into cakes, often with fresh herbs, and dried in the sun. Stored like a cheese and re-ported to taste like salty cheese, spirulina was eaten with *tortillas* or could be crumbled on various dishes.[1] This sounds like *queso añejo*, so spirulina might have been its earlier equivalent.

Whatever the reasons, Mexicans made cheeses in the Spanish-Mediter-ranean style. The following are the main styles. *Crema* is a soured cream that comes in two main versions: a sweeter one that is like *creme fraiche* and *crema agria*, a true sour cream with more bite than ours. *Panela* is a fresh cheese, lower in fat than others, that is also known as *Tuma*. It is good for frying by it-self, when done correctly—crusty on the outside and tender on the inside. *Cotija* is a hard, dry, aged cheese that is used for grating or crumbling on sal-ads, beans, *tacos*, and anything else that the cook thinks could use a little bite. *Manchego*, the great Spanish cheese from La Mancha, is usually made from cow's milk in Mexico, unlike the sheep's milk used in the homeland. *Asadero* is semi-soft, easily melted cheese with very mild taste, rather like a mozzarella. *Blanco fresco* is something like a Muenster cheese; fresh but not crumbly, it can be eaten alone. It has more bite than its U.S. counterpart. *Queso añejo* is an aged, salty, sharp cheese that can be crumbled on dishes or melted. It is widely available in the United States and is a must for many Mexican dishes. *Oaxaca* refers to a style of semisoft braided cheese that comes in many flavors. One is a "belted" cheese that is more like a flavorful, powerful string cheese. *Chihuahua* style is based on the cheeses made by the Mennonite communities around Chihuahua. Like a mozzarella in consis-tency, it should be more acidic and saltier than that Italian standby. It is the melting cheese *sine qua non*. Monterrey Jack is not too dissimilar, but be sure to get a good, sharpish one if you are substituting. Mexican producers also make French-style cheeses, although in much smaller quantities than their own "national" types. Still, nothing compares to the down-home varieties we found in our travels through Michoacán.

From our current location, near the town of Quiroga, it was best to drive along the east side of Lake Pátzcuaro to get to the small city of that name. That meant going through a town we had intended to visit the next day, Tzintzuntzan. Since we were right there, we stopped to see and shoot part of the town. This town was once the capital of the Purépecha state. It is also where Christianity took root among that people. The great apostle was a Franciscan friar named Vasco de Quiroga, also known as "Tata" Vasco, or "Father" Vasco to the *indigenas* to whom he devoted his life. Born in Castilla in 1477, Vasco de Quiroga was trained as a lawyer in Valladolid, and at the age of fifty went to North Africa when the Spanish monarchy conquered Oran. There he saw the enormous mixture of cultures in the Islamic lands and realized that peace and conversion could only be brought by assimilating other cultures. In 1530 he was sent to Mexico as a judge in the colonial government. From the very beginning he was a paternalist who was concerned with the good of the oppressed indigenous peoples. A scholar educated in the Renaissance style, he had read Sir Thomas Moore's *Utopia* and decided to put some of its tenets into practice. One of these was to establish a society that was just and where the people were happy. Could the indigenous people now sunk in servitude benefit from such treatment, he asked? The method he employed was to create a town where native youths, newly well-educated in the Catholic faith, could live a civilized and just life. That place was Santa Fé de Mexico (near Mexico City), founded in 1531.

Later Quiroga became the bishop of Michoacán and took his social experiment to the Lake Pátzcuaro area, at Santa Fe de la Laguna. An extended family formed the base of that society, which was headed by a father of the family. These fathers elected the village chief and served as the town council. There were no servants and everyone had to work, but no more than six hours each day. Everyone was to share their work time between the fields and artisan work. For this reason, Quiroga is thought of as the father of all the many craft traditions of Michoacán. For example, there was wood carving at Capula, beaten copper at Santa Clara, ceramics at Tzintzuntzan and Patambán, and in Paracho guitars and violins, and many more. Many of the craft traditions remain in these same villages today. Profits gained from their production were pooled and then divided equally among all citizens. Medical care was free and all luxuries were banned, as was liquor. Only the hospitals owned goods that they could distribute. In this system, the *indigenas* were treated as responsible human beings and not as lesser beings to be either enslaved or protected.

Quiroga was responsible for founding ninety hospitals, all along the lines of his Santa Fé original. His main goal, however, was saving souls. The Indians had to be converted to the true faith (not to the new Protestant ones that had just appeared in Europe). To do this, he had to preach to the native peoples, but they were reluctant to enter churches. If they would not come in, then missionaries should go out, Quiroga reasoned. Churches were being built and attached to them were open-air chapels. Most of these are large niches set on an outer wall, the "extenta" type fully functioning mini-churches. Sometimes the large courtyards in front of the church or cloister would have *posas*, or corner chapels set at the four corners. During processions, the worshippers could stop at each chapel. We saw many of these open-air chapels in Michoacán, including in Tzintzuntzan.

Right in the center of town there is a crafts market with some fine local pottery and very good woodwork (too big to bring home, we told Dudley, who lusted for it). On one side there is a famous archaeological site, on the other side is the church complex. Named for Saint Francis, the church's foundation dates to the time of Bishop Quiroga. It is said to be the oldest in Michoacán, although every town claims that honor. The Platersque-style church, with its open-air chapel, is at one end of a large enclosure. Adjacent to it and surrounded by a wall is the hospital, a long building that looks a little like a barracks. The complex holds another church, also dating from the seventeenth century, and chapel. The buildings are in need of some plaster and paint and looked spare compared to the riotous baroque we had seen earlier in the trip. But some visual compensation came from a row of beautiful leafy olive trees in the open area. They are obviously old, so much so that local legend holds they were planted by Bishop Quiroga himself The story goes that olive trees were once planted in many parts of Mexico, but that Spanish authorities commanded them to be removed to protect the mother country's monopoly on olive oil. To this day, Mexico produces little of this valuable liquid. The Tzintzuntzan trees are some of the few survivors of the cutting (if not desecration) of these trees. They are large, with hollowed-out boles so large that a person can stand in them. Jan said that I had to do just that while describing what these were on camera. Unfortunately, the hollows seem to serve another purpose—that of privies. Stepping into one was like standing in a latrine. Needless to say, we did not pursue the on-camera discussion, but it did make our "out-takes" reel. What would the bishop have to say about this use of his precious reminders of his homeland?

Whatever Quiroga might think of what has happened to his original dream, he and those religious men and women who followed him succeeded in converting the original native peoples and the new *mestizos*. How deeply that conversion went is another matter. Three major orders contributed to the conversion process in all the varied regions of Michoacán: the Franciscans, the Augustinians, and the Jesuits. All three used the same methods of attracting people to the Church. It began with the catechism, the short course on Christian principles, which was imparted by direct preaching, with the help of didactic sculpture and paintings. A boom in religious construction followed, with the churches at Pátzcuaro and Tzintzuntzan as examples. Religious costumes—the ornamented dress of the bishops and priests—brilliant church decor, music, dance, and festivals all moved toward the same end: each element was to remind the native peoples of their own rituals, and in town after town patron saints replaced the old deities. However, "merged with" might be a better term, since so many non-European practices also transferred into common use. That became especially true when Michoacán's local parishes were formed in 1570. Independent of the more rigorous monastic orders, local customs began to flourish and they surely account for the many local varieties of religious observation, and, in part, for the region's folkways and art styles. As always, it is diversity that makes Mexican culture and its food so intriguing.

Once again we set off for Pátzcuaro and arrived in time for a late lunch after checking into our hotel. Bill had told us how picturesque the town was, and, as usual with things artistic, he was right. Set against hillsides that slope upward from the lake (it is not on Lake Pátzcuaro itself), the town features meandering cobblestone streets and tile-roofed, adobe-walled houses. It has some fine early buildings: the *Templo de la Compañía* (sixteenth century), the famed House of the Eleven Courtyards (a seventeenth-century convent), a Museum of Popular Arts (the building was an old Jesuit school, originally founded by Vasco de Quiroga himself), and the public library with murals by Juan O'Gorman, among others. The main squares are surrounded by arcaded buildings under which are shops, hotels, and restaurants. Most of the old structures have that Mexican air of weathered age; they are lived-in places that the inhabitants take as perfectly ordinary. Pátzcuaro is very much an Old World town, a place to settle in for a time. Later all of us would explore, but first we had to work . . . exploring the region's most famous dishes.

José Leo de la Rea, Pátzcuaro's director of tourism, had arranged a lunch for us at a hotel called the San Rafael Hostería just on the edge of town. Rea, a very jovial fellow who was full of energy and enthusiasm, took us everywhere in his region, cracking jokes while imparting all kinds of useful information. (He once introduced Dave, still beset with a few intestinal problems, as "Mr. Beans.") Situated in a beautiful old mansion, the San Rafael is an equally handsome hotel that also serves fine food. To enter it we passed through an archway onto a flowered patio shaded by old trees. The guest rooms, all newly redone in knotty pine, were arranged around the open space. Evidently this had been the stables area, now hosting human

"Another little fish (michin *in Nahuatl*)?"

and not equine guests. We were greeted by the very agreeable Maldonado family who own and run the hotel. Señora María Estella Maldonado, its elegant patroness, had arranged a demonstration of how to make *sopa tarasca* that would be followed by two of Lake Pátzcuaro's natural treasures: *pescado blanco* and *charales.*

Sopa tarasca is one of Mexico's most famous dishes and can be found on the menus of many Mexican restaurants at home and abroad. This version was made by placing in each bowl crispy fried *tortilla* chips, shredded cheese, *pasilla* chile, and a fat dab of sour cream. Then stock made with tomato, onion, and garlic was added and all was topped with some crumbled *añejo* cheese. It was excellent. The dish is a classic mixture of Indian and European ingredients. . . truly *mestizo* Mexican, even though the recipe may be no more than fifty years old. We discovered that any number of restaurateurs claimed themselves or their restaurants as the inventors of the recipe (actually, there are many recipes). After nosing around for a while and talking to many food people, Dudley discovered that the real creator was none other than José Leo de la Rea's father-in-law, Felipe Oceguera

Iturbide. José's wife, Catalina, also a splendid cook, described it as a special dish made for the opening of a new hotel in Pátzcuaro after World War II. Seeking something different from the usual regional dishes, he came up with this recipe, naming it for the indigenous people, the Púrepecha, or, as the Spanish called them, "Tarascans."

Pescado blanco is less controversial. It is a pale white fish that comes from the freshwater lakes in this part of Morelia. Whitefish come in several measurements. The full-sized versions are about trout size, perhaps smaller. Preparation almost invariably means a light batter coating, then quick frying, and the dish is usually served with a sauce. *Tiro* are minnows about the size of smelts and not very different in flavor. They are often dried, then prepared with sauces in varieties of ways. *Charales* are even smaller; these are usually deep fried, either with or without batter. Each of these appeared on the table and served as an introduction to the local cuisine. Everyone liked the *pescado blanco*; it was delicate and drizzled with butter and lemon, as one might eat a brook trout or sole. The *charales*, served with freshly made *tortillas*, were less popular because they have quite a strong flavor, not sweet like smelts, but fishier. Carol suggested that it was difficult to eat something with its eyes still intact. Dudley and I packed the little fish into *tortillas*, loaded them with green sauce, and did our usual thing. To tell the truth, I would not order these regularly, but when in Pátzcuaro, do as the Pátzcuarans. In all, though, it was a fine meal and all of us declared that if we returned this is where we would lodge. (It is quite reasonably priced.)

One local specialty we did not eat was *achoce* or *axolotl*, a kind of salamander. Dudley did when he paid a visit to Pátzcuaro later in the year (staying at this same hotel and meeting Catalina Oseguera de la Rea again). *Axolotls* are amphibians that resemble immature lizards because they have smooth skins and legs. They were a pre-Columbian specialty and were used especially in vegetable soups. Live *achoce* are available in the town market because according to the locals, they must be freshly prepared. For better or worse, like iguana, they must be prepared while still living. The seller takes a living *axolotl* from his tank, slits it quickly, and peels the skin off. The meat is then placed in the already boiling soup and cooked further until tender. It sounds disgusting, but it is not so different from the Japanese habit of cutting up live fish to eat raw, or the way that snake and eel are prepared in Cantonese cookery. Dudley discovered that the *axolotl* skins are used for stews and that in earlier days, nuns made a cough syrup from it because of its special affinity for the lungs and throat. The taste of *axolotl*? Dudley claims that is was a bit slimy, but that the flavor was good, almost like fish. That sounded suspiciously like the old standard: "It tastes like chicken." Perhaps for our stomachs' sakes it was better that Dudley, not we, got to eat this amphibian.

Mole Verde

This version of a famous preparation from Michoacán was devised by Kisella Sotomayor, whose daughter, also named Kisella, is the manager of the *Casa de las Artesanías* (the museum and shop where artisans from all over the state display their work) in Morelia. It is a little like the *pipián verde* recipe given earlier, but richer.

¼–½	C.	cooking oil (light olive would be good)
5		*poblano* peppers, seeded, deveined, and chopped
4		*serrano* chiles, seeded, deveined, and chopped
4		*jalapeño* chiles, seeded, deveined, and chopped
8		*tomatillos*, peeled
1	C.	Italian parsley
1	C.	fresh cilantro
1	t.	fresh thyme
		a handful of pumpkin seeds
10		almonds
8		leaves of romaine lettuce, washed
1	lb.	pork loin, cubed
		chicken stock
1		bay leaf
¼	t.	ground cloves
		salt and freshly ground pepper, to taste

The sauce is prepared in three separate steps. First prepare the chiles. Heat 1–2 tablespoons of oil in a heavy skillet and sauté the chiles until soft. Remove them from the pan and set aside. Second, reheat the oil, adding more if necessary, and sauté together the *tomatillos*, parsley, cilantro, and thyme until the *tomatillos* are soft. Remove the mixture from the pan and set aside. Third, reheat the oil, adding more if necessary, and sauté together the pumpkin seeds and almonds until the pumpkin seeds are lightly browned. Remove the mixture from the pan. Place the three mixtures—the chiles, the herbs-*tomatillos*, and the pumpkin seeds-almonds in the bowl of a food processor bowl (a *molcajete*, or grinding bowl, is really much better). Add the lettuce leaves and process until blended. Set aside. Meanwhile, sprinkle salt and freshly ground pepper to taste over pork cubes. Heat 2–4 T. cooking oil in a deep, heavy pan. Add pork and brown over medium heat. When browned, add enough chicken stock to cover. Stir in the prepared sauce. Add bay leaves. Cook over low heat, simmering, until the liquid is reduced to about half its volume. Stir in ground cloves at end and adjust salt and freshly ground pepper. Serve the fresh tortillas.

Serves 4

Sopa Tarasca

(Sr. Felipe Osegura Iturbide, Pátzcuaro, Michoacán)

This is one of Mexico's most famous "traditional" dishes. In reality it was created by Sr. Osegura, who ran a hotel in Pátzcuaro, the Hostería San Felipe. Made for the opening of the hotel, Sr. Osegura gave this dish the Spanish name for the indigenous peoples of the region, *los tarascos*. These people usually call themselves the *Purépecha*, as we have throughout the book. The story of the name *tarasca* is that it means "son-in-law" in *Purépechan*, a good example of the mixture of Spanish and native languages. This dish, then, is aptly named because it shows both influences and has undergone many transformations in the hands of chefs over the past forty years. This is the "original" version.

6	T.	canola oil
1		whole onion, finely chopped
2		cloves garlic, finely chopped
1	C.	tomato purée
8-½	C.	water
4		whole bay leaves
4		sprigs fresh thyme
2		sprigs marjoram
4	C.	chicken stock
1	t.	freshly ground pepper
6		whole *ancho* chiles, julienned
¼	C.	or more canola oil
10		whole tortillas, cut into strips and deep fried
12	oz.	*fresco* cheese
1-¼	C.	sour cream
1		avocado, peeled and cubed

Heat oil in a deep soup pot. Add onion and sauté until transparent. Add garlic and tomato purée. Heat to simmer and cook for 3 minutes. Stir in the chicken stock, herbs, and black pepper. Heat to simmer and cook for 10 minutes. While the soup is cooking, heat canola oil in a deep, heavy skillet. Add tortilla strips in batches and fry. Drain on paper towels. Place 1-½ cups of the soup in the bowl of a food processor or blender. Add ⅓ of the julienned *ancho* chiles and strips from one of the fried tortillas. Process until mixture forms a thick purée. Stir this purée into the soup and mix well. Simmer for an additional 5–10 minutes. To serve: Place remaining julienned *ancho* chile strips, *fresco* cheese, and cubed avocado on a serving plate, along with a bowl of fried tortilla strips and a bowl of sour cream. Place tortilla strips and sour cream in each bowl. Cover with soup. Garnish with julienned *ancho* chiles and cubed avocados. *Serves 8*

Sopa de Frijol

(Catalina Oseguera de la Rea, Pátzcuaro, Michoacán)

Felipe Osegura Iturbide's daughter is also a fine cook who gave us some interesting receipes. *Sopa de frijol* is a simpler version of *sopa tarasca* and is in fact, its ancestor. The preparation is strongly reminiscent of Spanish black bean soup, though Spaniards did not get black beans until their discovery of them in the New World. The Spanish preparation usually has cumin in it and is served with a spoonful of sour cream in the center.

1–2	T.	olive oil
½		onion, chopped
6		cloves garlic, crushed and chopped
1	lb.	black beans, raw (equals 4-½ C. cooked)
1	t.	fresh oregano
1	t.	white pepper
2	t.	unsalted butter
1–2	t.	kosher salt
		grated *fresco* cheese

If using raw beans, first heat olive oil in a large soup pan, add onion and garlic, and sauté. Add beans and cook according to "Preparing Beans" section (p. 244). When done, allow beans to cool a bit and remove from pan. Reserve the water for thinning the soup. Then place the beans in the bowl of a food processor with a little of the bean water. Purée together with oregano and white pepper. Pour the bean purée in a large strainer and force it through to make a finer purée. Return the resultant fine bean purée to the soup pan and heat gently. Add butter and stir into the beans. Add bean liquid to thin the soup to the desired consistency. Adjust salt levels to taste at end.

Serves 6-8

Note: Ten *epazote* chopped leaves and a pinch of cumin make a good substitute for the oregano and white pepper.

Aporreadillo de Charales

(Catalina Oseguera de la Rea, Pátzcurao, Michoacán)

We had almost forgotten about breakfast in the lake region. The Patio Restaurant and many others make an omelette using their favorite little fish, *charales*, or whitefish. Whenever we ate them it was always the dried version, and they had a powerful fish flavor that takes some getting used to. In testing our recipes, a few of our cooks liked them no matter how they were done. If you prefer to use fresh fish, then smelt will do, although they are much sweeter than *charales*. Closer to the original are the small dried fish that can be found in Asian markets. Or, you could try dried shrimp as an experiment.

2	T.	canola oil
2	C.	dry *charales*
6		whole eggs, whipped
1		large tomato, diced
½		medium onion, finely chopped
1		clove garlic, chopped
1		*serrano* pepper, chopped
5		sprigs cilantro, chopped
1	C.	hot chicken broth
		kosher salt and freshly ground pepper, to taste

Heat the oil in a large, heavy skillet over medium heat. Add the dried fish and fry for 2 minutes. Stir in the eggs, tomato, onion, garlic, and *serrano* chile. Cook until set, stirring occasionally. Add chopped cilantro and chicken broth. Bring to a simmer and allow to cook for 15 minutes, uncovered, or until liquid is mostly absorbed. Season with kosher salt and freshly ground pepper, if desired.

Serves 4

Note: Serve in warm *tortillas* topped with a fresh red salsa.

Lake Pátzcuaro, Tzintzuntzan, and the Night Market

Lake Pátzcuaro

The next day we planned to go out onto the lake to shoot something we hoped would be a highlight of the documentary: fishing with butterfly nets. While this was interesting, the idea of seeing working *chinampas* held a greater interest for me. We had taken a quick scouting trip to the lake the evening before and were anxious to come back for a more complete tour. Because we would have to be on the lake by 6:00 A.M., most of us went to bed early. Dudley, who was rooming with Bill, told us to wake him so that he could go along. But he (and we) had not counted on his social proclivities.

That night Dudley and Bill encountered some interesting art people and ended up chatting and snacking with them for some time. Pátzcuaro has a wonderful climate, not too hot, because of the lake. But in the early morning hours, the lake becomes not just cool but cold. Of the entire crew, only Dudley had thought to bring anything like a warm jacket. The rest of the crew would have to borrow some warm clothing from Sr. de la Rea, who was chaperoning us throughout the whole shoot. When we were ready to go, Jan asked Ralph to wake Dudley. He crept down the row of rooms to Dudley and Bill's door and tapped gently. No answer. He tapped louder, but still no response. Not wanting to wake up all the guests, he returned and reported back to Jan. Never one to brook any delays in action, and with a hot temperament to boot, Jan pounded down the corridor and smashed her delicate little fist on Dudley's door. Only then did a groan arise from within. "Dudley, let's go," she announced. There was a silence followed by, "Dudley, *we're late!*" Then came Dudley's immortal line, a phrase we have never let him forget: "I'm not goiiiing. . . ." "Good," Jan replied, "then give me your jacket." Several moments later, Bill opened the door and handed out our prostrate friend's jacket, while he lay in bed still groaning. Jan turned with a big grin, saying, "I was hoping he wouldn't get up!" Everyone else also grinned, knowing that a cold director is not a happy one.

Lake Pátzcuaro is several miles from town. There are docks on the mainland with large tourist boats taking visitors to the lake's islands, especially the island of Janitzio, which bears an enormous statue of Morelos. Most of the butterfly fishermen were at the southern and eastern ends of the lake, where they worked among the *chinampas* and fish-breeding pens. Because of heavy overfishing, the unique *pescado blanco* has become an endangered species. The state's government intervened and established severe limits for how much and what kind of fishing can be done. In addition, it has built breeding areas that are restricted zones. These measures have worked well enough to allow *pescado blanco, charales*, and other regional fish to appear once again on the menus of all the region's restaurants. One of the restrictions is on the overuse of butterfly fishing nets. The state marine biologist happened to be on site at the time, and when he saw the boats and their nets, he pulled out his own camera and began shooting. In all the time he had worked on the lake, he had never seen them. We did, and they were as wonderful as advertised.

A morning mist rose from the lake like a thin cloud bank, and then, where the white haze met the gray-green water, a line of brown pointed shapes slowly emerged. They were the prows of dugout canoes; presently, whole canoes appeared, long narrow shapes with paddlers upright in the center and gossamer wings on either side. They moved in silence, eerie in the morning light, like hovering dragonflies. The wings were fine mesh nets attached to a long handle and cross brace in two wide arcs. The fishermen were small, nut-brown men who silently—since all fisherman know that talk will frighten the fish—dipped their nets into the water, waited, and then pulled on the net itself, taking it in a little at a time. They worked methodically, slowly, and without much reward. Then, after three-quarters of an hour, one fish managed to get itself caught. It was a fine specimen, about eight inches long, and it brought cheers from the assembled boatmen. Once fishermen such as these made a good living from the many fish they caught; today they farm as much as pursue their ancient prey.

Where the lake dwellers farm is on the lake's edge and on *chinampas*. Around the lake's perimeter were gardens, some attached to small houses, others in what were obviously allotments. Corn, beans, greens, squash, and tall flowers all grew in abundance. The plants were so verdant that we could hardly see the houses nestled behind them. *Chinampas* are floating artificial fields that are usually associated with the lakes on which ancient Tenochtitlán, the Aztec capital, was built. (see Chapter 2, p. 54.) They are made from bottom mud, reeds, grass, and animal and human wastes (in pre-Columbian times). Exceedingly fertile, *chinampas* were a splendid invention, an essentially closed ecological system that fed huge numbers of people. I had read much about them, and here they were, lying in long rectangles just off the shore. Our own motor-driven boat eased its way around and into the channels between them so that we could get a good look. There were not any crops on the *chinampas*, only wild greens, cattle, and birds. Gliding by, we saw black-and-white Holsteins grazing on the rich plants and could see why the local fresh cheeses were so good. How the cattle got to the artificial islands puzzled us at first, but after seeing several wading offshore, up to their necks in water, it was apparent that they swam across the sort distance. The idea of cows swimming still seems odd. Another time, a white heron stood on the back of one wading beast, scanning for any small fish that its hooves might have churned up. The whole scene was idyllic: a rich environment, so very different from the landscape just a few miles inland. As the sun rose higher moment by moment, the air grew warmer and the mist burned off the waters. More and more canoes appeared from the tiny slips leading down from the houses along the lake. Men and women together paddled off on their daily business. It is one of the best commuting systems, and positively the most economical. But it reminded us that we had to be off, back to Pátzcuaro for a long day.

We were going back to Tzintzuntzan to visit the archaeological site that was once the seat of the Purépecha kingdom. But before that, José de la Rea told us that we had to visit the traditional medicine center not far from our hotel. We walked there quickly. An old, dilapidated building that was obviously once a grand house or cloister, the center is on Vasco de Quiroga, (literally) down the street from the museum of popular regional arts. We walked through a wide doorway, and the ancient wooden door swung open for us. Inside was the usual courtyard with rooms around it on two levels. A doorway passed through that section opening onto an unkempt garden area behind the building that was littered with stray bricks and building materials. But the centerpiece was a garden planted with a profusion of medicinal herbs of various types. Each had a handwritten wooden sign staked next to it, telling what the herb was in both Spanish and Purépecha. Each was symptom-specific, and more than one was said to cure chronic Mexican complaints of *vómito y diarrea*. Other herbs were for liver ailments, the heart, the lungs,. . . just about anything that ails human beings. Most were native American plants, although a few, like chamomile, had been imported from the Old World. We had seen dried versions of these in markets, so there is a wide interest in "natural" medication in Mexico. However, there was more to see in the center itself.

De la Rea led us up to the building's second level where the clinic was located. But this clinic was not for a conventional medical practice. Out of its door came a tiny, Purépechan woman, all smiles, who shook our hands with great vigor, introducing herself as Señora Agapita. Our guide explained that she is the "medicine woman" for the clinic, a healer who has practiced her craft for fifty years. She hardy looked it, appearing to be only in middle age. Were any of us in need of cures, she asked? Not really, said our director, but filming a demonstration of how she worked might make for a good segment in our program. Of course that would be possible, Agapita said, just come into my "office." That meant I would get the treatment and Dave would shoot it. No spectators were allowed while Agapita performed. Wait, said the tourism officer, did we really want to do this? The *señora* is famous for dealing with serious problems; perhaps her therapy would be too severe under the circumstances. Don't worry, came the lady's reply, this would simply be a general tune-up to protect against any future mishaps. With that assurance, we entered through a curtained arched doorway.

The room was as decrepit as the rest of the building, dark save for light from many candles and small windows high up on the exterior. A table at one side of the room held bundles of fresh and dried herbs, dark liquid-filled bottles, candles, and framed pictures of the Virgin and Jesus. The first step was an overall scrubbing with a large bunch of green tarragon leaves that Agapita then threw on the bare stone floor. Why she chose this herb the practitioner would not say. It is not native to Mexico, but it has always been used medicinally, especially to "freshen" breath and body. Maybe it is its slightly anise-like pungency that allows it to be used this way. Next, Agapita energetically rubbed me all over with an egg while chanting religious formulae; Christian invocations to the Holy Trinity and other saints. The egg, she said, was used to divine evil spirits and remove them from the body. Next, she chose a bottle from the table, had me open my shirt, and rubbed my chest with the elixir that came from it. It was wonderful, rich in herbs and flowers. When I asked what was in it, she replied that it was a secret formula of seven plants that were sovereign protection against any external evil. If she were more commercially minded, the liquid could be bottled and sold for a good deal of money. I can smell it still! Finally, she demanded that I crush all the tarragon underfoot and, when I began to falter, insisted on more spirited stomping until all the leaves were thoroughly mashed. As I did this Agapita told us that she had learned the craft from her mother, who had learned it from her mother, and so on backward into generations now forgotten. What she did, on reflection, was something we had seen in the drawings and paintings from the villages in Guerrero, and so is clearly part of a vital tradition. Did the cleansing work? Absolutely. I felt great afterward and, discarding those pink tablets, ate everything in sight without ill effect. When I reported this to our friends, they all promised that if ever they returned, a visit to Señora Agapita would be on their agendas.

Tzintzuntzan

Our schedule beckoned, so we left the medicine center before anyone else could get a similar treatment and headed back to Tzintzuntzan. That day we were going up to the archaeological site to explore and discuss the ancient Purépecha kingdom. Modern Tzintzuntzan is set on the shore of Lake

Pátzcuaro and, as is so common in Mexico, hills rise behind it. We approached from the hillside and from its crest we could look out over the lake from behind the ruins of the ancient palace complex. We stopped there to examine the scene and do a little shooting. The road at that point spirals downward—down the hill and around the bend onto the valley floor. At the top we saw what had now become familiar, crosses in memory of *los accidentos*. As Dave and Ralph were setting up, José de la Rea knelt down on one knee near the crosses, we thought to say a small prayer. Instead, he began clearing away a little dust and then stood up holding a small object. Beckoning us over, he showed what he had found: a slim, black stone blade. It was a pre-Columbian tool made from obsidian; this beautiful flake tool was struck from a core and was as sharp as if it had just been made—sharp enough to cut into the chest of a sacrificial victim, for that is the substance from which the priests' knives were made. The discovery of one blade must mean more nearby. Dave and Ralph handed the camera to me, saying that they would only be a moment. Before long they and everyone else were loping along, bodies bent to the ground, searching for blades and bits of ancient pottery. Ah, the allure of archaeology! After half an hour of this and a few handsome flake blades later, we finally got the treasure hunters back to work. But there was something in what had happened: the mixing of remnants of a dead civilization among memorials to the more recently departed, all together on a sunlit Mexican hill top.

We got to the site itself,[2] finding it set on the southeast edge of town on a hill top with a panoramic view of the lake. All of us walked to the edge of the hill and imagined ourselves as the *Kanonsi* or priest-king, surveying his vast domains. The archaeological zone is more than two square miles in extent, and the public section is only a small part of the whole. Nonetheless, it is a park setting with trees that is bounded by major standing buildings (much reconstructed) facing the lake and other excavated building foundations off to the side. It is an impressive place, especially the huge platform (1335 feet long and 600 wide) upon which rest five *yácatas*. Rectangular at the base, each *yácata* is a pyramid built in steps, connected by a step to a round structure. The *yácatas* are constructed of basalt block and once had facings of basalt slabs fitted neatly together and mortared in place. Like the pyramids in other parts of Mexico, these, too, were built in layers, one over another.

The pyramids' architecture is unique in all Mexico, the method of construction closer to that of ancient Perú than to the Mexican models closer at hand. That these pyramids might have been influenced by far-away Perú has been suggested by some scholars. That argument has been given apparent reinforcement by the problem of the language spoken by the rulers of this place, one that is still spoken in some Michoacán villages: Purépechan or

Tarascan. Many think that it has no linguistic relatives anywhere, except for Quechua in highland Perú. After all, if tomatoes came to Mexico from South America, why not bits and pieces of its culture as well, or so the argument goes. More recent work on language suggests, in fact, that Purépechan is distantly related to other languages in northern Mexico. Still, the site and the people are exotic even in a land that is full of surprises.

Excavation of some of these massive edifices shows that they were ceremonial centers, temples, and burial places for kings, and perhaps palaces. Who were these great kings? We know something about the kingdom from a work left by Vasco de Quiroga, apparently a translation of writings in the native language, called the Relacion de Michoacán."[3] The story goes something like this. Michoacán has a long prehistory that begins with small farming or food-gathering communities located all over the state's many regions. That included the lakes, which were much higher then (and, in fact, still were well into the sixteenth century) than they are now. People from Teotihuacán came from the Valley of Mexico and established trading posts in the state before 650 A.D. along with some urban centers that looked just like their big brother to the north. Tingambato and its ball court, mentioned earlier, was one of the centers. After the great city fell, other small states appeared, probably created by people who spoke Nahuatl. Farming and fishing were the base of this economy and when the Purépecha appeared, there were plenty of resources available for them to build their state.

According to the Relación, the Purépecha migrated from the north sometime around 1200 A.D. A warlike tribe, some of their chiefs eventually gained power over the Pátzcuaro region by around 1325, and from there eventually conquered almost all of Michoacán, with much of the expansion carried out by a legendary king named Tariácuri. His death led to the kingdom's divisions into three major areas and capitals: Tzintzuntzan, Pátzcuaro, and Ihuatzio. All three were allied in war and trade and were so powerful that they were able to repel invasions by the Aztecs around 1450. However, the Purépecha resembled the Aztecs in many ways. They collected tribute from their subjects, enslaved people, practiced human sacrifice, had kings who were deified, and supported artisans who created brilliant art. It was a highly stratified society where the wealthy elites lived next to the poor who labored for them. All of that was lost—the kingdoms destroyed and the chiefs and nobles reduced to peasants by the all-conquering Spanish. But after the Conquest, the poorer peasants continued to live much as they had in the past.

Villages lived on, farming and fishing, hunting and gathering. Even when much of the land was given over to European plants and animals, the villagers shifted their practices to accommodate them . . . but they always grew corn and made *tortillas*. Their crafts also lived on. In the old kingdom, each town specialized in a craft according to the available resources in its area. In some it was wood, in others it was stone carving; weaving of *maguey* threads and cotton; copper, silver, or gold work; turquoise and jade carving; pottery; and more. When Bishop Quiroga set up craft villages, he followed a well-established pattern. Those villages are still there, some Purépecha, others Nahua or other groups, and many *mestizo*. Most still specialize, producing wonderful work and some terrific food. We were anxious to see them.

The Night Market

A long day deserved a good night. Carol had read about the local specialty, "Plaza Chicken." Since it featured her favorite food, potatoes, she was ready to go. This time, Señora Catalina de la Rea, the tourism director's wife and a fine cook, came along as our guide. Although Pátzcuaro is a small town, it has several street markets with food everywhere. Earlier in the day when we returned from Tzintzuntzan, Jan needed some batteries for a piece of equipment. Dudley and I went out to find them, searching through the small storefronts and at the same time exploring the nooks and crannies of this quaint town. Unfortunately, since it was getting on to evening, street-food vendors had begun to emerge. Dudley clapped eyes on one that seemed interesting: a pushcart serving *carnitas* and *cabrito*. He had to stop, get some, and stuff himself. As sauce dripped from his merry face, he looked up and, suddenly remembering that I existed, offered me some. I declined, worried about fulfilling our errand before the stores closed, and only commented to Dudley that now I knew why Mexicans are chronically late for everything, except meals.

After dark we walked to the Plaza Gertrudis Bocanegra where food sellers rimmed the square under nylon awnings. We walked past long rows of candies from Morelia; *dulces de leche* are my favorite because, unlike many, they are not tooth-sticking like the oversweet *morelianos*—thick fruit jellies. Much of the cooking is done on one side of the square where some permanent stands are located across the narrow sidewalk from the portable ones. The soft, yellow light was suffused with smoke and steam from cooking, along with smells that made the gastric juices flow. Here we found Plaza Chicken. It is made in an interesting way—in a large copper *comal* with a concave center and a wide rim. The center is set over the flame, oil or lard is added, and the chicken, cubed potatoes, carrots, and onions are cooked in it. Once cooked, each ingredient is pushed up on the flat edges where they are kept warm. A place is also left open for the small *enchiladas* that are served with the chicken portions. It was a properly greasy treat, just what one expects in good street food. We saw *tamales de harina*, made from wheat flour, some with blackberries in them that had been cooked to a jelly-like consistency. Corn on a stick, *tacos*, *empanadas* filled with pumpkin (called *chilacayotes*), and sherbets with flavors such as guayanaba, pistachio, peanut, watermelon, and zapote negro, as well as many more delectable items were all available. The best *carnitas* in town were not far away in a stand belonging to Raul Majia Coria.

Off the square and up a small street was a long row of clothing and shoe sellers. They all had handmade blankets, embroidered shirts, the usual *huaraches*, typical Michoacán farmer hats (many states have their own distinctive styles), and handmade *rebozos* (shawls). The last were so handsome that we all got some, the women wearing them throughout the rest of the trip. We were only sorry that it was not a full market day where we would have found *cayarcta*, the small lake bird that is a local delicacy. Nor did we see the display of pre-Columbian cooking tools with particularly fine *molcajetes*. When Dudley returned a few months later he bought a batch of good ones—each weighs a good ten pounds—and brought them back for friends. When we worked out the recipes for this book, we often used one: it definitely makes the food taste better. But then, so does the food in the open-air market; it is something like a permanent picnic.

Michoacán is famed in Mexico for its dairy industry and its ice cream; the leading chain of ice cream shops is named for the state. The following recipe is not from that chain and is hardly what we would think of as ice cream today (although it does resemble U.S. recipes from the 1930–1940s era). *Nieve de pasta* shows just how sweet the Mexican dessert tooth can be.

Nieve de Pasta

(Sra. Lolita González, Pátzcuaro, Michoacán)

2	qts.	whole milk, boiled
1	can	evaporated milk
1	C.	sweetened condensed milk
1-½	C.	sugar
½	t.	cream of tartar
¼	C.	cold water

Have ready an ice-cream-making machine or churn. Place the milk in a large pan over medium heat. Bring it to a gentle boil and turn down the heat immediately, so that it does not overflow the pan. Stir in the sugar a little at a time while keeping the milk at a simmer. When the sugar is blended and melted, allow the milk mixture to simmer for 20–30 minutes. Stir in the evaporated milk and sweetened condensed milk. Mix together the cream of tartar and cold water in a bowl. Pour a tablespoon or two of the hot mixture into it, and stir until thick and smooth. Slowly stir this mixture back into the simmering milk mixture. Return the liquid to a simmer and allow it to cook for at least 1 hour. Stir it constantly (about every 5 minutes) in a circular motion, so that it does not burn on the bottom of the pan or become lumpy. After it becomes thick, about the consistency of a thin custard, remove the mixture from the heat. Allow the mixture to cool at room temperature. When cool, pour it into the bowl of an ice-cream maker and process until it becomes very thick, like an ice cream. Serve or freeze.

Serves 6–7

Note: Nuts can be added to the mixture before freezing; in Mexico these are usually pistachios, pecans, or peanuts. Also, the dessert goes well with almond cookies.

Pollo Placero

Plaza Chicken is a relatively simple recipe. It is best made in the giant pans used in Michoacán, in which all the operations are done except the sauce. Lacking one of these, try a large cast-iron pan or even a large wok. There are three steps to the procedure—the sauce, the chicken and vegetables, and the *enchiladas*. The sauce can be made while the chicken is cooking, of course.

Chicken

1	medium whole chicken
	bouquet garni (mixture of oregano, basil, thyme, and laurel leaf, tied in a bag)
	kosher salt and freshly ground pepper, to taste
½ C.	canola oil
3	medium potatoes, boiled and chopped into large squares
3	large carrots, chopped into large squares

Sauce

1	medium onion, finely sliced
3	large tomatoes, peeled and chopped
1 T.	sugar

    1 C.   chicken broth, from cooked chicken
           oregano to taste
    1   head romaine lettuce, finely chopped

Enchiladas

    3   *ancho* chiles, deveined, seeded, and soaked in hot water
    1   large tomato, toasted or roasted and peeled
    1   garlic clove
    1 C.   *queso fresco* or *ranchero* cheese, crumbled
    1 C.   canola oil
    8   fresh corn *tortillas*

To Prepare the Chicken:

Place whole chicken in a large pan and add enough water to cover. Add *bouquet garni*, kosher salt, and freshly ground pepper, to taste. Bring to a boil, reduce the heat and simmer for about 1 hour. Remove the chicken from the pan and set aside to drain and cool. Reserve the broth. When ready to cook, cut the chicken into 6–8 pieces and have the chopped potatoes and carrots ready. Heat the canola oil in a large heavy skillet or wok until hot. Add the chicken and fry quickly until browned. Remove it from the pan and keep warm. Add the potatoes and carrots and fry until lightly browned. Remove them from pan and keep warm. While the chicken and vegetables are cooking, make the *salsa* and then the *enchiladas*.

To Prepare the Salsa:

Heat 1 tablespoon canola oil in a saucepan. Add the sliced onion and tomato and cook until the tomato becomes a thick sauce. Add the sugar, kosher salt, and freshly ground pepper, to taste. Pour in 1 cup of the reserved chicken broth, bring to simmer, and allow to cook until thick.

To Make Enchiladas:

Soak chiles in hot water until very soft. Toast or roast the tomato until the skin blisters and peel. Place the chiles, tomato, and garlic in the bowl of a blender or food processor (or *molcajete*) and purée. When done, strain the sauce. Heat 1 teaspoon canola oil in a saucepan. Pour in the sauce and cook until slightly thickened. Season with kosher salt, to taste. Heat a deep, heavy skillet or *comal* and add 1 cup of canola oil and heat until hot. Dip each *tortilla* in the oil and fry lightly. Remove it from pan and dip in the *enchilada* sauce (not the *salsa* described previously. Fill with crumbled cheese, fold in half, and place in hot oil. Fry until lightly golden. Remove from the pan and drain.

To Serve:

Place the chicken pieces on a large platter and surround them with the cooked vegetables. Pour the *salsa* over the chicken. Sprinkle with oregano and decorate the top with shredded lettuce. Serve with the *enchiladas.* *Serves 4*

Artists and Artisans

The next day, we were going to visit a mask maker, Bill's friend Juan Orta, and then on to Santa Clara del Cobre, the famous copper village. After a fine breakfast at the nearby Patio Restaurant—hot cakes, *machaca de charales* (eggs with white fish), *huevos divorciados* (fried eggs, one in green sauce and the other in red sauce with *chilaquiles* in the middle), and plenty of Mexican coffee—we were off.

First we wanted to get another overview of the arts and crafts of the region in addition to some information about the archaeological finds in the immediate area. Have we mentioned the *Museo Regional de Artes Populares?* The building, in which the museum is housed is simple in design and decor and was originally a jail built by particularly cruel Spanish *conquistadores* for their Indian prisoners. Taken over by Bishop Quiroga in about 1540, the jail was turned into a school. It is located on the site of a spring that is said to have been brought forth miraculously by Quiroga. Its nine rooms are filled with collections of handicrafts and popular arts from all over Michoacán. The rooms begin with pre-Columbian artifacts, move through the Spanish colonial period, then on to religious art, and finally end with a series dedicated to traditional objects of everyday life. Fine green pottery from Tzintzuntzan (which is still made there; especially fine is the ware made by Consuelo Saldivar with fish, deer, and rabbit motifs) and Santa Fe de Laguna, copper work from Santa Clara, and textiles, wooden products, and much more are on display. For us, the best displays were the mask collection and the pre-Columbian ruins. About fifty years ago when the museum was founded by the National Institute of History and Archaeology, the authorities expanded into the back garden area. There they discovered the ruins of an ancient temple, and now it stands on display at ground level. Above it, just as it would be in a stratified archaeological site, is a traditional Michoacán house called a *troje*. These are still to be seen in the state's villages. Made of wooden planks (reminding us of the Michoacán forests), they resemble Swiss chalets done in a Mexican style with carvings on posts and the exterior. *Trojes* descended from native houses, when pre-Columbian styles mixed together with Spanish and perhaps other European traditions. If visiting Pátzcuaro and the museum, be sure to see these displays: the masks and buildings in the rear.

We were bound for the village of Tocuaro west of Pátzcuaro and south of the lake. The village is well known for its fantastic masks, and no carver is more renowned than Juan Orta. When you read about the masks of Tocuaro, the references are likely to be this artist, his sons, or his cousins. Tocuaro is a small village of white-walled houses, a rutted dirt "main" street, and earthen side streets. Each house was more like a compound, as we had seen in many parts of the country, with workshops, domestic quarters, and ancillary buildings set behind a white-washed wall. Bill had known Juan and his family for many years and had helped him arrange showings of his work in the United States. We entered the compound at about lunch time and, as is typical of Mexico, were invited to dine with the family. It is a large one: five sons, all of whom have taken up the art of mask making. Two, Orlando and Ugo, have married and set up independent households, but the others still live at home, and all remain in the village. Juan's wife Enedina, was making a lunch of ham, eggs, and beans in *tortillas*. Naturally, everything was made by hand and from scratch. That meant taking whole kernels of corn soaked in lime water and grinding them on a *metate* into a *masa*, or dough. From these she slapped out fresh *tortillas* and toasted them on a *comal*. The method of preparation was so interesting that we filmed it in a darkened room lit only by a fire so that as Enedina moved back and forth, she cast a shadow on the wall. It was an eerie scene and was meant to convey the antiquity and continuity of life in the village. The lunch was delicious, as was almost all the Mexican village cooking we tasted.

Short, stocky, but not fat, and with thick, powerful hands, Juan looks decidedly more indigenous than Spanish, and his art reflects these roots. After we looked over his showroom and marked the masks each of us would buy, we set Juan before the camera and asked him to carve a mask on the spot. With Enedina and Juan's boom box radio playing Mexican tunes in the background, Juan got out his tool kit. It contained a wide array of chisels, gouges, small machetes, borers, scrapers, and others wood carving instruments. Most had been designed and created by the artist himself. Taking a chunk of soft wood, he chopped into it, shaped it roughly, and then worked on it with the various tools. Before long, he had shaped a double-faced mask with serpents or lizards running from the eyebrows to down around the chin. He had

Grinding corn

not even sketched the design beforehand, having evidently envisioned it in the wood from before he began. When asked about the designs, he said that they are sometimes altered depending upon the qualities of the wood he is using, but usually he has a vision of what he wants before he begins. It was an extraordinary display of dexterity and craftsmanship; we hardly understood how the shape had come about, even though we watched the process closely.

Juan Orta makes many kinds of masks. A few are decorative, but most are designed to be used in traditional dances. Bill says that the first one he got was a cow with an articulated jaw that was made from the real jawbone of a cow. Most of the ones we saw and acquired are used in two of Mexico's most celebrated dances: the *danza de los viejitos* or *huehues*, and the devils from the *danza de la pastorela*. If there is one dance that is associated with Michoacán in general and Lake Pátzcuaro in particular (although it does appear elsewhere), it is the old man's dance (*la danza de los viejitos*). The dancers' costume begins with a *sombrero* woven from palm with colored ribbons that flop over the edges and onto the dancer's face. The mask is of a smiling, pink-faced old man who has some teeth missing, a sunken face, and a hooked nose. Today the mask is made of wood; in days past it was of *maguey* paste. Each dancer wears a shawl of bright colors around his neck with a white overshirt and wide cotton pants. The shirt is embroidered with designs particular to the village from which the dancer comes. The *viejito* carries a cane made from tree root that is shaped like a fist or a deer head. The dancers come from larger groups of young men who act like their elders. When they appear before the audience, they limp and then walk with difficulty, with one hand on their canes and the other behind their backs. As the dance progresses, they speed up and begin to pound their canes and stomp their feet rhythmically, their ribbons whirling around their heads. Inevitably, they tire and retire from the scene as quickly as they appeared. The dance is very popular and fun to watch with its pounding rhythms and coordinated action. But it does have a meaning beyond the surface.

The dance is a very old, once dedicated to Huehuetéotl (hence the word—*huehues*), the ancient god of fire who was represented by a smiling old man holding a brazier. There are many more meanings attached to other symbols of the dance, among them the fact that it is young men who are the performers. The old man represents the end of life, the lighted brazier may symbolize rebirth and the light of a life still to come, and the young men begin anew the endless cycle of life. Today some of the old meanings are remembered and the figures do exemplify the past and traditional ways of life, but the dance is really more about having fun and poking fun than anything else.

Juan' s other masks are also spectacular. They come in many shapes and colors, with twisted forms all over them. Some have faces like iguanas, with snakes and other reptiles all over them; others have double and triple faces and are fantasies from an imagination that is rooted in folklore. The *danza del diablo* is a dance about devils in its own right, but devils also appear in many other dances, in particular, the *danza de la pastorela*. This is one of the most important of the Christian dances, and it is danced mostly by girls and women. It is the nativity story, the Adoration of the Magi. If the dance has to do with such gentle themes, why are devils used? In Mexican culture, the devil is not just evil, but also a clown and a teller of dirty jokes, someone who keeps everyone amused. He is, like Judas in the Easter festival at Taxco, the classic tricker and jokester of traditional folklore. Devils act as counterpoints to serious dances, and they are social safety valves for the celebrants. Devils can talk with impunity about anyone: criticizing, gossiping, and mentioning local scandals. They may say what they like, and none of it is taken seriously because it is spoken by, well, the devil-jokers. Because this character is supposed to be both horrible and funny at the same time, greater care is taken in creating his mask. Some are made to look like standard European devils; others look more like Juan Orta's and his sons' creations.[4]

We poked around Tocuaro for a little while and visited other mask makers such as Felipe Anciola. In the end, we all liked the Ortas' work the best and bought their place out. By now we were all demon shoppers. Dave stood before a double-faced mask for a long time, admiring it greatly. He then asked Juan if he ever did anything on commission, portrait masks for instance. Yes, indeed he did, said Juan, adding that he could work from life or from photographs. Well, then, how about a double-faced mask of Dave and Kim, he suggested. No problem, the artist replied. He asked it for a photograph to work from and a small payment and promised to send it within a week or so. Dave gave him the photo and address and paid him and we left.

Several weeks later, back home in Chicago, we were talking with our two friends and asked if they had received their mask. They had, they said, then, hemming a bit, added that it was not what they had expected. Dave looked more or less like himself, but Kim did not look like herself. We thought that perhaps Juan had made her into an iguana, but it turned out that it was simply not a life-like portrait of Kim, but of Mr. Data from the "Star Trek Next Generation" television series! "Do you want it?" Dave asked. "Oh no,'" Jan replied, "it is a piece of art that you should treasure." Dave rejoined, "No, I want you to have it." We went on like this for a period of several weeks. Finally, we called in a arbiter: Bill Goldman. "Well," he said, "it's not the most beautiful mask Juan ever made. . . ." That did it for Dave: "Take it," he said. So we did. It now sits on our mantlepiece and we regard it not as a realistic depiction, but as an interpretation of reality. . . or so we say.

After we left the Ortas we were off again, over the hills and into small valleys. Along the way, we passed farms and people farming, which we stopped to videotape. One shot was of a farmer standing next to his fields and walking his horses in a circle over a pile of what seemed to be straw. He explained that they were threshing oats. We might have seen this same process in medieval Europe. Later we passed a rough wooden ox-drawn cart near a field where some farmers were just beginning to plow the earth and sow corn in anticipation of the rains that would come in a month or two. The plows were wooden, with only a simple share to cut the soil, and were drawn by two horses. After the plowman made a furrow, his wife or children walked behind him and dropped in corn seed by hand. That same wooden plow might have been seen in sixteenth-century Spain, and the sowing technique was either medieval or pre-Columbian. Ancient indigenous farmers used digging sticks to create the holes, but the planting technique was the same. Down the road, a small herd of Holstein cattle meandered through a field. When we stopped to see them up close, we noticed that they were feeding on clover and oats, two plants that are as European as the cows themselves. What we saw in this very agricultural state reinforced what we already knew: that the conquest of Mexico was not simply a political, but also a biological event. And yet beneath all of that more recent history remains that indigenous layer, represented by corn and the *tortilla*.

We moved on. There are so many craft villages in the area that we could have spent weeks going through them. Santa Clara del Cobre (or Villa Escalante, as it is also known) would have to suffice for now. The town is about

The sowing

twenty kilometers south of Pátzcuaro along route 128. Much of it is a ribbon of adobe houses and shops along the main route through town with the town square just off to the side. The afternoon we arrived, all the shops had their wares out on the sidewalk for sale, and the square was filled with vendors. Everyone was selling the same thing—copper. There were pots, pans, tubs, cups, jars. . . anything one could imagine as a vessel or decorative piece was here on display, all of it handmade from copper. The whole town was copper and had been since the days of the Purépecha kingdoms. In those days, and later in the colonial period, there were large copper deposits in the vicinity. Purépecha artisans from this area turned out some of the best metalwork in all the Americas, the behest of their society's elites. When the Spanish came, they, too, appreciated the fine work, but they wanted the products made in a Spanish style. It is said that Quiroga, that veritable patron saint of Michoacán, taught the coppersmiths of Santa Clara to work in the new fashion. They have continued to do so ever since and have become world-renowned as a result.

José de la Rea, our guide, had picked out one style of artisanship among all the others for us to explore and film. The workshop was in a compound off the main street, along with the retail shop and houses of the Punzo family, headed by the artist, Abdón Punzo. We parked our bus on the street and entered through a nondescript door into a treasure house of copperwork. The place glittered with copper vessels, trays, animals, and wall and floor ornaments of ever description. All were the products of the workshop behind the shop. Before we could—what else?—shop, we wanted to see how the work was created.

Behind the main store was a courtyard surrounded on two sides by sheds running off the main buildings. At the far side stood a smelting furnace. Alongside that were forges and firepits for the preparation of heated-copper ingots, and further along toward the house were anvils for working the copper into the desired shapes. A dozen men and boys were working, stripped to the waist in the warm weather; all were members of the Punzo family. Abdón himself, a man in his late thirties, took us around the shop and told us about the forging process. Did they use local copper, we asked. No, because there is none left in the mines. Everything is made from scrap, he replied. We then saw one of his men pounding a pile of old copper wire with a sledgehammer to prepare it for melting. The Santa Clara smiths' skills are so great that it pays to have scrap hauled in from everywhere in Mexico and who knows where else.

Abdón asked if we would like to see the actual forging, since they were about to do some work. We did, but only after Dave returned from his now-habitual detour. Forming the copper is a multi-stage process. First the smiths melt fireproof ceramics full of copper and pour them into a round, flat mold in the ground. When the long copper ingot, about three feet in diameter, has cooled sufficiently, two men with long tongs take it to the furnace and thrust it into its mouth. The furnace is wood fired and spews clouds of smoke and sparks everywhere. When the ingot is red-white hot, the men remove it and quickly lay it on a flat forge. Then comes the interesting part. Everyone in the place drops whatever they are doing and grabs a long-handled sledgehammer, surrounding the blazing-hot ingot. On a signal, first one, then another and another raises his hammer above his head and smashes it onto the metal surface in sequence. More join in until eight men are pounding in perfect rhythm, never missing a beat. It was like playing an instrument: it became more and more musical as the metal cooled and chimed with each hammer strike. When the men had finished, the disk had grown wider and had semicircular hammer marks in it. Now we knew where that kind of copper design originated. The process was a spectacular bit of showmanship and looked wonderful in the final documentary. All of us who witnessed it still sometimes speak of it in awe.

We also filmed Abdón and his young son hammering away at individual pieces to form them into handsome vessels. That is the way the father learned from his father, and now his son was learning from him. After that, we got to shop. Hanging on the shop wall was a large certificate showing that Abdón had won first prize at a recent annual silversmith's contest in Taxco. No wonder everything in the shop was so interesting. The family was especially fond of braided designs on large vessels, a design that was somewhat Moorish in style. Dave, Dudley, and even Ralph, who was determined not to indulge in the shopping frenzy, had to have pots, both large and small. I wanted to find some copper cookware, but this family did not make them. Jan, however, settled on a slightly globular copper flower container that was chased with silver flowers and birds: it was a stunning piece at a remarkable price. Here was another place everyone swore they would visit again: another example of how deep are the veins of cultural continuity in Mexico.

The day grew old as we made our way back to Pátzcuaro. We were scheduled for a dinner at a fancy hotel with state and local tourism officials as well as some local political people. The Posada de Don Vasco was a handsome place that had been completely refurbished by one of the major hotel chains. We were to dine in the large open patio area. The evening was cool when we arrived, but fortunately the patio had large fireplaces and braziers set around; they were all blazing, so we were quite comfortable. The setting looked like something from a banquet scene in a movie epic about Old Mexico or old California. We expected Zorro to appear at any moment, but instead of black masks, we met people wearing dark glasses, reminiscent of film-land "heavies." Bill's old friend Martín came down from Morelia to see how we were getting along. With him were two "journalists" from Morelia newspapers; both were glowering, thickset men who were wearing sunglasses even though the night was pitch dark. We noticed and remarked under our breaths about the bulges in the armpit areas of their jackets. Mexico was currently in the midst of some political turmoil, we knew, but how deep that went became apparent to us only at that moment. A little frisson went through our group as we contemplated what might happen. . . . What happened was that both men took out notebooks and began to interview us about what we were doing, interspersing their questions with educated comments about Michoacán history, prehistory, and geography. And, sure enough, a few days later stories about our documentary appeared in the Morelia newspapers. Maybe journalists in Latin American countries have to be armed these days!

As we began to drink our usual beers, we were served Mexican wines; they were red wines from the Baja California region and not at all bad, about the equivalent of mid-level Californian cabernet-merlot blends. After a while, everyone became very merry. Catalina de la Rea, the local food authority, had excellent English and told us about the food. The meal was creditable, beginning with a vegetable soup and followed by something we had come to expect in and around Pátzcuaro: *charales*, deep-fried. These always have a very strong fishy flavor that resembles dried anchovies. Then came another local trademark dish: *pescado blanco rebozado*, white fish lightly battered and gently sautéed. After that we sampled some thin steaks grilled and topped with refried beans and cheese, a good classic Mexican dish, and then *chiles rellenos*, another standard dish in a well-flavored version. After all this, we were treated to a display of traditional dance and music. The music was *mariachi*, native to Jalisco. The dance was the very same one for which Juan Orta had made masks: the *danza de los viejitos*. A group of fully costumed dancers hobbled onto a stage set up on one side of the patio. Starting off slowly, and accompanied by music, they picked up their pace, tapping and stamping in a coordinated dance. By now, most of us diners were doing a very Mexican thing. Bottles of *tequila* were set out on the table, together with plates of cut limes and salt. Shot glasses were filled and, after appropriate toasts, downed, accompanied by bites of lime and salt. The *tequila* made the dance and the whole evening merrier than ever. It was as good a way as any to end our stay in Pátzcuaro.

Pescado Blanco Rebozado

The preparation given here is the preferred way to make *pescado blanco*. Since you are not likely to find this fish outside of Michoacán, try smaller, ordinary whitefish or whitefish fillets. The portions should equal about ½ pound per person.

8		whole *pescado blanco* (whitefish) cleaned and cut in half lengthwise
2	oz.	lime juice
½	C.	all-purpose flour
		kosher salt and freshly ground pepper, to taste
6		large egg yolks
6		egg whites
2	C.	vegetable (canola) oil

Wash the fish and pat it dry with a paper towel. Sprinkle lime juice over the fish. Place the flour on a plate and season with salt and pepper. Dredge each piece of fish in the seasoned flour and set aside. Separate the eggs carefully, making sure no yolk mixes into the whites. Place the whites in a large bowl and whip by hand or with an electric beater until they become fluffy, but not too stiff. Gently stir in the beaten egg yolks. In a deep, heavy skillet add ½ cup of oil and heat until quite hot. When ready, dredge the fish in the egg mixture, then set in hot oil. Fry until golden brown. Remove the fish from the pan when done and drain. Add more oil as needed for the rest of the fish. *Note*: Serve the fish on a bed of romaine or red-leaf lettuce, radishes, slices of purple onion, and slices of limes. *Serves 4*

Chiles Rellenos

Stuffed chiles are one of the great Mexican dishes; several varieties are presented here, although the cook can improvise almost anything.

6	large *poblano* chiles, toasted, peeled, and seeded
3	eggs, separated, with the yolks beaten
	flour
½ lb. or more	*panela* cheese, cut into thick strips about 1-inch long
	salt and pepper, to taste

Making chiles rellenos (*stuffed* chiles)

    oil for frying
    red sauce

Cut a slit in the side of each prepared chile and fill it with cheese. Carefully close the slit and roll each chile in flour. Beat the egg whites until stiff and then fold in the beaten yolks. Add salt and pepper to taste. Dip each chile in the egg mixture and fry it in hot oil at least ½" deep. Turn the chile and brown on all sides. Remove from the pan and drain well. Place the chiles on a serving plate and serve with the red sauce.   *Serves* 6

To Make Sauce:

1	small onion, chopped
1	clove garlic, peeled and finely chopped
3	medium tomatoes, peeled, seeded, and chopped
2	*serrano* chiles, seeded and chopped (optional)
1–2	sprigs of fresh coriander, finely chopped
	kosher salt, to taste
1–2 T.	canola oil

Heat the oil in a saucepan. Add the onion and garlic and sauté until transparent. Add the tomatoes and, if you are using them, the *serrano* chiles. Bring to a boil, reduce the heat and cook until a pulpy sauce is formed. If you want a smoother sauce, place the mixture in a blender or food processor and purée. Stir in the cilantro and adjust salt.

Carne a la Mexicana

There are two ways to make this dish: either fry the steaks quickly in a pan or grill them, also quickly. At the Posada Don Vasco they were grilled, as they are at many Mexican restaurants.

6		skirt steaks, about 4–6 oz. each
1	C.	red wine vinegar
5		*ancho* chiles, seeded and soaked in warm water
1		medium onion, chopped
4		cloves garlic
		kosher salt and pepper, to taste
1–2	T.	canola oil
1		large green, red, or *poblano* pepper, roasted, seeded, and sliced into strips
1		large onion, sliced
		boiled black beans (see Basic Recipes p. 244)
½–¾	C.	*panela* cheese, shredded

Marinate the meat in the vinegar for at least an hour. Grind the *ancho* chiles, onion, garlic, salt, and pepper in a blender or the bowl of a food processor with a little of the chile water to make a puree. When the meat is ready, heat a grill. Grill the steaks quickly over high heat, making score marks on them if possible. Remove them from the grill and set aside. Have ready a heavy saucepan. In it heat 1–2 tablespoons of canola oil. Pour the chile puree into the pan and fry for 2–3 minutes. To serve the steaks, spoon the chile mixture on top of each and cover with beans (to taste), the green, red, or *poblano* chile slices; the sliced onion; and the shredded cheese.   *Serves 6*

Zamora and Taracuato

The Trip to Zamora

Arturo Olivares from the *Casa de la Artesanías* in Morelia joined us in Pátzcuaro for our journey to a village in the high country to the west: Taracuato, by way of Zamora. Arturo, a slim, elegant man, is filled with enthusiasm for the artisans of the state he knows so well. He made the arrangements for our visit because it is in precisely these villages that he has worked for some years, and he speaks the language, Purépecha. As we drove northwest, we rolled over more hilly country and wider valleys as we got closer to Zamora.

Along the way, Arturo talked about the history of the Purépecha kingdom and sites where remains of it were to be found. It was better than any book we could have brought because he knew the connections between the old art and crafts and the new, and how the Indian peoples had lost so much of their heritage. Arturo is one of that happy band who are seeking to preserve what is left of the traditional arts in Mexico. They are part of a worldwide movement that, in these times of rapid change and increasing cultural uniformity, wants to sustain some of the differences that make us humans interesting to each other. "You will love Taracuato," Arturo said. "They are excellent people. " Bill Goldman agreed, since he had been there before to photograph the women working on their handicrafts. Bill's photographs had been published in an art book and it was because of them that we were going to Taracuato in the first place. But first, Zamora.

When planning the trip, we had asked Bill how long the journeys were from place to place. On the map and by the direct routes shown, all the places we wanted to visit looked fairly close to one another. Our friend then imparted this wisdom, based on thirty years' experience traveling in Mexico: "Nothing in Mexico is ever direct." Since we planned to spend some time in Taracuato, we realized that it would be best to stay in a town close by. Zamora, to which none of us had ever been, was the closest. We expected very little of Zamora, expecting it to be just an ordinary small city, but we were in for a surprise.

As we drew closer, the land became more level and verdant. We saw more fields growing produce and more and more trucks hauling fruits and vegetables. The small city of Zamora turned out to be a major agricultural and regional trade center. We realized now why the Valleys of Zamora were so well known in Mexico. The city is on a branch of the Río Lerma that connects to a large body of water, the Laguna de Chapala. The water and a warm climate make the area ideal for farming, something the Spanish discovered early on. They set up sugar cane plantations south of Zamora and brought in labor from sub-Saharan Africa to work them. Interestingly, the Africans got along well with the Purépechas, who regarded black as a fortunate color because it was related to the gods. Over several centuries the sugar cane industry became less important in Michoacán, and the African-based communities were absorbed into the general population. When we asked, we were told that in some villages people looked vaguely *negrito*, but nothing more. The Africans are remembered, however, in a famous dance, a vigorous one called the dance of the *negritos*, that is performed here but most often in the state of Puebla. Zamora has a more interesting history than we had suspected, but there was no time to linger. After we checked into our hotel for the night, we left immediately for Taracuato where we were expected for lunch.

Taracuato

As we drove south, we climbed higher and higher into the hill country. This was the Montañas Occidentales zone, an area less fertile than the valleys and its towns not so prosperous. Up the winding roads we went and finally reached our destination an hour or so later. Taracuato is another prosaic town; it is strung along a road, with its enclosed walls lining it. We pulled into a deeply rutted side street and then turned down a steeply slanted street that was even rougher then the first. Small houses and enclosures were located on either side of it. Women householders popped their heads an out of their doorways to see what the commotion was all about—just the usual bunch of tourists, Arturo explained. We walked through a small door set in a wall and entered another world: the compound of the Castro family. It was not large; the main housing units were set against the wall and along another at ninety degrees to it. The rest was open courtyard with the front paved with flat stones and the rest dirt. Against the far wall was a thriving herb garden with plants that we had seen in the herbal medicine clinic in Pátzcuaro. The other wall to the north was covered with a tin roof that was held up by thin wooden posts. This was the outdoor kitchen, cupboard, and dining room, the latter set up with a long trestle table and benches. The whole place was immaculate and well ordered, and so were the activities of the women of the house.

Purépecha women command their households, and none do it better than Marcelina Castro, the matron of the Castro family. A very tall (taller than almost all of us) woman with noble bearing, she had the features of the native peoples of Perú or perhaps even of North America. She was an extraordinary-looking person, as were her daughters and nieces. Arturo told us that she was a classic Purépecha type. No wonder some people think that the Purépecha originated in South America. The half-dozen members of the family who were there to see us were dressed in handsome traditional costumes. They all wore blouses embroidered with multi-colored geometric or flower designs, multiple petticoats, and heavy skirts bunched into large pleats in the back. All wore the aprons that are the sign of marital status: that is, black aprons mean the women are widows and white aprons mean they are married. Around their waists were heavily embroidered wraparound belts. As Marcelina and her daughter showed us, dressing takes some time, since the wearer needs assistance to get the belt on correctly. To do it, one person holds an end and the wearer turns around until it is wound around the body. Why is it so long? The belt is a key to status: the higher the level of respect, the longer and more decorative the belts. We thought that perhaps the family put on these costumes especially for us, but they said, no, this is what they wear every day. Marcelina added that she would not feel comfortable in anything else. Yet the children of the family did not wear the traditional clothing, but ordinary dresses or jeans. When they are old enough, we learned, they too will acquire the same splendid costumes, although one wonders if the custom will continue that long.

The family's women practice the craft of embroidery. Their work is well known in the state and can be found in artisan shops in major cities. Their designs reflect the natural world around the village, especially the floral patterns. Some motifs are geometric and based on *yácatas*. Arturo mentioned that the oldest designs were almost entirely geometric and had changed with outside influences on the style. Other things have changed as well. The thread used now is commercial cotton or even nylon, where once it had been made and dyed by the embroiderers themselves. Most of the cloth upon which they work is now commercially made. In the past the village weavers, all men, made it for them from tree cotton (from the cottonwood tree), but now only one man in town does it and, even then, sporadically.

The dress itself is not exactly pre-Columbian. Like so many supposedly traditional costumes in Europe, these are really late-eighteenth or nineteenth century in origin. Prehispanic peoples wore simple shifts that might have been embroidered. The women's blouses certainly date from the latter era and so do the petticoated skirts. Maybe only the wonderful belts are older. Still, this was a traditional extended family. For example, in Taracuato, Purépecha women wear their hair in a long single braid. Women in other villages wear two or style their hair in other ways. The embroidery also differs in style from village to village and from family to family, so everyone knows how they and what they make fit in. Not quite like us North Americans.

The meal the women made for us was also traditional, and its preparation was perfect for the documentary. Naturally, every step of each operation was done by hand. Not only was it done by hand, but it was done with the precision of a military operation. Everything is done in its correct order, from grinding corn to slapping out and making *tortillas* and more. We started with snacks of fresh toasted *tortillas* with *guajes* (the thin, snow pea-like pods), lots of coarse salt, and *salsa* freshly ground in the *molcajete*. Apart from the salt they were excellent; the *guajes* were just crunchy, and there is no substitute for fresh *tortillas*. Meanwhile, large clay pots of beef and chicken were boiling on the open fires. All the preparation and cooking was done in the shed area on a stone-lined hearth or on the large clay stove set against the outer wall. While one woman tended the meats, others set about making *corundas*. This is one of Michoacán's signature dishes. They are thick, unfilled *tamales*, often flavored with wood ash, that are wrapped in corn leaves and steamed. Another kind of *corunda* is like a bread, raised not with yeast but with the beerlike *pulque*. This *corunda* is also wrapped in corn husks and steamed. They are used as a bread to be eaten with stews or soups. We watched as some teams made the round loaves while others wrapped them, piled them in big pots, and then put them on the stone hearths.

As they worked in teams, the women chatted in their own language, laughing while grinding, patting, and slapping away. They all became teary-eyed, not from sadness, but from all the smoke from their cooking fires. So did we. When something was ready, they went to their pantry to get a pot. The pantry was a partition wall between the kitchen and dining area where about fifty pots of varied sizes were neatly piled one atop the other. Most were globular in shape and were made for boiling liquids. Why so many pots, we asked. Because, they replied, this is the way they usually cooked for the large family when the men came home from the fields and business. Also, every pot had its own special use. None was used for any other kind of food or dish than that for which it was designated. The same went for the large spoons and spatulas. The pots came from different regions of Michoacán and were used according to the nature of their material. More porous ones were used for steaming and the solid pots were used for real boiling. The pots' glazes, too, made a difference in the cookery done in them. That clay pot cooking technique made for first-rate food, we thought, along with the smoke flavors and the simple joy of eating in the open air. Whatever it was, we discovered that in both its seasonings—at once subtle and distinctive in flavors—and in its techniques, village cooking is more sophisticated than one might think. Taracuato and the cookery done there turned out to be one of the real treasures we found in Mexico.

Preparing corundas

After we had gorged ourselves once again, guess what we all did? Shopped. The women brought out samples of their work for our inspection. Fortunately, they were low in stock because a shipment had just gone out to the *Casa de las Artesanías*; otherwise, no one would have had any money left. We snapped up blouses and belts. As handsome as all of them are, most have hardly been worn since because the design and cut does not really match the rest of our wardrobes. Such are the perils of mixing souvenir and clothes shopping. Sated with food and loot, we took our leave and headed back toward Zamora late in the afternoon. This time we took a different route through deep-green pine-cloaked mountains that dropped down into fertile valleys. The mountains were strange, truncated cones, clearly extinct volcanoes in a region that is still volatile. Again, we marveled at the tremendous varieties of landscapes that Michoacán holds within a small area.

Zamora

By the time we got back to Zamora, it was growing dark. Dinner had been arranged at a local restaurant and that gave the more adventurous of us only a few hours to explore the city. It is a busy place with plenty of shops intermixed with food stands that would be worth visiting one day. Several squares stand not far from the main road into the city and two interesting churches are located there. One is the *Catedral Inconclusa* (the Unfinished Cathedral), which, true to its name, has never been finished. It is built in a Gothic style, with nicely pointed arches, and it is very spacious inside, because it has no roof. Nearby is a little gem of a church dedicated to San Francisco. It is a simple design: simply decorated and well proportioned with handsome entrance archways. A service was being held at the time we saw it and the interior was lit with myriad candles. It was everything one imagines a Mexican church to be. By now the squares were sprouting food stands and other stalls. It was too bad we had to leave. There are other interesting structures in the city as well as Opeño, an archaeological zone with some pre-Columbian tombs that I wanted to visit, but dinner called and it was well worth the detour.

We were taken to the Mesón de San Fernando restaurant across the street from our hotel. Like other restaurants we had visited, this one was in the patio of an old mansion and was more intimate than the others. The owner, Fernando Bustamente, had created a gorgeous restaurant and an interesting menu; in fact, it was one of the best meals we had in Mexico. The walls were gold colored and it was decorated with fine Puebla pottery, live parrots in an enormous cage (Mexican Redheads as Jan, a bird enthusiast, told us), plants everywhere, and a rear garden wall covered in ivy. We sat at a large, old wooden table with a giant *molcajete* filled with fruits and flowers in its center. The proprietor, an energetic young man who spoke excellent English, said that he had spent some time in California at a university and working in restaurant management. Some of the restaurant's motifs reflected a California sensibility that was carried over into the recipes. They were something like *nouvelle* Mexican, as we had seen in Mexico City, but with a more traditional Mexican regional accent. For example, the *guacamole* (this part of Michoacán is the heartland of the fruit) had a *tomatillo*-based sauce mixed into it. It was thinner than standard *guacamole* and it combined the sharpness of the *tomatillos* with the creamy qualities of the avocado to create a surprising and excellent combination. The rest of the meal followed along the same lines.

Taquitos are small *flautas* (literally, "little flutes") filled with roasted chicken and a zippy, chunky red sauce. For Carol, the best part of the meal was a dish with tiny potatoes, freshly harvested, slow-roasted with garlic, and served with a sensational cilantro sauce and a red sauce. She and the rest of us wolfed these down and would have been happy dining on potatoes alone. Next out was a huge, handsome pottery platter with *cecina* (thin strips of beef jerky), fresh avocado slices, bean *enchiladas* made with cheese, delicate little *gorditas* with fresh, crisply cooked vegetables and cheese, and light, delicate *uchepos* (fresh corn *tamales*) made in the local style with strips of *poblano* chiles. The whole meal was composed of these small dishes, a kind of Mexican degustation that was in keeping with the restaurant's style. Even the expected *flan* at the end of the meal was light and had just the right amount of caramelized sugar; it was neither too sweet nor too heavy. Were we doing a restaurant review, the Mesón de San Fernando would receive high marks. It alone would make a return trip to Zamora worthwhile. Next time, we all said.

Mole de Cosecha

(from Jiquilpán, Michoacán)

Dudley collected this recipe from a small town in the Michoacán hills. It is something like the dish we had at Taracuato, but with some unusual ingredients. The sour prickly pear can be found in Mexican markets; use unripe ones, or you can omit them entirely. The fruit gives the dish a "sour" flavor that you may or may not like. Many of our recipe testers did not love it on first bite, but the next day found it more interesting.

8	C.	cold water
2-¼	lbs.	beef stew meat
5		*xoconoxtles* (sour prickly pears), peeled and diced large

1		whole *chayote* fruit, peeled and diced large
2		whole carrots, diced large
1		whole potato, peeled and diced large
3	C.	warm water
½	lb.	*ancho* chiles, toasted
½	lb.	*pasilla* chiles, toasted
3		cloves garlic
1	t.	freshly ground black pepper
3		whole cloves
½	C.	corn flour (*masa*)
		kosher salt, to taste

Place the 8 cups of cold water in a deep pan and add the meat. Bring to a boil, reduce the heat and simmer for 20–30 minutes. During the cooking process, skim any surface matter from the top of the water and discard. (Actually, village cooks stir this back into the liquid because of the nutrients in it.) Add the sour prickly pears, *chayote*, potato, and carrots. Continue to simmer. Meanwhile, place 2 cups of warm water, the chiles, and garlic in a separate saucepan. Bring to a boil, reduce the heat, and simmer for 10 minutes or until the chiles are soft. Remove the chiles from pan, and stem, devein, and seed them. Reserve 1 cup of the liquid. Place the chiles and garlic, along with the cloves and pepper, in the bowl of a food processor or blender and purée. Add about 1 cup of the chile water to make the mixture smooth. Add the chile mixture to the beef and vegetable pan and continue to simmer for at least 20 minutes—the vegetables should be tender and crisp and the meat should be tender. Mix together the *masa* flour and 1 cup of warm water, incorporating the flour slowly so that it does not form lumps. Slowly stir the flour-liquid into the meat-vegetable mixture to thicken. Season with kosher salt, to taste.   *Serves 4 or more*

Note: Serve this with *corundas* or *tamales*. (See below.)

Corundas

While we have made efforts to keep fat to a minimum in these recipes, especially "bad" fat, some dishes must have it in order to be authentic. Traditional *corundas*, one of Michoacán's signature dishes, should be made with lard. If you must, use vegetable shortening, but the flavor will not be the same. Like *uchepos* (p. 210) this is another of the "wrapped" dishes that characterize pre-Columbian cookery.

½ lb.   *masa* (*tamal* dough)
1 C.   lard
½ C.   milk
1 t.   baking powder
12   green tomatoes (*tomatillos*), peeled
½ t.   baking soda
1 C.   water
20   fresh large corn leaves (*milpa*)
½ lb.   cooked black beans, boiled with *criollo* avocado leaves
1 C.   wood ash

Place the green tomatoes (*tomatillos*) in a pan with the baking soda and a small amount of water. Bring to a boil and cook until the tomatoes are soft. Allow to cool. Sieve the mixture to make ½ cup, place in a bowl, and stir in the milk. Place the lard in a mixing bowl and beat until it turns fluffy-white. Gradually add the *tortilla* dough, *tomatillo* milk mixture baking powder, and wood ash a bit at a time, until all the ingredients have been blended. The mixture should be fluffy. Wash the *milpa* leaves and drain well. Tear long, thin strips from the exterior corn husks for use as string when tying up the packets. Remove the veins from the middle of each leaf, leaving two pieces. Fold over the wide end to make a flap. Place the dough on each leaf and add a table-

Making tamales nejos (*with beans*) *with banana leaves, or* telolotzin

spoon of beans in the center along with some green tomato sauce. Fold the dough into a triangular shape and tuck the thin top end of the leafs into the large fold at the bottom. Tie with corn strips. The *corunda's* shape will be triangular. Place on steamer rack and steam about 1 hour or until the *corundas* come away from the wrappers.

Makes 20 small corundas, *serves about* 10

Tamales de Harina

The other kind of *corunda* we ate at Taracuato was made with wheat flour and raised with sediments from *pulque* following a pre-Columbian technique. These *corundas*, or *tamales de harina*, are also found in the Lake Pátzcuaro region, and are often eaten on Easter Sunday. In the market at the Gertrudis Bocanegra Plaza you can see a line of giant *cazuelas* used as steamers set over wood fires, where the cooks shout out, "¡*Tamales de harina!*" Since you are not likely to find *pulque* in North America, we have used yeast as the leavening agent. The preparation is much like the *corunda* recipe given above.

¼	oz.	(1 pkg.) dry yeast
1-¼	C.	warm water
		a pinch of sugar
3-¾	C.	all-purpose flour
1	t.	salt
20		corn husk leaves (*milpa*)

In a small bowl, dissolve the yeast and sugar in a ¼ cup of warm water. Allow to proof (bubble up) for about 5 minutes. Mix together the salt and flour in a large bowl. Pour the yeast mixture into the flour, followed by the rest of the water. Knead by hand or by machine until a soft dough has been formed. Cover the mixture with a towel and allow to rest for 10 minutes. Place the dough on a floured board and knead the mixture for at least 5–8 minutes until it develops a soft, elastic consistency. Place the dough in a lightly oiled bowl, turning it over so that all sides are slightly coated. Cover the bowl and allow the dough to rest for 1–1-½ hours in a warm place or until the dough has doubled in size. When ready, spread out the corn husks. Tear long, thin strips from the exterior corn husks for use as string when tying up the packets. Wash the *milpa* leaves and drain well. Remove the veins from the middle of each leaf, leaving two pieces. Fold over the wide end at the bottom, making a flap. Form small balls of dough and place one on each leaf.

Fold the packet into a triangular shape and tuck the thin end at the top of the leaf into the large fold at bottom. Tie each packet with corn strips. Place on a steamer rack and steam about 1 hour, or until the *corundas* come away from the wrappers.

Makes 20 tamales de harina and serves about 10

Note: These *corundas* should served with *atole negro* or hot chocolate, but are also wonderful with soups and stews.

Uchepos

Uchepos take a little practice, but once the technique is mastered they are easy to make. You might omit the sugar if the corn is fresh and tender. Do not overcook the *uchepos*; otherwise, the purée will become like paste and stick to the corn leaves. Tender corn really takes only a little cooking. The dish is often served with sauces, recipes for two of which, butter-*ancho* and *asadero* cream, follow. The emphasis on dairy ingredients reflects Michoacán's famed industry.

6		whole ears young, tender corn (*xilote* in Nahuatl)
2	T.	unsalted butter, softened to room temperature
1	T.	granulated sugar
1	t.	salt
6		whole fresh corn husks from the fresh corn

Have ready a steamer rack and water in the bottom of a pan. Husk the corn and cut the kernels from the cobs. Discard the cobs and save the husks. Place the corn kernels, butter, sugar, and salt in the bowl of a food processor and purée. Select the largest and most tender of the interior corn leaves for wrapping. You may need to fill in spaces with the smaller corn leaves. Tear long, thin strips from the exterior corn husks for use as string when tying up the packets. Using a tablespoon, spread the fresh corn mixture along the bottom of a leaf. Fold the leaf over vertically (left to right), and then from top to bottom to form a packet. (Be sure you do not overfill the leaf with corn mixture.) Using the strips from the husks, tie the packets, once at the top end and once at the bottom. If you run out of the larger interior corn leaves, use several smaller ones to cover the larger bottom ones. You should have about 12 packets when finished, perhaps more. Stack the *uchepos* upright in the steamer and place it over boiling water. Steam for 15 minutes or until the corn husks can be easily removed. To serve, remove the husks and arrange the warm *uchepos* on a plate. Serve with butter-*ancho* chile sauce or *asadero* cream sauce. *Uchepos* can be eaten warm or cold, but are better warm. *Serves 4*

Butter-Ancho Chile Sauce

1–2 *ancho* chiles
¼ C. (or more) butter

Soak the *ancho* chiles in warm water until soft. Remove the seeds and veins. Squeeze them dry and place them in a food processor or a *molcajete*. Grind into a paste. Melt the butter in a saucepan. Stir in the *ancho* chile paste until well blended. To serve, drizzle the butter-*ancho* chile mixture over *uchepos*. *Serves 4*

Asadero Cream Sauce

1 pt. heavy whipping cream
¼ lb. *asadero* (quesadilla, *ranchero* or *Chihuahua*-style cheese)
1 spring *epazote*
a pinch of nutmeg
a pinch of salt
queso fresco, crumbled

Mix all the ingredients together in a small saucepan and heat very gently until the *asadero* cheese is melted. Remove the *epazote* sprig. To serve, spread over *uchepos* and top with crumbled cheese. *Serves 4*

Urupán

"Who says you can't drink the water in Mexico? In the town of Uruapan you can. . . from the Cupatitzio river. In the Indian language the name Cupatitzio means 'the river that sings through its falls.' The water is said to be the purest in all Mexico. . . ."—from the documentary "Hidden Mexico"

The route from Zamora to Uruapán, seventy-seven kilometers to the south, passes through the range of volcanic mountains that stretches lengthwise through the center of Michoacán. Once more we noticed how odd they looked with their truncated tops often cloaked in dark-green pines. The road passes through Paracho, another of the state's famed artisan villages; this one is composed of guitar-makers. Our luggage compartment was already full, so we did not stop for another buying spree. As it was, Dave thought we needed an education in how guitars are used in popular culture and had our agreeable driver José pop a tape into the bus's cassette deck. It was some group called "The Crash Test Dummies" who sounded exactly like the kinds of events for which they are named. "Appalling stuff!" I cried out. "Especially in this glorious countryside." "What," asked our friends who are attuned to popular tastes, "You don't like that?" I gave my standard response to pop music fans. "It ain't Mozart." So, to compromise we put on a tape of Mexican folk music that Gonzalo, the cultural attaché in Chicago, had given us, and listened to music that went with some of the masks, costumes, and dances we had seen on our travels.

We passed the Tancitaro National Park where the former volcano Paracutín stands. In 1943 a farmer plowing his field felt the earth move under him. Soon a fire-spitting hole appeared in the ground. Although the local farmers tried to stop it up, it got bigger and began to swell up out of the ground like a giant boil. At that point, everyone in the vicinity fled; it was a good thing that they did, because the hole turned into a volcanic cone that spewed lava, volcanic bombs, and ash all around. It buried the village of San Juan Parangaricutiro, leaving only the top of its church above ground. Paracutín remained active until 1952, and the area around it still shows deposits of gray ash. Would that we could have stopped to take the horseback ride from the village of Angahuán up to the crater! Yet another "next time."

We arrived in Uruapán and drove immediately to our hotel. The Hotel Mansión del Cupatitzio sits adjacent to the Eduardo Ruíz National Park and is as beautiful as its neighbor. Built around a wide, landscaped patio with a heated swimming pool in the middle, this hotel was the best we stayed in. The handsome rooms and excellent service made us want to lengthen our stay in the area. The whole town had the same effect. Since the town is set on a plateau, its climate is perfect and the landscape is literally a garden. The pure waters of the Cupatitzio made the whole place into a small Eden. No wonder the name Uruapán means "forever springtime." Better, still, Ralph could do his usual morning five-mile run without wheezing. Although its area is small, the city numbers over 200,000 people, many of then dedicated to agriculture and handicrafts. It was founded on an indigenous village in 1533 by Juan de San Miguel, who laid the town out in square blocks like a chessboard. In front of the cathedral there is, as always, the *zócalo* that is really three small squares connected to one another. Next to the *zócalo* is a fine small museum called La Huatepera. It is a sixteenth-century building made in several styles including the decorative *Mudéjar* (a mixture of Gothic and Arabic). It houses a collection of regional artisan work, including splendid lacquerware and pottery figures in many unusual forms. The museum is a good place to get a bird's-eye view of the local art.

Before we went to the square, our guide from the tourism office, Señora María del Rosario Salinas (who was one of the best guides we had), walked us over to the national park. The section we entered was a narrow strip of steep bank surrounding the small river, with paths and small terraces on either side for pedestrians. We walked down the path to a small iron bridge and turned back to see a small waterfall surrounded by huge-limbed trees. Monster banana trees grew up on the river's edge and formed a canopy over much of the waterfall. Had we not known that we were in Mexico, we might have mistaken the scene for China, or at least a pastoral Chinese painting. Our guide informed us proudly that the river was pristine because it wells up from natural springs that have never been polluted and that it is one of the few places in Mexico where water can be drunk straight from the river. We did not test the hypothesis, since at the time the river was filled with teen-aged bathers. These boys were having a great time leaping from the steepest banks into the water under the falls, screaming and showing off their budding *machismo*. Bill, the old public school teacher, cast a sour eye upon them, saying that had these louts been in his classroom their behavior would have been different. We all smiled, knowing that he was probably the most genial of teachers. But even Rosario commented that the tourism authorities would like to have stopped the frivolity, but they did not have the power to do so. Nevertheless, the whole setting was lovely, and Dave and Ralph got plenty of good shots that later appeared in the documentary.

Since we were doing food history, our guide asked whether we might like to visit an experimental agricultural station where some older species were being preserved and some new ones developed. Why even ask, we said, and set off to the north and east of Uruapán for a visit to the Vivero La Alberca. From the road the station did not appear to be as advertised. A small building fronted the road with a cleared area for cars in front and behind. We pulled in and were immediately greeted by the proprietor, José Carlos Bautista. Slim, sun-tanned and loquacious, Sr. Bautista had lived in California where he worked in agricultural science before returning to his native city to pursue his research. As we walked behind the main building, we saw row upon row of orchards, each tree labeled, and all growing something different. Trees bearing peaches, pears, and avocados in several varieties were familiar to us, but another was not. On it were smallish red "fruits" with knobby exteriors. They looked like lychee fruits from Asia. "Oh, no," said our host, "although we could grow them. These are our great experiment: macadamia nuts." We knew that the macadamia nut was one of Hawaii's specialties, but not Mexico's. Sr. Bautista quickly sketched its history as we walked along nut-tree shaded paths. The tree is native to Australia's coastal forests; in fact, it is the only native Australian plant that has developed into a commercial crop. Its name came from a nineteenth-century botanist who named it for his friend, a certain Dr. MacAdam. Macadamias came to Hawaii's Big Island in 1882 and took off from there. Volcanic soils and tropical climates suit the nut well, so why should it not succeed in Uruapán? Interest in macadamias has grown rapidly around the world and, as shoppers know, they bring good prices. Eyeing the world market, Sr. Bautista began planting seven years ago. Since then, he has produced good crops and has been busy introducing tree stock to other growers in his area of Michoacán. While we were walking, we munched on the excellent macadamia-nut cookies that the Vivero makes, followed by some *chía*-seed cookies that were just as good. Maybe one day we will be able to get these at home.

Sr. Bautista led us up a small tree-topped hill and pointed to the trees there. All were avocados of different varieties—and there are many. One set of trees was particularly interesting. They bore small, round green fruit that looked a little like avocados. They were. Called *criollo*, these fruit are as close to the native wild avocado as exists today in Mexico. Unlike the usual variety of avocado, Haas or alligator, these have edible skins and much smaller pits. After they are plucked from the tree, they have a distinct avocado flavor, although it is not as "meaty" as that of their larger cousins. Dudley asked if we might try one of the leaves. There are a number of sauces that use avocado leaves as flavoring agents; they give food a sharpish quality. In years past, Dudley always asked Jan to have her parents, who live in Florida and have avocados, send him packets of leaves for various sauces. He also knew that the *criollo* leaf has a different flavor. When we tasted the freshly broken leaves, we understood what Dudley meant: they have a distinctive licorice-anise flavor. A certain flavor in black-bean-filled *corundas* now came to me, as well as subtle anise undercurrents in other dishes we had eaten. We were told that visitors can drop in and buy some of the products made in the Vivero, including avocado oils, macadamia nuts and cookies, and other goodies, all at very reasonable prices. As we were leaving, Sr. Bautista mentioned that his sister had a restaurant in Uruapán that drew upon products from the station. We didn't have time to go there, but Dudley went there on a subsequent trip. There, at the Macadamia Restaurant, Hilda Bautista Villegas prepared avocados stuffed with trout and cod, trout with macadamia butter and roasted nuts, and peach and macadamia nut pie. All of us who heard about this meal later were deeply envious.

Once back in Uruapán, we were on our way to the main plaza. We had passed by early in the day and saw the pottery sellers setting up. First, though, we had an appointment with one of Uruapán's most celebrated artisans, a woman named Lucina Tulais. We had seen her on a poster at the *Casa de las Artesaniás* in Morelia, where she was depicted working on her specialty, a lacquered dish. We arrived at her small house not far from the center of town, where the seventy-nine-year-old woman sat in the interior courtyard before a low table. The tools of her craft were at hand: paint brushes, engraving tools, bowls of crushed mineral pigments and fats for mixing them. As she worked in front of the camera, she told us that she had begun working at her craft at the age of twelve and was considered the paradigm for the regional style.

That style is mainly black- or red-bodied gourds and pots or dishes with colorful floral patterns on them. The style itself is called *embutido*, or encrustation. In this process, the crushed mineral or vegetable matter is first mixed with animal fat, usually an *aje* made from crushed insects, and laid on the object to be decorated. Then dried designs are cut into it and the lines are filled with different colors. Later, thinner layers of lacquer are used to cover and seal the whole piece. Lucina still does some of this, but these days works more with paint. The technique, including the floral designs, are said to have been influenced by Chinese lacquerware, but the same has also been said of the products of Olinolá in Guerrero. Whatever the case, the Uruapán style is vivid and justly famed. Once again, fortune smiled on us. The artist had just sent almost all of her work for sale in Morelia and had only two or three pieces left for sale. Dudley got the largest, a big gourd covered with multi-colored flowers. I told him that the style was not to my taste; it was too flowery and reminded me of the kinds of heavily ornamented objects that my Russian relatives always kept on their mantlepiece. Then we dragged him away before he collected more.

Next we were off to the *zócalo* to walk through the open-air market and then visit a specialty market. When we arrived, the small tree-lined park that makes up the main plaza area was filled with vendors, their wares spread on portable tables and on tarps lying on the pavement. Most of the goods for sale were pottery in the local style: brown and green wares used for practical, everyday cooking. Shoppers strolled through the park buying this or that pot in which to make, we now knew, a delicious stew. It was so scenic that we decided to shoot the opening of the program here. Once we got rid of a sound truck blasting commercials for an appliance store, we filmed the scene. Looking at the footage later, I realized how diverse the people in that market were: from *indigenas* to Spanish and everything in between. What an interesting-looking people, we all reflected later, just like their culture and their food.

Rosario then led us across the street and down a small street to one of Uruapán's best attractions. The Mercado de Antojitos is just that, an array of *fondas* that serve mainly snacks. The tourism office had arranged a welcome for us. The *fondas* are arranged on a large U-shaped platform with steps leading up from a small sunken square in front of it. The eating part is covered

Eating bread (of the dead) with atole

with a red-tiled roof that is supported by brown-painted wooden posts The building looked very much like a Chinese pavilion. Against the back wall hung a large white banner welcoming our television crew from Chicago. In honor of our visit, the vendors were decked out in regional costumes. Women wore brightly embroidered blouses and traditional skirts. Even those vendors not in costume wore standard restaurant jackets and white caps, as required by the market's health code. The *mercado* was as neat and clean as anything we had seen and it was filled with families of parents and children sitting at the *fondas* and eating and drinking the homemade dishes. It made for a homey, friendly atmosphere.

Dave shot everything, including the roasted chickens displayed standing upright with lettuce "wings" attached to them. Red and green *tamales*, *uchepos*, several flavors of *corundas*, *cecina*, many chicken dishes, stews of all kinds, and a wonderful green sauce made with whole ears of corn were all on display. If we wanted to show the characteristic foods of this region of Michoacán, the Mercado de Antojitos would be the place to start. Dudley ran from stand to stand sampling the most interesting preparations and jotting down notes. Meanwhile, Carol and I settled at an *atole* stand where the proprietor, Rosa Tajimaroa Espinosa, put on a spectacular display.

Throughout this book, the word *atole* has popped up; it has an important place in Mexican cuisine. It is a kind of thin porridge made of corn that has been boiled, ground, and mixed with either cornstarch or *masa*. It is, in short, virtually a liquid cornstarch. A*toles*, however, are mixed with a variety of flavoring ingredients so that drinking it—and it is almost invariably drunk warm—is akin to taking in an uncooled pudding. A*tole* is commonly eaten at breakfast, where it is seasoned with *piloncillo*, cinnamon, and almonds or fruit; sometimes it is mixed with eggs and milk instead. In pre-Colombian days, *atole* was combined with beans or herbs and eaten at any time of the day. It still is in rural Mexico, in something like its original form, or in a simple sweetened and flavored version. It is definitely an acquired taste.

Rosa Espinosa put on a great show for the camera. A*tole* is usually served in a pottery pitcher and the viscous liquid is then poured into cups. First the *atole* has to be cooked and strained of its thick lumps, and then it is slightly cooled. The cooling was done by Sra. Espinosa; holding two large cups in either hand, one full of *atole*, the other empty, she poured the *atole* back and forth from one cup into the other. As she poured, her arms drew apart so that the stream of liquid between the cups grew longer and longer, until her arms were as wide apart as she could get them. Her performance was swift and she hardly looked at what she was doing, so adept was she. We wondered how she managed not to spill a drop, until we realized how thick *atole* really is.

We finally stopped shooting and, after some sightseeing in town, returned to the Hotel Mansión de Cupatitzio. Everyone was ready to hop into the pool. After two weeks of steady shooting and tramping over the countryside, the crew deserved it. Even in Acapulco no one had had time to sit out on the beach, much less dive into the water. We had to rest anyway, because the hotel restaurant's chef was putting on a special meal for us. The restaurant is known as one of the best in Uruapán, and for good reason. It is made up of several comfortable rooms that look out over the landscaped countryside. We sat around a long table drinking down the usual beverages and becoming very merry. Dudley had spoken with the chef, Sergio Uribe Jeytud, and the two would eventually swap chef stories, exchange recipes, and generally become professionally friendly. Jeytud is a pastry chef by training, but now headed the hotel's banquet kitchen. That he was trained in the French tradition became apparent, but it was clear that he was also creative with Mexican ingredients. Our table sauce was excellent. Dudley and I argued about what was in it, before we finally discovered that it was made with *chipotle* and *pasilla* chiles, *guajes*, olive oil, onion, and garlic. The meal began with— what else in this country?—*guacamole* made of tree-ripened, freshly picked fruit. That was followed by fine cold avocado-cream soup and crepes filled with *huitlacoche*, that splendid Mexican fungus, with a creamy green *habas* (lima bean) sauce. Most of asked for *chiles rellenos*, but Jan and Dave, carnivores both, got *Chateaubriand*, medium rare, with an excellent *chipotle* sauce. In all, it was a fine meal that fit the surroundings well.

Uruapán was a fitting conclusion to our journey through Mexico. It was too bad that we had not been there on October 24, when a huge folk fest, the *Festival de Coros y Danzas*, is held. Folk music and dance groups from all over Michoacán come to perform (and eat) their regional specialties. By all accounts it is a colorful event. . . yet another "next time." After all we had done, the trip back to Morelia (only about 140 kilometers) felt like a return to the previous year, and Acapulco seemed an eternity in the past. We stayed over in the Michoacán's capital without incident, eating in the market and shopping some more in the markets and in the *Casa de las Artesanías*. Then we set off for the airport and another adventure. We arrived at Morelia's airport with all of our purchases and equipment, said goodbye to José, our affable driver, and moved our mountain of luggage up to the check-in desk. The reservations clerk examined our tickets, checked his computer screen, and declared that he had no reservation in our names. We would have to wait until maybe tomorrow, or the next day, to get back home.

"What?!" we shrieked in unison. Every one of us had to be back at work the next day. "Call Chicago and get Chris López (the airline manager there who had arranged everything) on the phone," we demanded, as we pulled out letters from the Consul General and the Secretariat of Tourism that requested that we be treated decently. Jan leaned across the counter as far as she could, fixed the representative with her best death-stare, and hissed, "Point me to the border; I'm walking!" The poor fellow did not know what to do. All of the airline employees conferred and began to telephone the head offices in Mexico City, Chicago, and other places unknown. No luck, their deepest regrets, but there was still no room on the plane. Now, we thought, we know what it is like to be stranded on a foreign shore.

At the moment of our greatest despair, who should turn up but the director of promotions for the Secretariat of Tourism in Michoacán, Sr. Edmundo Villalobos Castillo. We had met him several times in Morelia and Pátzcuaro and found him to be friendly and helpful—just how friendly and helpful we were about to discover. He walked up to the ticket counter, pulled out his many credentials, and asked if there might not be places on the flight after all. We were from a television station in Chicago, a place where so many people from Michoacán now lived, people who regularly returned home for visits; we were doing the state a good turn, and who would not want to give the best service possible to visitors, the Director asked. Furthermore, he would take it as a great personal favor if we were allowed to leave on this flight. The airlines staff nodded understandingly and said that they would see what they could do. Within a few minutes, we headed toward the airplane ramp and got on board. Our gratitude to our benefactor overflowed. We thanked him for coming to the airport to see us off. "Oh no," he replied, "I just happened to be here. Our victorious football team is arriving in a few minutes, and I had to be here to celebrate their latest victory in the Cup competition." Sometimes fortune smiles upon the undeserving! By the way, when we got home and told Chris López about the problem we had, he said, "It was in the computer all the time, they just didn't know how to access it . . . new staff, you know, and everything is all fixed now." He still owes us dinner at a Cuban restaurant for that one.

We cite two *atole* recipes, the first easier to make, and the second typical of the way that it is done in the Mercado de Antojitos in Uruapán. Some of the ingredients are a little general, for example three bunches of anise greens or *epazote*, because much of the seasoning depends on individual taste. When making the *atole*, be careful to add the thickening agents slowly and not to overcook them, otherwise, they will turn to glue.

Atole de Grano

10		ears of fresh corn, kernels removed from the cob
5–6		anise seeds, ground, or 1 T. chopped dill
3	qts.	water
4	T.	corn flour
½	C.	warm water
		salt and pepper, to taste

Shuck the corn and set it aside. Bring a large pan of water to boil. Strip the corn kernels from the cob, place them in the boiling water, and return to a full boil. Boil until the corn is just tender, about 3–5 minutes, depending on the freshness of the corn. Drain the corn and reserve the water. Mix the ground anise or dill into the water and add the cooked corn. Return the mixture to the stove for simmering. Dissolve the corn flour in ½ cup of warm water and simmer until a thick consistency like a gravy is obtained. Season with salt and pepper, to taste, and serve hot. *Serves 8*

Note: Serve in soup bowls accompanied by green *salsa*.

This version of *atole* calls for cacao peel which is available in Mexico and in some Hispanic markets in the U.S. It is the outer husk of the cacao bean that is discarded in the chocolate-making process. If you can find it, use this recipe as is. If not, substitute cocoa powder.

Atole Negro

(Rosa Tajimaroa Espinosa, Mercado de Antojitos, Uruapán, Michoacán)

1 C.   cacao peel, toasted until black (or substitute ½ C. unsweetened cocoa powder)
½   stick cinnamon
½ t.   ground anise seeds
4 C.   water
½   piece *piloncillo* or cane sugar, grated (or substitute ¼ C. brown sugar)
⅛ lb.   *masa*, dissolved in warm water

Heat a large skillet or *comal* until hot. Place the cacao peel on it and toast until black. Place the toasted peel (or cocoa powder), cinnamon, and anise seeds in the bowl of a food processor or blender and grind to a fine consistency. Add the water to a saucepan or clay pot (*olla*) and heat to a simmer. In a separate bowl dissolve the *masa* in 4 ounces of warm water. Stir in the *cacao* mixture into the water in the sauce pan. Then slowly stir the dissolved *masa* into the mixture until it is well blended. Stir in the *piloncillo* or brown sugar until it is melted and incorporated. When the mixture is well blended, strain it and cook it gently until the *atole* becomes thick, but not gelatinous.

Note: *Atole* is an excellent complement to tamales de harina (see p. 204).   *Serves 4*

Alternative Instructions: If using cocoa powder, skip the toasting instructions. Mix the powder with the cinnamon and ground anise seeds and proceed with the recipe.

Crema Fría de Aguacate

This easy-to-make soup is something like a modern *gazpacho* because it is not cooked and is served cold. The flavor is subtle, but is made somewhat piquant by the *serrano* chiles. They may be omitted, but the result is an almost totally cream flavor and texture. For maximum flavor, freshly picked avocados are best. By avocado, we mean Haas, the dark green alligator-skinned type. The soup is best when made just a few minutes before serving. The recipe can easily be increased.

3   avocados, peeled and pitted
2 C.   whipping cream
2 C.   chicken broth, cold
2   *serrano* chiles, chopped
2 C.   crushed ice
         salt and freshly ground pepper, to taste

Place avocados in the bowl of a food processor or blender and purée. Add whipping cream, chicken broth, *serrano* chiles, and ice. Liquify. Season to taste with salt and freshly ground pepper.   *Serves 2–3*
    Note: Serve with garlic-bread croutons or medium-diced *tortilla* croutons and diced avocado.

La Macadamia is the Bautista family's restaurant in Uruapán. It is a place where the produce of the Vivero La Alberca can be tested by a superior cook, Hilda Bautista Villegas. The following recipe calls for macadamia butter. This delicious and delicately flavored product may be difficult to find, so you may use unsalted butter in its place. Trout, incidentally, is being raised on farms in Michoacán and is thus becoming more widely available in Mexico.

Trucha Tarasca

(Hilda Bautista Villegas, Uruapán, Michoacán)

1-½ C   all-purpose flour
 ½ t.   kosher salt
 ¼ t.   freshly ground black pepper
 6   rainbow trout fillets
 ½ C.   canola oil
 6 t.   macadamia (or unsalted) butter
 ½ C.   macadamia nuts, oil-roasted and crushed

Season the flour with the salt and pepper and lightly dredge the fillets in it. Heat the oil in a deep, heavy skillet. When ready, sauté the fillets until golden brown on both sides and set aside on a plate. Spread a teaspoon of macadamia or unsalted onto butter each fillet, and sprinkle the nuts on top. Serve at once.   *Serves 3–4*

5

INGREDIENTS AND TECHNIQUES

Ingredients

This small survey of ingredients and cooking procedures typical to Mexican cuisine is nothing like an exhaustive study of the subject. An encyclopedia-sized volume would be needed for that. The products mentioned here almost exclusively relate to the recipes used in this book. We omit, for example, plantains and many of the other fruits we found in Mexico. Mexico is so rich in foodstuffs that it makes a comprehensive survey impossible in this limited space. The same applies to its cooking techniques, so here we offer a simple guide and some tips on how to prepare the recipes found in these pages. Some of the recipes are specialized and have their own sets of instructions. See those specific recipes for details on their preparation.

Two notes before beginning. Coarse salt is standard in Mexican cooking On the coast, sea salt is used and if you can get it, use it. If not, use coarse or kosher salt, available almost everywhere. Sea salt is "saltier" (and has more trace minerals) than the other varieties, so you may need to use less sea salt than the amount called for in the recipes. Second, we use the Spanish spelling for chile peppers, *chile*, not "chili," because that is the Mexican usage. Besides, to us, "chili" means a kind of bean and meat dish.

Most of the ingredients used in this book's recipes can be found in typical North American food stores. That was not always the case, when even a few years ago cilantro was hard to find in Chicago and commercial *salsas* were all but unknown. Happily, the North American palate has been expanding, and now formerly "exotic" ingredients have made their ways into many of the nation's pantries and refrigerators. Naturally, any place with a large Hispanic population is likely to have stores that cater to south-of-the-border tastes. There you are likely to find the foods mentioned in these pages, and if they are not fresh, at least you can get canned, frozen, or refrigerated versions. Some of the ingredients listed are not likely to be found in the United States at all and where this seems to be the case, we have suggestions for substitutions.

On the other hand, some ingredients have no real substitutes. One important herb, *epazote*, is not always found fresh in Mexican markets, much less in any other market (although it grows wild all over the United States and can be gathered). Jumiles (the insects from Mt. Huixteco in Taxco) are not going to be found on the standard grocery shelf (although Mexican markets may have them frozen or dried), and they also have no substitutes, unless you use iodine in the *salsa*! If you cannot find some of these foods, one more suggestion might help: look in Asian or Italian markets if they are available to you. Some of the vegetables and herbs used in these cuisines are interchangeable with the Mexican items. Or, you can try to make do by "fixing" ordinary North American ingredients. For example, if you cannot locate *chorizo*, then a good-quality pork sausage with spices, *annatto*, and lots of fat might do. Lastly, if you are really interested in "authentic" Mexican food, get a field guide to wild edible plants, go outdoors, and gather some. That is exactly what many Mexican families do in the spring when *quelites* are collected for the cooking pot. E*pazote* is only one of these plants; *verdolagas* (purslane) is another. And while gathering, remember the stories about Quetzalcóatl!

Corn or maize is the foundation of the ancient Mexican diet, and come to that, of the modern Mexican diet as well. As you will see in the recipes, it is used in a variety of ways, most often ground into meal or flour. In traditional cookery, this is done by soaking dried corn kernels in lime water and, when soft, grinding them on a flat stone called a *metate* with a rubbing stone called a *metlapil*, or *mano*. As the flour is ground, more water is added to make a dough—*masa* in Spanish, *nixtamal* in Nahuatl. This was the primal stuff of ancient Mexican cooking. Today's *tortillas*, *tamales*, and most *antojitos* are part of that tradition. Preparing *masa* from scratch is a process few would want to undertake: obtaining lime, boiling the corn, rubbing off the skins by hand, and then grinding them on a *metate* is grueling work. However, for sheer flavor, this is the preferred way to make *tortillas*. If you are fortunate enough to be near a tortilla bakery, then often fresh *masa* will be available, usually at low cost. They are almost always good. There is also a ready-made flour, often sold as "corn flour," "*tamale* flour," or simply *masa*, that is now sold in many markets. The instant version most widely distributed is that made by the Quaker Oats Company under the name *Masa*. Dough can be made by simply adding water to this product. Incidentally, do not mistake cornmeal for *masa*; they are not the same thing and cannot be used interchangeably.

If you cannot find corn flour, then normal wheat flour (preferably unbleached or even whole-wheat flour) will have to do. Mexicans, especially in the northern part of the country, use lots of wheat flour to produce pastries, raised breads, and *tortillas*.

Tortillas

Tortillas are not very difficult to make if you have the correct tools and a little patience. In the event that you have neither of these, prepared *tortillas* made of corn or wheat are always available. In non-Mexican food stores they are often refrigerated or frozen. When using this kind of *tortilla* we always buy Azteca (made by Azteca Foods, Inc. in Chicago), not just because they are friends, but because they make a good and sanitary product. For those who are worried about the amount of fat in their diets, one Azteca label, Buena Vida, is fat free. Write to the company and they will send you fat-free recipes (5005 South Nagle Ave. Chicago, IL 60638).

In cities where there are large numbers of Mexicans, there is sure to be a *tortilla* bakery. Chicago has a number of these, and we often use their *tortillas* when cooking. There is nothing quite like the smell and feel of freshly made tortillas, hot when they arrive from the "factory." When shopping for *tortillas*, let experience guide you as to brands. The best have a light color and mealy texture, while the worst are yellow and rubbery. In either case, if you are using refrigerated or bakery-made *tortillas*, you may need to be make them more flexible. To soften prepared *tortillas*, simply place them on a hot griddle or frying pan for a few seconds or steam them very, very briefly.

Beans

Frijoles or beans, are the second staple of ancient Mexican fare. They are everywhere in modern Mexican cuisine and are an important source of protein, especially when combined with a grain. Apart from their use as ingredients in main dishes, beans are often served as a separate course in a large meal. In this case, they are boiled and served in their own thick liquid, or they are boiled, mashed, and fried (called *refritos*, meaning "well fried"). Of the many different kinds of beans, only a few are called for in this book, since each region of Mexico usually specializes in one type of bean. Pintos, for instance, normally characterize the northern parts of the country, while in Guerrero and Michoacán black beans are more typical. The beans called for in the recipes here are black, small pink, and *habas*, or lima beans. All of these are commonly found in dried or canned form in most supermarkets. The dried variety is recommended over the canned product, since the cook will have more control over the taste, texture, and vitamin content of the final dish. Canned beans often contain additives and tend to be mushy.

Herbs and Spices

Most of the seasonings used in Mexican cooking can be found in the spice section of any supermarket. They are usually packaged in small cans or bottles and often are not as fresh as they might be. For instance, to get the best flavor, black pepper should be freshly ground from peppercorns. Some herbs dry well (oregano and basil), while others are best used fresh (cilantro and dill). The best place to buy these items is a store specializing in spices and herbs, fresh ones if possible, or a good Mexican food store. In the latter location, the shopper uninitiated into Mexican cuisine may be overwhelmed at the variety of condiments found there, but with patience and a spirit of adventure, can discover all sorts of new tastes and smells. One word of advice: Spices and herbs should smell strong and fresh, so let your nose be your guide in shopping.

The spices and herbs most commonly used in Mexican foods that are also familiar in the United States include bay leaf, basil, cinnamon (usually available in stick form, as in Mexico), cloves, coriander seeds, cumin, garlic, marjoram, mint, oregano (there are several Mexican varieties from which to choose, all of these stronger than our usual variety), parsley, and saffron (Mexican *azafrán* that differs from European saffron). A Mexican herb less commonly used in North America is *achiote* (annatto), which comes from the seeds of the tropical tree of that name. The reddish pulp surrounding the seeds is used as a seasoning and coloring agent for some meat (mostly pork) and fish dishes, but it is used most often to give rice a rich yellow color. When *annatto* is unavailable, a mild American paprika can be used for meat and real saffron for rice.

Two other herbs are important to genuine Mexican cooking, and one is more commonly found than the other. Cilantro, or fresh coriander, is widely available in most supermarkets. We grow it at home where, even in Chicago's abysmal climate, it does very well. Fresh coriander leaves and stalks are a must for sauces and other major dishes because they lend them a fresh "green" taste. Coriander leaves do not dry well but will keep for several weeks in the refrigerator if stored properly. If you can, buy coriander with the roots still attached. Wash the leaves and, while they are still wet, place the stalks in a plastic bag and seal it. Check the leaves occasionally, removing the yellow ones as they appear. If the coriander does wilt, place it in fresh cold water for a few minutes before use.

Epazote is likely to be the most difficult Mexican ingredient to obtain commercially, although it grows wild all over the United States. Called pigweed, wormseed, goosefoot, or Mexican tea (*Chenopodium ambrosioides*) in the United States and *pazote* in Spain, this herb is a must for bean dishes and is also widely used in *tortillas*. If you cannot gather *epazote* in its wild state, then the dried variety may be found in good Mexican food stores and often in shops that specialize in herbs and teas. It dries quite well and can be stored for some time. But the flavor of dried *epazote* is not the same as the fresh herb. Do not be put off by the initial "musty" smell and flavor of *epazote*—just use it.

Chiles[1]

Chiles have been an integral part of the Mexican diet since long before the beginnings of agriculture in the New World. New World chiles (*Capsicum*) are often called chile peppers although they are not at all related to the Old World *Piper nigrum*, whose seeds are the common black pepper. All chiles belong to the same genus and to a score or more separate species. The two main species are C. *annuum* and C. *frutescens*. Within these species are many, many varieties of chiles. Popular lore in Mexico has it that there are ninety-nine, though the types may number anywhere from sixty to over a hundred in Mexico alone, and many more in other parts of the world. To make matters even more confusing, the names for the same chiles differ from place to place, so that what is a *chile ancho* in one place is a *chile mulatto* or a *chile pasilla* in another. Fortunately, only a few types of chiles are used in this book, and often the differences among the chiles are so slight that only a dedicated connoisseur could distinguish them.

Not all chiles are extremely "spicy hot." They also include sweet varieties such as bell peppers, the *Güero*, and others with rich, pungent flavors. On the whole, though, it can be said that the smaller the chile, the hotter it is likely to be. However, there are many shades of hot, and a *poblano* chile might range from mildly *picante* to perfectly sweet; in fact, any two from the same plant might be different! Chiles change colors as they ripen or as they dry. Green bell peppers, the kind usually found in United States food stores, are really immature fruits which would turn red if permitted to remain on the vine. Red, brown, orange, and yellow are the normal colors for dried chiles. To complicate the matter even more, in Mexico the immature and dried chiles bear different names, hence the *poblano* chile, the one usually stuffed in various recipes, turns into the *ancho* chile when dried.

Fresh Chiles   Probably the best-known chile in the United States is the *jalapeño* (from Xalapa in Veracruz). It is almost always available canned or bottled, either pickled or packed in oil. Pickled *jalapeños* are relatively mild and may be used as an ordinary table condiment, but when they are preserved in oil they tend to be hot. *Jalapeños* are also fairly often found on produce counters in many markets around the country. The fresh chile is dark green and stubby in shape, measuring about two-and-a-half inches in length and one inch in girth. When dried and smoked it becomes the *chipotle* pepper (the mature pepper) and *morjta* pepper (immature); the former is often canned or bottled in vinegar. The *jalapeño* is used in the United States in a number of commercial pastes and sauces, while in Mexico the *chipotle* chile finds its way into many stews and other dishes. If you want to substitute, the hot varieties of Italian pickled peppers resemble the *jalapeño*.

The *serrano* ("from the mountains") is a small chile, roughly an inch-and-a-half long, that is commonly used in hot sauces. The flesh provides a vibrant flavor and the seeds are medium hot. When fresh, the *serrano* chile is a rich green color that changes to a red or orange when dried. (Dried *serranos* are often called *chiles japonés*). Usually found in Latin markets, the *serrano* also comes pickled (*en escabeche*) in bottles and, while these are perfectly useful, their flavor is not the same as that of the fresh chiles. *Serranos* are commonly used in *salsas*.

The *poblano* chile ("people's chile") is rich in flavor and may be the most popular of the fresh chiles in Mexican cooking. It is the base for *chiles rellenos*, or "stuffed chiles." Its dried version, the *ancho chile*, enjoys almost equal popularity. In its fresh form, the *poblano* is a long, triangular chile with a deep green to black color. *Poblanos* are almost invariably found in Latin food stores, but, if you cannot find them, then bell peppers or other large chiles grown in California and called either "California," "Anaheim," or "New Mexican" may be substituted, although with a certain loss of authentic flavor. The small, sweeter Melrose pepper, found in Italian markets in season, also works for stuffing, although the flavor is not the same. My all-time favorite chile, the Hungarian Wax, can be stuffed if large enough. This one ranks about the same on the heat scale as the *poblano*. All these chiles are very mild, but some *poblanos* can be a bit hot, so the substitution amounts for different chiles in recipes may not be exact.

Found in many supermarkets in the United States are varieties of small, fresh chiles usually identified merely as "hot peppers." In their sharp flavor, these are similar to the Mexican *chile de árbol*, or "tree chile," although they are not really related to that wild Mexican plant. "Hot peppers" come in many shapes: the long, thin *puya*, a fatter green one that resembles the *jalapeño* or small round chiles; and the *costeña* and the *pequín*, ranging from orange to red in color. The latter has several names, including the "bird chile" of southeast Asian cuisine. I grow them as ornamentals outdoors in the summer and indoors during the colder months (until the cats get to them). They are very hot and rate at the top of the heat scale. Any of these chiles can be used in place of the *serrano* or other hot chiles, but be careful.

We should mention also the hottest chile that you are likely to encounter: the *habanero* chile (the Asian "bird chile" comes the closest to it). It is found bottled, *en escabeche*, usually from the Yucatán, and in this guise should be eaten only by those who have a developed taste for the truly *picante*. However, this chile does have a fine flavor and appears in many cuisines and, increasingly, on North American store shelves in the form of sauces.

Dried Chiles   *Chile ancho*, the dried version of the *poblano* chile, serves as the basis for many chile sauces, including the authentic *chile con carne*. It is a broad, wrinkled chile that resembles a large prune and ranges in color from deep red to almost black. When soaked, it usually turns a rich red in color. Close in shape and color is the *chile mulatto*, a chile that is a dark brown in color. Both the *ancho* and *mulatto* possess delicious rich flavors, with the latter perhaps a bit stronger than the *ancho*. Both exude a splendid rich fragrance that resembles prunes or dried fruits. These particular varieties of chiles are becoming more widely available in ordinary food stores in North America, or they can be ordered from specialty catalogues.

The *pasilla* chile ("little raisin") is a long, thin chile, dark brown, with a flavor more *picante* and less rich than the first two. It is often confused with *an-*

chos and *mulattos* and, if obtained in their place, should be seeded before use (unless you want a hotter sauce). The fresh version of this chile is called the *chilaca*, a red chile that does very well in cooked or fresh sauces.

The *chipotle* and the similar *morita* are two of Mexico's greatest chiles. Their smokey flavor reminds us of the cooking fires of Mexican villages. Often found in pickled form, usually sliced into strips, these chiles are mildly hot, less so than the dried *pequíns* and *cascabels*. We use them in their natural dried state in several sauces. Try using them in a barbecue sauce if you wish to experiment.

The *cascabel* and *guajillo* chiles are in the *mirasol* family. *Guajillo* chiles are about four inches long and range from medium-bright to dark red in color. *Cascabels* ("little bells") are round and of similar color. They are medium hot with a marvelous flavor. As noted previously, the *guajillo* is the distinctive chile of Guerrero. Both these dried chiles are also eaten green in sauces, very much like the *serranos*.

Powdered Chiles   Many, if not all, of the chiles mentioned here will not be found in ordinary food stores. Most markets do stock powdered chile of some kind, and these may do instead of the whole dried chile. Powdered chiles may be pure *ancho* or *pasilla*, cayenne or "red pepper with cayenne," paprika (which is really a powdered, ripe, sweet chile), Spanish paprika (a hot chile preparation), or ordinary commercial chile powder that has been mixed with other seasonings. The last of these is not recommended for use in these recipes.

Mexican cooks often use powdered chiles in place of whole ones, and Mexican stores will normally have a stock of pure chile powders. It is notoriously difficult, however, to give exact quantities of whole chiles in recipes, because the chiles vary in size; that problem is compounded when the chiles are powdered. But based on the average size of various chiles, some relationships between powdered and whole chiles have been worked out. In general, one tablespoon of powder is equivalent to a whole large chile such as the *ancho*, *mulatto*, or *pasilla*. The smaller, hotter chiles, such as *pequíns*, might be replaced by cayenne pepper or Spanish paprika in the amount of one-eighth teaspoon per chile. Of course, equivalents depend on the individual's taste and tolerance for heat. Therefore, as in many recipes, experimentation is in order.

Storage of Chiles   Dried and powdered chiles can be stored in a cool, dry place for months on end, although it is not a good idea to keep them out in the open; excessively dry air, typical of North American homes during the winter, tends to make the chiles too brittle and causes them to lose flavor. A plastic bag or container will do nicely for storage. Any moisture in a batch of dried chiles will encourage rotting; therefore they should be examined occasionally and the bad ones thrown out.

Whole, fresh chiles may be kept in the bottom of a refrigerator for several weeks but not in plastic bags—they tend to promote rotting. Make sure that the chiles are dry and check them for mold from time to time. Chiles for stuffing, such as *poblanos,* may be frozen for later use if they are first toasted and peeled (see "Preparing Fresh Chiles and Sweet Peppers," p. 242). When frozen unprepared, *poblanos* lose their flavor and texture entirely. Other chiles may be chopped raw, packed in plastic bags, and frozen, as long as they are cooked when used later.

Cheeses and Dairy Products

Many Mexican dishes include cheese, as one might expect in a country that today raises so much cattle. Several types of cheese are used in this book's recipes. One is *añejo* (aged cheese), a dry crumbly type that is grated atop beans, *enchiladas,* and other such dishes. *Cotija* is a similar cheese. *Queso fresco* (fresh cheese), a moist white cheese with a crumbly consistency, is usually found in Mexican food stores and is the everyday cheese of the Mexican household; it can be used in many ways, such as in stuffings or atop various *tortilla*-type dishes. One should be careful with this cheese when it comes from Mexican shops because some varieties are excessively salty. If the cheese is to be cut from a large block, ask for a taste first. Otherwise, you will have to take your chances with the small packages labeled *queso blanco.* A reasonable North American substitute is farmer's cheese, a commercial variety that is available in standard supermarkets. A number of companies produce a *Chihuahua*-style cheese under various labels, including *Ranchera,* *Enchilada,* and so on. This type of cheese should be a wonderful yellowish cheese with a mild flavor and have, when cooked, a fairly stringy consistency. As noted, it comes from the Mennonite communities in the state of Chihuahua. The cheese is vaguely like mozzarella, but if you need to substitute, try Monterrey Jack. *Asadero* is a semi-soft melting cheese, very mild, more like mozzarella than *menonita.* *Panela* is fresh cheese, lower in fat than others, and also known as *tuma.* Oaxaca has styles of string cheese that take many forms, all widely used throughout Mexico. You may find it in specialty stores, but if not, use Chihuahua-style cheese in recipes that call for it. *Crema* is soured cream that comes in two main versions: sweeter *crema* that resembles a *crème fraiche,* and *crema agria,* a real sour cream with more bite than ours. All of these cheeses feature in the various dishes we ate in Mexico and are reflected in the recipes given here.

Cooking Fats and Oils

Pork lard is the traditional Mexican medium for frying and to capture authentic flavor it must be used. If you want pure, unadulterated lard, a visit to a local butcher who makes it is the best bet, otherwise the commercial product will have to do. Of course, lard can also be made at home by rendering fat from any kind of pork. Vegetable shortening is also a useful substitute, especially when a fluffy consistency in flour products is required. We call for canola oil in many recipes, rather than lard or other vegetable oils. Canola oil is low in polyunsaturated fats, unlike lard, and therefore reputed to be better for one's health. In fact, Dudley and I often use olive oil for cooking because of its flavor. Mexicans rarely use butter in village cooking, although they have good-quality products (usually from cultured cream, as in Europe), especially in the cattle-rearing regions of the country.

Fruits and Vegetables

Most of the fruits and vegetables used in the recipes will be familiar to the North American reader, but some are more exotic and harder to obtain outside of Latin American markets. Among the ordinary vegetables are green beans, broccoli, spinach, radishes, chard, and others that are grown the same way on both sides of the border. These can be obtained fresh almost everywhere. Freshness is critical in at least one item used in Mexican cooking: tomatoes.

Tomatoes   Summer is the best time for all produce in northern cities and, as any shopper in these places knows, in the winter good ripe tomatoes are hard to come by. This fruit is usually picked while green in California, Florida, and Mexico and ripened off the vine during its transit to urban distribution points. Sometimes for cosmetic effect, the unripe tomatoes are treated with a gas that turns them from their natural green to an ill-hued red. It need hardly be said that the texture and taste of these truncated monstrosities leaves much to be desired. Even in the summer tomatoes such as these appear in food markets. In the event that ripe tomatoes are not available, use canned ones instead. Most brands of Italian-style plum tomatoes will serve since they are less acidic and meatier and have fewer seeds and a better flavor. You should experiment with several brands to obtain the least acidic kind. If you want to be more authentically pre-Columbian, use cherry tomatoes in place of the more conventional types.

Corn   There is nothing quite like the taste of just-picked sweet corn, which is very different from corn in its husk that has been picked several hours or days before eating. The reason is that corn rapidly loses its sugar content (it turns to starch) after picking. Unless you have access to a field of ripening corn or a farmer's market, it is unlikely that you will be able to enjoy this wonderful treat. In reality, we rarely saw anyone eating fresh sweet corn in Mexico. All the dishes were prepared with dried kernels, and when the corn was eaten on the cob, roasted and sprinkled with chile powder, it was fairly old. Use fresh corn if you can, and in one recipe fresh corn is a must: *uchepos*.

Onions   Mexican cooking calls for onions in numerous dishes, but these are not the yellow onions ordinarily found in North American markets. In Mexico, a small- to medium-sized knob onion, a white bulb with the green stalk still attached, is used. It has a tangy flavor that is unlike that of the yellow onion. These onions can now be found in many supermarkets and are almost always available in Italian or Mexican produce markets. Occasionally red or large yellow "Spanish" onions will be called for in fish dishes or in salads, and these delicious mild varieties may be found everywhere, although at a premium price.

Lettuce   Lettuce appears in many Mexican dishes, often shredded over *tostadas* and *tacos*, as a thickening agent in sauces, and in salads. But the variety used is almost always romaine lettuce, not the usual iceberg. If one were to follow a simple nutritional rule of thumb, it is this: the greener the vegetable, the more vitamins and food value it will have. That holds absolutely true for lettuce. Neither Dudley nor I ever use the tasteless white head of iceberg lettuce at home and blanch to see it in what passes for salads in many Mexican-style restaurants.

Avocados   This fruit is indigenous to the New World and was one of the main sources of fat in the pre-Columbian diet. It is used in salads, sauces, soups and is, of course, the basis for *guacamole*. Almost every food store in North America carries avocados at all times of the year. Use the dark green Haas ones with the bumpy surfaces, which usually have a better flavor and texture then the other varieties. When buying avocados in parts of the country to which they are not native, pick those that are firm but not too soft. Since avocados, like tomatoes, are shipped green, you will likely have to buy them while they are fairly hard. To ripen them, leave the fruit out in a warm place. When ready for eating the avocado should have a firm, yet soft flesh, a slightly greasy texture, and a rich aroma.

Tomatillos   Frequently called "green tomatoes" or *tomates verdes*, these small green berries (*Physalis ixocarpa*) are distant relatives of our familiar tomatoes.

Tomatillos are covered with a paper-like brown skin that must be peeled off before they can be used. Washing may also be necessary because of a sticky substance that lies on the berries' surfaces. They have a delicate light flavor that comes out only when cooked and are typically used in wonderful green sauces. If fresh *tomatillos* are unavailable and they cannot be found canned, do not use green tomatoes in their place.

Huazontle   Fresh amaranth can be found in more and more Mexican markets, especially around Easter time. It also grows wild in the United States, though usually with smaller seed heads than its Mexican version. If you want to find them, get a field guide and start hunting!

Verdolagas   The same things said of *huazontle* also apply to this class of "greens," or purslane. Considered a weed, it is routinely pulled out and thrown away by gardeners. Its small, bulbous leaves are slightly mucilagenous and when prepared should be treated like cactus leaves (see *nopales* below) with light boiling and washing. They are usually eaten in a salad.

Nopales   The flat green leaves of the prickly pear cactus are found fresh in Latin markets or canned in the specialty sections of many supermarkets. They make a crisp addition to salads, can stand as a vegetable on their own, and are useful in egg dishes and soups. If you find them fresh, buy the smaller and more tender leaves. To prepare them, peel off the thorns very carefully, place the leaves in a small amount of water, and simmer them until tender; after cooking, wash any sticky residue from the leaves.

Tunas (Prickly Pear)   These are the fruits of the *nopal* cactus, usually called simply the "prickly pear." In the United States the fruit is usually reddish, but in Mexico they range in color from dead white to deep red, each with a different degree of sweetness. The *tuna* is an utterly delicious fruit that may be eaten plain or served with other fruits and/or cream. In local tradition it is said to cure diarrhea, the ubiquitous Mexican affliction.

Guava, Papaya, Mango, Zapote   These fruits are found everywhere in Mexico, sold on street corners by vendors and in restaurants and markets. The *guava* is made into a sweet paste and commonly eaten as a dessert; the papaya is found on the breakfast table; and the mango is eaten as a delicious snack. The papaya is rich in vitamins and valuable enzymes and has a subtle sweet flavor. It is served at breakfast peeled, cut into chunks, and accompanied with slices of lime squeezed over it. A good sweet papaya is usually cut in half, seeded, and eaten like a cantaloupe. When you buy a mango, make sure that it is firm but soft to the touch, with a reddish tinge to the skin. To eat one, thrust a fork into one end of the fruit, then feel around until the pit, which is long and thin, slides between the tines. Once secured, peel the skin gradually as you eat the mango. The *zapote* (from the Nahuatl *tzapotl*) is an oval-shaped sweet fruit that comes in several colors and grades of sweetness, from white to black. It is used in fruit drinks and desserts and is wonderful eaten plain.

Chayote   This pear-shaped fruit takes its name from the Nahuatl word *chayotli* and is often called a vegetable pear because it is almost always served cooked. *Chayote* grow on vines and there are several varieties; the usual sort found in North American markets are light green and smooth skinned. These *chayotes* are not the best because they tend to be less flavorful and watery when cooked. (You might as well use a rutabaga instead of these.) If you can find the deep green *chayotes* with prickly exteriors, buy them and use them in a salad, peeled and lightly boiled.

Jícama   The *jícama* resembles a turnip with white flesh and tastes very much like a water chestnut, with which it may be used interchangeably. The *jícama* has a sweetish flavor and a crisp texture that is rather like an apple, and it may be sliced and eaten raw with lime juice or served in a salad.

Limes   Mexicans normally use limes (*limón*) where North Americans use lemons. The lime has a lighter flavor and contains less vitamin C than other citrus fruits. If you are substituting lemons, be sure to take into account its stronger flavor.

Squash Blossoms   The *flor de calabaza* is made into a famous soup and is a popular filling for *quesadillas*. It is not usually found in ordinary food stores, but is available in Latin markets either dried or in cans. The best brand we have found is Herdez—they also make great sauces. Otherwise, get fresh ones in season and use them accordingly.

Huitlacoche or Cuitlacoche   Corn fungus, as we have already mentioned, is one of Mexico's "gourmet" foods. It is the black rust that grows on corn late in the season. The flavor cannot be described, but must be experienced. Finding it not easy, but Herdez cans an excellent version. There are other companies that pickle it, but these are not the best versions to use in *quesadillas* or in the other dishes mentioned in the book.

Guajes   Looking something like snow peas, *guajes* (*Leucaena esculentia*) are tree-born pods usually about four to six inches long. They have thin skins and large seeds and range in color and depth of flavor from light green to dark red. They are used in sauces, *moles*, and fritters and make a wonderful filling in *quesadillas* or small *tacos*. Sometimes the seeds are ground and used in place of dried shrimp in seasonal Lenten dishes. No substitute for *guajes* exists, but they are becoming increasingly common in Mexican markets in North America—in Chicago we can always get them in our outdoor market. If you can find them, *guajes* are worth trying.

Nuts and Seeds

Nuts and seeds, both ground and whole, are often found in Mexican recipes. Pumpkin seeds (*pepitas*) and peanuts are native to the Americas and were used in sauces before the arrival of the Europeans. Sesame seeds and walnuts, introduced by the Spanish, are equally used as thickening agents in *moles*, desserts, and candies. Nuts and seeds also make wholesome snacks by themselves, once they have been hulled and toasted. All seeds are toasted before they are used in sauces. To do this, spread the seeds on a cookie sheet and set them in a preheated (350°) oven. Bake them for about twenty minutes or until all the seeds are golden brown. Be sure to shake the pan every so often to prevent the seeds from burning. Seeds may also be toasted on an ungreased frying pan, but they must be shaken constantly to prevent scorching. This procedure takes only a few minutes. *Pepitas* are the basis of that great style of sauces, the pipiáns.

Chocolate

Chocolate has a long history in the New World. The cacao bean was used by the ancient peoples as a medium of exchange, and in ground form it served as both a delicacy and a medicinal drink. Soon after the Conquest, chocolate drinking became the rage in Europe (the first stimulant beverage!), and one has only to taste the wonderful hot chocolate mixtures of Mexico to see why. Commercial North American hot chocolate pales by comparison. To gain an appreciation for Mexican chocolate, the next time you are in Pátzcuaro, go to the chocolate shop, where you can get chocolate ground together with sugar, almonds, and cinnamon. Barring a trip to that most interesting of towns, Mexican chocolate can also be purchased in cake form in the United States under several brand names.

Beverages

There are few beverages more strongly associated with Mexico than *tequila*. It is true that beer is usually associated with Mexican cuisine, since spicy food and cold beer seem natural companions. Beer has replaced *pulque* as the

"Pulque, tequila, *or* atole?"

mildly alcoholic beverage of choice throughout the country, but nothing can replace the stronger liquids made from the same juice as *pulque: tequila* and *mezcal*. Both are distillates of the blue *agave*. Spaniards brought the art of distillation from Europe (yet another invention of the Islamic world), where it had been used on wine to make brandy. Using *pulque* was a natural extension of the technique. *Tequila* comes from the towns of Tequila and Tepatitlán in Jalisco state, near Guadalajara, where the volcanic soil produces what are said to be the best varieties of the succulent *agave* plant. *Tequila* is made by chopping and steaming the leaves and fruits of the plant, traditionally in wood-lined pits similar to a barbecue. The cooked leaves and fruits are then pressed and the juices are allowed to ferment for two days. *Tequila* is fermented twice in copper and the first batches are very potent, more than 100 proof. After the *tequila* stands for about a month, water is added to it to reduce it to "normal" strength. The first run of *tequila* is called silver or white. Other batches are aged in oak for nine months, thus achieving title of "gold." The best *tequila*, *añejo*, is aged three years or more. The older the *tequila*, the smoother it is, so that when you are drinking the best brands, such as our favorite, Herradura, you hardly realize it is a spirit.

Mezcal is made much the same way, but it is hardly ever aged. Produced in various parts of the country, Oaxaca in particular, *mezcal* routinely comes with a *gusano*, or *agave* worm at the bottom of the bottle. North Americans may be disgusted at the thought, but these are great treats, the prize at the end of the bottle. One other Mexican drink deserves note. *Charranda*, an alcoholic beverage is distilled from sugar, is a Michoacán specialty. The people of Michoacán say that the *charranda's* flavor goes perfectly with meats. When one goes into regional restaurants, there are always bottles of *charranda* on tables in much the same way that *tequila* can be everywhere else.

Miscellaneous

Tamales are made using husks of corn or banana leaves, the latter ingredient used especially in the southern parts of Mexico. Latin American markets will normally carry either corn or banana leaves or both. Corn husks are sold dried and have to be soaked before using. In the summertime you may find fresh ones or can use the husks from ears bought to make corn on the cob. Banana leaves are usually found fresh and may be kept for several months in the refrigerator, provided they are kept wrapped and free from mold. If you cannot find either of these, use parchment paper to wrap *tamales* for cooking.

Many prepared sauces, both hot and mild, are sold in the United States. Some are fairly authentic, and others are merely hot. You may do best to look for brand names imported from Mexico, especially Herdez, whose products we have used successfully in many dishes.

Utensils

The traditional Mexican kitchen that is still found in country village homes, is filled with the same cooking tools that would have been used in a similar household centuries ago. Such a kitchen would have included a primitive stove, various ceramic pots and pitchers (*ollas* and *jarras*) glazed in bright colors, a grinding stone and rubbing stone (*metate* and *metlapil*), a mortar and pestle made of rough basaltic stone and used for grinding spices and herbs, (*molcajete* and *tejolote*) an earthenware or cast-iron griddle (*comal*), and various wooden implements for stirring and serving. Many of these utensils have passed out of use in the modern, urban Mexican kitchen that resembles, for the most part, nothing more than the standard United States style of kitchen. Nevertheless, some of the items mentioned here are quite useful in preparing Mexican dishes, especially if one is interested in traditional cooking methods. Many of these special utensils can be purchased in Latin American or specialty cookware shops. We strongly recommend a *molcajete* because the sauces made in it simply taste better. If you do get one, season it in the following way: grind dried beans in it until they are powdered, then continue to grind until the powder is well ground into the pores of the vessel. After using the *molcajete* to grind foods, just rinse it out, but do not scrub it.

Blender

The blender has replaced the various grinding and crushing tools of the old Mexican kitchen. It is best to have one with a detachable base and small blending jars for preparing small amounts of chiles and spices.

Food Processor

The food processor is really a large blender. It is an invaluable tool for Mexican or any other kind of cooking, which is why it is used in so many restaurant kitchens and, in a smaller version, has appeared in millions of households the world over. The food processor will do most of the chores required in Mexican cooking. Want a smooth sauce? Properly chopped (not ground) meat? *Moles*? The food processor will save time and effort. We cannot give an adequate guide to the full capabilities of food processors here. There are several fine books on the market that deal with this subject and, of course, the manuals that come with most machines are also useful.

Comal

This earthenware or metal griddle is useful for making *tortillas* and toasting various other foods. In Mexico these are made to fit over the burners of a modern stove Griddles of this type are available in the United States, both in Latin American shops and in some hardware stores.

Casseroles (Cazuelas) *and* Pots (Ollas)

These pottery vessels come in many shapes and sizes. The *cazuela* is a wide, round dish that can be used for cooking, mixing, and serving, while *ollas* are excellent as soup and bean pots. Both should be made for use on top of the stove as well as in the oven. They are usually attractively decorated and can go straight from the oven to the table. One word of warning: The purchaser should inquire about the lead content of all pottery, since much of it is meant only for decoration and may therefore have high levels of lead in its paint. Down in Michoacán, we asked Arturo Olivares about this. He claimed that most Mexican pottery has very little lead and that, even if it did have lead, the lead would cook off after a few uses. We'll leave the argument there. I use *cazuelas* made by a Chicago-area potter, Dolores Fortuna (of Artworks in Oak Park), who previously worked in Mexico. She makes wonderful pots that

I use on the stovetop, just as they are used in Mexico. Food always tastes better when cooked in pottery this way.

Pans

A well-seasoned cast-iron frying pan is the best kind of frying pan to use for reasons of taste and health. (It adds iron to the diet.) Every kitchen should have at least one ten-inch frying pan and a ten-inch iron chicken fryer, that is, a high-sided pan with a tight-fitting lid. A heavy pan with a fitted lid is indispensable for making good rice. For ease of use, good cooking qualities, and aesthetic value, I use a heavy enameled saucepan for this purpose. A wide metal pan for making *paella* (assuming you do not have a wide *cazuela*) is yet another useful item. It closely resembles an oriental wok. If you happen to own a wok with all its accoutrements, consider it for Mexican dishes in which large amounts of fried food are required or for steaming vegetables, *tortillas*, and even *tamales*. A double boiler is also a useful when making *flans* and puddings. Finally, a pressure cooker cuts out an enormous amount of the time required for preparing beans, both of us use ours often.

Grinder

A small grinder can be used for grinding nuts, seeds, and spices that are best not put in a blender. (For example, cinnamon is so strong that it will leave a permanent flavor in a blender jar). Aside from using a mortar and pestle, an alternative is a grinding dish that is sold in Latin American and Asian markets. This is a shallow bowl with a heavily scored bottom against which nuts, softer seeds such as sesame, and spices may be crushed with a pestle.

Steamer

Tamales are made by steaming, and if you intend to make them regularly, a steamer is a great convenience. Otherwise, a steamer can be improvised by placing a rack of some kind in the bottom of a large pan with a fitted lid. Make certain that the rack is high enough to keep the tamales out of the water and to permit circulation of the steam around them.

Tortilla Press

Making *tortillas* by hand takes a lot of practice and considerable skill; one always admires the dexterity of Mexican women who regularly make them in the time-honored way. If you intend to make *tortillas* at home, a press is a virtual necessity. Presses are made of aluminum and come in various sizes. We recommend the six-inch size for most uses. *Tortilla* presses are relatively inexpensive and may be found not only in Mexican shops, but also in Chinese food stores. (The press is also used for making the delicious Chinese *moo shu* pancakes.)

Special Utensils

Cookie cutters, serrated edging tools for pastries, and many other specialty tools are adaptable for Mexican cooking. Latin American cuisine is famous for its *empañadas*, or turnovers. These come in many forms and sizes, with an almost infinite variety of fillings. One of the quickest of making these delectable dishes is with a Tartmaster. The round device is a kind of press, something like an automatic cookie cutter. To use it, dough is rolled out into a sheet, filling placed on the appropriate areas and a covering sheet of dough set on that. The Tartmaster is placed over each filled circle. Press down on the spring loaded handle and the pastry is sealed and crimped, ready for cooking. It saves a great deal of time and the result always looks good. Chef Dudley uses them all the time.

Tartmasters come in several sizes and are low-priced. They are available in specialty stores, or directly from the manufacturer: Kitchen Connection, 8405 W. 45th Street, Lyons, IL 60534; or telephone 1-800-233-5132.

Cooking Procedures

Mexican cooking leaves much room for improvisation, as might be expected from a syncretic and basically peasant tradition. However, some methods of preparation special to Mexican cooking are described in the following pages. Those readers who are experienced in Asian cooking may recognize some similar techniques, especially shredding, chopping, quick frying, and the application of sauces.

Frying

The word "fry" as it appears here means to cook something in more oil than it takes to sauté. That is to say, sauteing means to cook in a small amount of oil fairly quickly; frying means to. . . well, fry it until browned. To fry, bring lard to the point of boiling and oil to the smoking point; the high temperatures ensure that the cooked ingredient does not take on the flavor of the lard or oil. If you use a light oil such as safflower or olive, be careful not to use intense heat or it may burn. We almost never use lard because it is loaded with polysaturated fat. Unfortunately, much authentic Mexican cooking calls for lard. . . it does taste good!

Chopping and Cutting

Some recipes, mainly sauces, call for ingredients to be chopped in a blender or processor and, in this case, "chop" means that the ingredients are not to be puréed but churned into a pulpy mass. Most ingredients, tomatoes for example, need to be quartered or sliced before they are chopped by machine. If you intend to make sauces without the benefit of mechanical aids, you should chop the ingredients finely and cook them until they form a lumpy sauce. For chopping, we recommend a Chinese cleaver of middle weight or a French *sabatier*-style knife. When cutting herbs, always use scissors to bring out the best flavor.

Preparing Tomatoes

Several methods are used to prepare fresh tomatoes for sauces and other dishes and to reduce their acidity. The first is to place the tomatoes one at a time into a pot of rapidly boiling water. Depending on the thickness of its skin, leave the tomato in the water from ten to sixty seconds. Remove each tomato and drop it immediately in cold water. The skin should then peel off easily. To remove the seeds, cut the fruit in half and gently squeeze them out.

The other method is much the same as that used to peel chiles. Put the tomato over an open fire such as the burner of a gas stove or onto a heated, ungreased frying pan. The skin will begin to blister. Remove the tomato from the heat and peel the skin. This method creates quite a mess, and an alternative is to broil the tomatoes in a baking pan until the skin begins to pucker. Then it can be peeled and seeded. Dudley's recipes often call for roasting or toasting of tomatoes and chiles.

Removing the skin of the tomato wastes a valuable supply of vitamins and minerals, so you may want to use the whole tomato, in sauces at least. However, normal tomatoes used in this way produce more juice and acid than one might wish. To prevent that, seed the tomatoes first by slitting them in half and scraping out as much of the seeds and juice as possible. Or, use Italian plum tomatoes, which are far meatier than other varieties. Processing tomatoes in a food processor will break down the tough skin.

Preparing Onions

These are always chopped finely and gently fried until they are transparent, not brown. The same rule applies to garlic.

Preparing Dried Chiles

Most dried chiles are prepared in a way similar to tomatoes. (The smallest ones need only be smashed with a blunt instrument.) Place the chiles on a heated, ungreased griddle or frying pan or gently toast them in an open flame. Be careful not to burn them or the result will be quite bitter. After they are singed, cut open each chile and remove the seeds and veins, then soak them in enough water to cover until they are somewhat soft. Puree the chiles in a processor or blender, adding a few at a time with a little of the water in which they have been soaked. Do not permit the machine to run for long periods or some of the chiles' flavor will be lost.

A word of caution here: in handling hot chiles use rubber gloves or wash your hands with lots off soap immediately afterward. Chile juice in the eyes or an opening in the skin is painful.

Preparing Fresh Chiles and Sweet Peppers

Poblano and sweet peppers should be prepared for stuffing in the following way. Toast each chile over an open flame, on a hot griddle, or under a broiler. Turn each chile frequently so that it does not burn. When the skin develops blisters and begins to turn a light brown, remove the chile from the heat and wrap it in a damp cloth or place it in a paper bag. After fifteen to twenty minutes, remove the chiles from their wrappers and peel them with a small sharp knife. You may have to do this under running water to get all the skin from the chile. Make a slit in the side of the chile and carefully extract the seeds and veins. Wash the interior to remove any remaining seeds.

When preparing bell peppers for stuffing, cut around the top (the stem side), remove the innards, and use the top as a lid. Some chiles, *poblanos* in particular, are more *picante* than others. To dilute their heat, prepare the chiles as above, remove the seeds and white veins, and let them soak for about an hour in salted water to which a tablespoon or two of vinegar has been added. Dry the chiles before using them. When prepared this way, chiles may be kept frozen for some months without a loss of flavor, although soaking will remove a good number of nutrients, most notably the water-soluble vitamins B and C.

Preparing Moles

Moles are basic native American dishes that stand as an integral part of Mexican cuisine. The Aztec word *molli* originally meant a sauce, an accompaniment to some corn/bean dish, sometimes with meat. Now it refers to a sauce made from chiles and not just the famous sauce with a touch of chocolate from Puebla. *Moles* differ from other sauces in this respect: all the contents are ground into a paste and then cooked for a short time in lard. Cooked meats are added to the mixture, together with a little stock, and the whole is cooked just long enough for the flavors to blend. A good *mole*, which is often cooked in fat, is one of the glories of Mexican cookery. One note on this subject: the black *moles* from Oaxaca and Michoacán are black because the chile seeds are fried black. Indeed, everything in these *moles* is fried to that color, but never burnt.

Preparing Tortillas

Have ready a *tortilla* press, waxed paper or plastic wrap, a *comal* or heavy skillet, and *masa*. First, make the *masa* according to its package directions. Usually that is two cups of corn flour to 1-⅓ cups of warm water and, if it is not already in the mix, about 1 teaspoon of salt. The *tortilla* dough must be somewhat crumbly and, never sticky. If it seems too dry or too gooey, carefully work in either more water or flour. Form the dough into 12 small balls of equal size, about the size of golf balls. Open the *tortilla* press and cover the bottom with a piece of waxed paper or a sheet of plastic wrap. Place one of the dough balls on the press and set it a little off center toward the top of the press. Cover the dough with another sheet of waxed paper or plastic wrap and pull down the lid of the press to form a thin pancake. Heat the griddle or frying pan over medium heat to the point where a small piece of masa pops and puffs slightly when dropped on it. (Although *comals* are always ungreased, you might grease a frying pan very lightly.) Remove one of the sheets of paper or plastic wrap from the *tortilla* and place the *tortilla's* raw side on the griddle; remove the sheet from the other side. Toast the *tortilla* for only about 2 minutes on each side or until it begins to brown slightly. The *tortillas* should be neither thick nor soggy, but flexible and soft. They will remain warm for hours if stacked and wrapped in a cloth or if wrapped in foil and kept in a warm oven.

Tortillas made from wheat flour are very common, especially in northern Mexico, and are compatible with North American palates that are used to that famous North American-Mexican dish, *burritos*. To make them you will need 2 cups of unbleached all-purpose flour, 1 teaspoon of salt, ¼ of cup lard or vegetable shortening, and approximately ½–¾ cup of slightly warm water. Sift the flour and salt together. Cut the lard or shortening into the flour or work it in quickly with the fingers so that is thoroughly distributed, and add enough water to make a stiff dough. Form 12 balls of equal size and let them rest on a floured board for about half an hour. Then, either roll out each ball on a floured board or pastry cloth with a rolling pin until it is paper thin, or place the balls in a *tortilla* press and flatten using the same method as with the corn *masa*. Toast on each side for about 20 seconds on a hot griddle or frying pan, and serve at once or keep warm in a cloth. Wheat *tortillas* are wonderful hot off the griddle and spread with good butter (preferably unsalted) or a soft cheese such as cream cheese.

Preparing Enchiladas

The *tortilla* dish par excellence, in terms of popularity and variety, is the *enchilada*. Basically, it is a tortilla that has been dipped in a sauce and filled with almost any conceivable kind of food, frequently in combination with cheese. It is either rolled up or folded and served with a garnish. The imaginative cook will be able to create all sorts of new combinations and virtually all of them will be "correct." Among the fillings, shredded meats, cheeses of various sorts, chiles, beans, and cooked vegetables are all standard, while toppings may include a red or green sauce and sour cream.

There are two methods of *enchilada* preparation. Old-style Mexican cooks will dip the tortilla in a prepared sauce, fry it quickly in hot fat, and then fill and roll it. This can get messy because the sauce spatters in the hot fat and, unless the cook is careful, the sauce will easily burn. An alternative is to heat the tortilla in a little oil first, then dip it in the sauce, and then fill and roll it up. The *tortillas* used in this kind of recipe must be soft, but not too, soft or else they can absorb too much oil or liquid and become soggy.

Preparing Beans

Beans are easy to cook, but take some time to do it, unless you use a pressure cooker. In that case, follow the manufacturer's directions. Typically, beans take about 20 minutes when cooked this way, but the timing depends on the type and size of the bean. Otherwise, follow these simple steps.

1. Wash the dry beans thoroughly and remove all foreign material. Place them in a large pan with enough water to cover, about 2 inches above the level of the beans.
2. For the best-tasting beans, do not soak them overnight. At best, soak them for 8 hours before cooking in enough water to cover.
3. Beans ought to be cooked very, very slowly in an earthenware pot, as it is done in Mexico.
4. It is best to begin cooking dry beans, without soaking, by placing them in a pot with water to cover. Bring the water to a boil and cook vigorously for about 10 minutes. Then remove them from the heat, cover, and let stand for at least 1 hour.

5. Drain the water and refill the pan with the same amount of water. Bring the water to a boil, reduce heat and simmer from 1–2 hours, depending on the size of the beans.
6. As the bean skins begin to shrivel, add a little fat or oil to pan. When the beans are almost done, add salt to taste.
7. Beans always taste better the next day, so cook them the day before or keep a prepared supply in the refrigerator.

Frijoles de la Olla

1	lb.	dried black beans
8–12	C.	water
2		cloves garlic, chopped
		a sprig of *epazote*
1		avocado leaf (*criollo* is best) (optional)
4–6	T.	lard, pork drippings, or canola oil
		kosher salt, to taste

Follow the directions above for soaking beans (steps 1–4). When ready, add garlic, *epazote*, and the avocado leaf (optional) to the water. Bring it to a boil, reduce heat and cook about 1 hour until almost done. When the beans' skins begin to wrinkle, add the fat or oil. When the beans are almost done (they will be *al dente*), add kosher salt, to taste. When the beans are soft, remove some of the liquid and about 3 tablespoons of the beans. Place them in a bowl and purée or mash thoroughly. Return the purée to the pot and continue to cook until the bean broth is thick. *Makes about 6 cups*

6

MORE RECIPES!

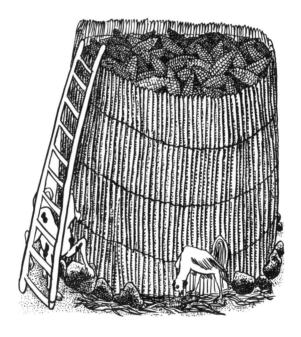

Not all of the recipes that Dudley collected during our travels appear in the chapters of this book. So, we thought that a mini-collection of recipes might be interesting as a quick way for reader-cooks to get some taste for the foods characteristic of Guerrero and Michoacán. Some special techniques are required for making several of the dishes; for advice refer to Chapter 5, Ingredients and Techniques.

"This is the life!"

Salsa

Sauces are fundamental to Mexican cooking and their many varieties are used in almost as many ways. Some are meant for table use as dips and condiments, while others are integrated into prepared dishes. Mexicans use sauces in or with almost any food, from soup to meats, and they can also be eaten with plain or fried *tortillas*. Almost all sauces are made with tomatoes, chiles, herbs, and spices, but the ingredients may be combined in an unending variety of preparations. These differences come partly from the different chiles' unique flavors that alter the character of the sauces in which they are used. Although we have given sauce recipes with some dishes (for example, *Huachinango a la talla* with *Salsa costeña*, see p. 83), the few sauces described here are basic and may be used in many recipes. For handling chiles, please read p. 242.

Salsa Roja

4		whole *chiles de árbol*, toasted and seeded
1	lb.	tomatoes, toasted or roasted
3		cloves garlic

¹/₂   medium onion, finely chopped
¹/₂ C. chopped cilantro
       kosher salt and freshly ground black pepper, to taste

On a hot *comal* or skillet, toast the *chiles de árbol* for about 3 minutes, then seed. Toast or roast the tomatoes until their skin blisters and blackens slightly. Place the tomatoes and chiles in the bowl of a blender or food processor and process to a medium consistency—they should be slightly lumpy. Stir the chopped onion and chopped cilantro into the mixture. Adjust kosher salt and freshly ground pepper, to taste.

Serves about 8

Burnt Chipotle Salsa

1   whole *morita or chipotle* chile, toasted and seeded
3   whole tomatoes, roasted or toasted
1   clove garlic
¹/₂   medium onion, chopped
¹/₄ t. ground cumin
       kosher salt, to taste

Toast the chile on a *comal* or a hot skillet until dark brown. Toast or roast the tomatoes on the same *comal* or skillet for at least 10 minutes. Place all the ingredients in the bowl of a food processor or blender and purée. Season to taste. Pour the salsa into a saucepan, bring to a simmer, and cook for 10 minutes.   *Serves 4*

Note: This sauce is good with *carne asada*, steaks, chicken, or fish.

Molcajete Salsa

This is Dudley's favorite sauce and, as the name indicates, it is best when made in a stone *molcajete*.

5   *serrano* chiles, toasted or roasted and seeded
2   ripe tomatoes, toasted or roasted
1   clove garlic
1 T. kosher salt, to taste
2   sprigs cilantro, chopped

Toast or roast chiles on a hot *comal* or skillet and seed. Toast or roast the tomatoes on the same *comal* or skillet for about 10 minutes. Place the chiles, tomatoes, and garlic in the bowl of a food processor or blender and process briefly. The sauce should be lumpy. Sprinkle in the cilantro and adjust salt, to taste. *Serves 4*

Pico de Gallo

"Rooster's beak" which is the meaning of this Spanish phrase, is a standard table sauce that can be eaten as is or added to other dishes. It is very good simply loaded into fresh *tortillas* and eaten.

4		ripe Italian plum tomatoes, diced small
½		medium red onion, diced small
2		*serrano* chiles, chopped
5–6		sprigs of fresh cilantro, chopped
2	T.	fresh lime juice
1	T.	olive oil
1	t.	kosher salt, or to taste

Mix all the ingredients together well and refrigerate until well chilled.

Serves 4

Salsa Endiablada

10		*pasilla* chiles, toasted, deveined, and seeded
½		large onion, peeled and toasted
1		whole head garlic, peeled and toasted
1	T.	cider vinegar
½	T.	dried marjoram
½	T.	dried oregano
½	T.	crumbled bay leaf
2–3		black peppercorns
1–2		whole cloves
½	C.	olive oil
		kosher salt, to taste

Toast the chiles on a hot *comal*, devein, and seed. Toast the onion and garlic. Place all the ingredients except the olive oil and salt in the bowl of a food processor or blender and purée. Pour the mixture into a large bowl and drizzle olive oil over it. Season with kosher salt, to taste. Variation: Use a *criollo* avocado leaf instead of a bay leaf.   *Serves 6–8*

Salsa borracha

Now Dudley says that *this* is his favorite sauce. Actually, almost every sauce is his favorite when he discusses and uses it. This one is particularly good.

6		whole *ancho* chiles, soaked, deveined, and seeded
1	C.	orange juice
1	T.	chopped onion
1	T.	olive oil
4	oz.	*mezcal* or *tequila*
		kosher salt and pepper, to taste

Place the chiles in warm water to cover and soak for at least 20 minutes. Devein and seed the chiles and place them, along with the orange juice, onion, and olive oil in the bowl of a food processor or blender. Purée. Pour the sauce into a large bowl, blend in the *mezcal* or *tequila*, season with kosher salt and pepper, to taste.   *Serves 6–8*

Salsa de Cascabel

Cascabels are the small round chiles that are described as "bell-like" because their dried seeds rattle when shaken. They have a distinctive flavor. This recipe calls for *tamarind* juice, which can be purchased in Hispanic or Indian markets.

4		*cascabel* chiles, toasted, deveined, and seeded
¼		onion, toasted
3		*tomatillos*, husks removed and toasted
1		clove garlic, toasted
3	T.	*tamarind* juice
1		pinch of dry oregano
1		pinch of dry cumin
1		pinch of thyme
1	t.	brown sugar
		kosher salt, to taste

Toast the *cascabel* chiles on a hot *comal* or skillet, then devein and seed them. Then toast the onion, *tomatillos*, and garlic. Place all the ingredients in the bowl of a food processor or blender and purée.   Serves 4
Note: This sauce is excellent with fish, *quesadillas*, and chicken.

Salsa Verde

8		whole *tomatillos*, husked and toasted or roasted
2		whole *serrano* peppers
3		cloves garlic
½		medium onion
¼	C.	chopped cilantro
		kosher salt, to taste

Toast or roast the husked *tomatillos*. Place all the ingredients except the cilantro in a saucepan with enough water to cover. Bring to a boil, reduce heat to a simmer and cook for at least 5 minutes. Drain the mixture, but reserve some of the water. Place the mixture, along with the cilantro, in the bowl of a food processor or blender and purée. Season with kosher salt, to taste.   Serves 4
Note: This is especially good with *barbacoa* and *carne asada*.

Salsa de Lago

(Pátzcuaro, Michoacán)

The last sauce is special. It is made with *charales*, the tiny fish from Lake Pátzcuaro, and *milpa tomatillos*. These are smaller than the standard *tomatillos*. You might substitute dried shrimp or other dried fish for the *charales* and regular *tomatillos* for the *milpas* if you can't find the required ingredients.

1	C.	*charales*, toasted
2	C.	*milpa tomatillos*
4		whole *serrano* chiles
3	T.	chopped cilantro
1	T.	kosher salt, to taste
		water, if necessary

Using a stone grinder (*molcajete*) or food processor, coarsely grind the *charales* and the rest of the ingredients, except the salt. Do not purée completely, but leave the sauce somewhat lumpy. Season with salt, to taste. Add water for consistency, if necessary. *Serves 4*

Notes: This sauce may be served in a *molcajete* with sprigs of cilantro around the sauce. It is also good with slices of *queso fresco* and fresh corn tortillas.

Salads

Acelgas con Limón

(Xalitla, Guerrero)

Greens figure prominently in Easter meals in Mexico. This salad is a recipe that Dudley picked up in the artists' village of Xalitla. It is not exactly pre-Columbian, but it is very good nonetheless.

2		large bunches Swiss chard leaves
2	T.	butter or margarine
1	T.	flour
		juice of 1 large lemon
		kosher salt and freshly ground pepper, to taste
4	T.	water

Place enough water to cover the Swiss chard in a large pan and bring to a boil. Add the Swiss chard, return to a boil, and cook quickly until the chord is just tender, about 1 or 2 minutes. Drain at once and rinse the chard under cold water to stop the cooking process. In a deep, heavy skillet, melt the butter or margarine. Add the flour and stir constantly over low heat until brown. Add the lemon juice, salt and pepper to taste, and the water; keep stirring. When the mixture is smooth, mix with the Swiss chard and serve immediately. *Serves 4*

Ensalada Nutritiva

(Coastal Guerrero)

The word "nutritious" is sometimes used for Mexican dishes that have a variety of ingredients, such as vegetables and fruits. This one is Spanish in origin, but with some regional changes.

4 C.	cauliflower florets
2 C.	fresh pineapple, chopped
1 C.	sugar
1 C.	raisins
1 C.	almond, slivered
1-⅓ C.	sour cream
1 C.	mayonnaise

Place the cauliflower in a large pan with enough water to cover and bring to a boil. Cook until the cauliflower is tender-crisp, about 5 minutes. Set aside to cool. Place the sugar in a deep, heavy saucepan over low heat and melt it. Add the pineapple and cook over low heat, stirring to coat the pineapple with sugar. When thoroughly coated and syrupy, remove the mixture from the pan and allow to cool thoroughly. Mix all of the remaining solid ingredients in a large bowl. Blend in the sour cream and mayonnaise. Add the cauliflower and pineapple to the mixture. Serve cold.   *Serves* 10

Note: To make this really "nutritious," use low-fat sour cream and low-fat mayonnaise.

Nopales en Chile Pasilla y Charales Secos

(Cuitzeo, Michoacán)

This is another recipe that calls for the tiny dried versions of the famed *pescado blanco* of Michoacán. If you cannot get them, try dried shrimp or other small dried fish, the kind usually found in Asian markets. The flavor will be milder than if *charales* are used.

2-¼ lbs.	*nopales* (cactus paddle)
3	whole *ancho* chiles, toasted, soaked, deveined, and seeded
2	cloves garlic
1	medium Spanish onion, chopped
¼ lb.	*charales*
1	sprig of fresh cilantro
3 T.	canola oil
	queso fresco, crumbled
	kosher salt, to taste

Prepare the *nopales* by peeling, boiling them in salted water, and washing. Cut the *nopales* into strips first, and then into small squares. Set aside. Toast the *ancho* chiles on a hot *comal* or hot skillet. Devein and seed. Soak in warm water to cover until soft. Place the chiles and some of the chile water in the bowl of a food processor or blender and purée. Heat the oil in a deep, heavy pan and sauté the *charales* for 2 minutes. Add the onion and cook until transparent. Stir in the *nopales*, cilantro, and the chile mixture. Bring to a simmer and cook for 15 minutes. Season with salt to taste. Allow to cool completely. Sprinkle with *queso fresco* and serve. *Serves 4*

Soups

Sopa de Milpa

(Tarímbato, Michoacán)

This is a corn-based soup whose recipe Dudley collected from the small town in Michoacán where we came across a delightful *fiesta* on Easter Sunday. Fresh *chilacas* may be hard to find; if so, try a medium-hot chile such as a ripe *poblano* instead.

1-¼ lbs.	tomatoes, toasted and peeled
2	*chilaca* chiles, toasted, seeded, and chopped (see p. 242)
1–2 T.	canola oil
	kernels of 6 ears of fresh corn
2	zucchini, sliced ⅛-inch thick
2	bunches of zucchini blossoms, chopped (or 1 can)
½	small onion, quartered
4-¼ C.	chicken broth
½ C.	sour cream, whipped

Toast the tomatoes on a hot *comal* or heavy skillet. Toast the chiles and seed them. Heat the oil in a heavy skillet. Add the tomatoes, chiles, and onions and sauté for several minutes until the onions become golden. Add the corn, the zucchini slices, and the zucchini blossoms. Sauté until the zucchini become slightly tender, 2–3 minutes. Add the chicken broth. Bring to a boil, reduce the heat to a simmer, and cook until the vegetables become soft. Remove from the heat, spoon into 4 soup bowls, and garnish each with the whipped sour cream. *Serves 4*

Sopa de Verduras

(Olinalá, Guerrero)

Olinalá is the famous lacquerware village in Guerrero. This soup, with all its colors, reminds us of the colorful boxes and plates made there. For "greens," Dudley uses Swiss chard or spinach.

4		medium tomatoes, halved
1/2		medium onion
1		whole garlic clove
2–4	T.	canola oil
1/2	lb.	carrots, sliced
1/2	lb.	potatos, chopped
1/2	lb	zucchini, sliced
1/2	lb.	green beans, halved
1/2	lb.	green peas
2/3	lb.	Swiss chard or spinach, chopped
1		*chayote* fruit, chopped
1		whole ear of corn, kernels removed and cob discarded
8-1/2	C.	chicken broth
		kosher salt, to taste

Place the tomato, onion, and garlic in the bowl of a food processor or blender and chop to make a chunky *salsa*. Heat the oil in a deep, heavy saucepan, add all the vegetables, and sauté until the Swiss chard or spinach is wilted. Add the *salsa*, bring to a simmer, and cook for 5 minutes. Add the chicken broth and salt, to taste. Bring to a boil, reduce the heat, and simmer until the vegetables are cooked tender-crisp.

Serves 4–8

Note: This soup is good served with *totopos*, or *tortilla* chips.

Sopa Huitzimangari

(Patzcuaro, Michoacán)

Here is a soup featuring an interesting mixture of vegetables and flavors. The name comes from the herbal medicine center, itself named for a famous Purépecha king. The *charales* give a potent and distinctive flavor to the dish.

Since these little dried fish may be hard to find, try substituting dried shrimp or other dried fish available in Asian markets.

4		medium tomatoes, halved
½		medium Spanish onion, sliced
1		clove garlic, finely chopped
2		*guajillo* chiles, toasted, soaked, seeded, and deveined
2	t.	canola oil
8	C.	chicken broth
1		sprig of *epazote*
8		small *nopales* (cactus paddles), peeled, washed, and julienned
2	C.	lima beans, cooked
2	C.	*charales* or other dried fish
		kosher salt, to taste

Place the tomatoes, onion, garlic, and prepared *guajillo* chiles in the bowl of a food processor or blender and purée. Heat the oil in a deep, heavy pan. Add the tomato-*guajillo* mixture and sauté for 2 minutes. Slowly stir in the chicken broth and *epazote*. Bring to a boil, reduce the heat to a simmer, and cook for 5 minutes. Add the prepared *nopales*, lima beans, and *charales*. Return to a simmer and cook for at least 15 minutes. *Serves 4–8*

Note: Like all Mexican soups, this one is eaten with fresh *tortillas*.

Appetizers-Accompaniments

Tamales Nejos con Frijol Negro

(Guerrero)

Tamales come in every shape, size, and flavor that Mexicans can imagine. This recipe is a standard—easy to prepare and typical of the Guerrero style of cooking, which is typified by the use of banana leaves and black beans.

1	lb.	prepared *masa* (see p. 224)
10 5" by 12"		banana leaves
½	lb.	black beans, boiled and pureed
10		sprigs of *epazote*, chopped
		kosher salt, to taste

Have ready a steamer, large enough to hold 10 *tamal* packets. Prepare the *masa* by mixing flour with water, or buy it prepared in an Hispanic market. Tear 10 long strips from the banana leaves, to be used later as ties. Set the banana leaves on a heated *comal* or skillet and toast lightly. Spread each leaf out flat. Divide the dough into 10 pieces. Form each piece of dough into an oblong, then flatten that into an oval shape and place one on each banana leaf, leaving wide margins on the edges for folding. Divide the bean purée into 10 portions. Spread the bean purée evenly in the center of the *masa* on each leaf. Sprinkle chopped *epazote* over the beans. Fold the banana leaves into packets: fold the bottom of the leaf to the top and press lightly at the edge to seal. Then fold the left end into the center and the right end into the center. Tie the bundles with a leaf strip around the center of the packet, with the knot at the folded edges. Put all the *tamales* in the steamer, either upright or stacked. Steam the *tamales* for 35 minutes at medium heat or until each *tamal* separates easily from the leaf. **Makes 10**

Note: These go well with *mole grasoso*.

Aguacates Rellenos

(Hilda Bautista Villegas, La Macadamia Restaurant, Uruapán, Michoacán)

La Macadamia is inventive in its use of avocados. The original dish upon which this recipe is based had fish in it, but this version is wholly vegetarian.

		kernels from 2 ears of fresh corn
½	C.	peas
½	C.	green beans
4		avocados
½	C.	olive oil
¼	C.	vinegar
		kosher salt and freshly ground pepper, to taste
		mayonnaise, to taste
		olives, halved (optional)
		leaves of ½ head of romaine lettuce

Bring to boil about 2 cups of water in a deep saucepan. Add the corn kernels, peas, and green beans. Reduce the heat and cook until just tender-crisp, about 5 minutes. Drain and place the vegetables in a bowl. Season the vegetables with oil, vinegar, and salt and pepper, to taste and toss together. Cut the avocados in half lengthwise and remove the pit. Fill the avocados with the vegetable mixture. Garnish with mayonnaise and olive halves. Place romaine lettuce leaves on a serving dish, arrange the stuffed avocados on top of them, and serve.

Serves 8

Note: You could also add cooked baby shrimp to the vegetable mixture.

Hongos de la Sierra

(Queréndaro, Michoacán)

As we have already noted, mushrooms play a larger role in Mexican cuisine than is usually thought by outsiders. Michoacán is particularly good country for fungi because of its forests and rainfall. This recipe calls for wild mushrooms, but shiitakes or Portobello mushrooms will also do.

2	C.	water
1/2	t.	kosher salt
1/2	lb.	wild mushrooms
1/4	C.	canola or olive oil
1/2	lb.	*pasilla* chiles, toasted, deveined, and seeded
2		cloves garlic
		kosher salt, to taste

Heat the water and salt in a deep saucepan and bring to a boil. Add the mushrooms, reduce the heat, and simmer for about 5 minutes. Remove the mushrooms from pan and drain. Heat the oil in a deep, heavy skillet, add the mushrooms, and sauté. Lightly toast the chiles on a heated *comal* or heavy skillet. Devein and seed. Place the chiles in a *molcajete* or the bowl of a food processor or blender with the garlic and purée. Add a little water to facilitate the grinding. Stir the chile mixture into the skillet with the mushrooms. Season with kosher salt, to taste.

Serves 4

Papitas Estilo Mansión San Fernando

(From the Mansión San Fernando Restaurant, Zamora, Michoacán)

This was one of the best restaurants we encountered in Mexico, and this is a wonderful dish. Easy to make, its does require fresh potatoes to duplicate the original flavor. In Zamora, a garden center, these are readily available.

Preheat oven to 225°.

2	lbs.	new potatoes, washed
5		cloves of garlic, creamed
1	C.	olive oil
		kosher salt and pepper, to taste
5		sprigs fresh Italian parsley, finely chopped

Arrange the potatoes on a cookie sheet. Make a mixture of the olive oil and garlic. Brush the potatoes with the mixture and season with salt and pepper, to taste. Set the cookie sheet in the oven, bake, and turn and brush the potatoes with the mixture every 15 minutes. Roast slowly for 30–45 minutes. *Serves 6–8*

Tostadas de Chícharo

(Guerrero)

Peas provide the basic flavoring ingredient in this easy-to-make but delectable dish. It can be served warm or cold.

½	lb.	fresh or frozen green peas
10		whole corn *tortillas*, or prepackaged *tostadas*
1	T.	kosher salt, or to taste
½	C.	canola oil
1	pkg. (6 oz.)	*ranchero* cheese, grated

Place green peas in a small amount of water in a saucepan. Bring to boil, reduce heat, and simmer until tender, about 5 minutes. (If using frozen peas, follow the package directions for cooking.) Place the cooked peas in the bowl of a blender or food processor (or *molcajete*) and purée; season with salt, to taste. To prepare *tostadas* from *tortillas*, heat the oil in a skillet and fry each *tortilla* until crisp. (You may need more oil.) Drain the *tostadas*. Spread each *tostada* with the green pea purée and garnish with *ranchero* cheese.

Makes 10 tostadas, serves 5–10

Specialties

Guasmole

(Chilapa, Guerrero)

Guasmole (*huaxmole* in Nahuatl) comes from one of those compound Nahuatl words that means something "with sauce." In this case, that something is *guajes* (*huax*) (See pp. 234–235.) The *guajes'* flavor is unique, so do not substitute for them.

1-¼	lbs.	pork center loin (or see note below)
1-¼	lbs.	pork center rib (or see note below)
1	T.	kosher salt
6	C.	water
6		tomatoes, roasted
2		*serrano* chiles, chopped
1	C.	*guajes*
5		sprigs of fresh cilantro, chopped
		kosher salt, to taste
2	t.	lard or canola oil

Cut the pork into 1-½-inch pieces. Place them in a large sauce pan, cover with the water, and add kosher salt, to taste. Bring to a boil, skim the froth, reduce the heat, and simmer until cooked through, about 45 minutes. While the pork is cooking, heat a heavy skillet or *comal*. Roast the tomatoes, then peel. Roast the *serrano* chiles, then coarsely chop. Open the *guajes* as if they were large pea pods. Remove the seeds and toast them on the *comal*. Place the tomatoes, chiles, and *guaje* seeds in the bowl of a food processor or blender and chop coarsely. In a large, heavy skillet, heat the lard or canola oil. Remove the pork from the saucepan, reserving the broth. Set the pork in the heated oil and sauté until golden brown. Add the tomato-chile-*guaje* mixture and two cups of the broth to the meat. Bring to a boil, reduce the heat and simmer, uncovered, for 20 minutes. Add more broth as necessary to create a sauce thick enough to coat a spoon. Add kosher salt, to taste. Garnish with cilantro 5 minutes before serving. *Serves 4*

Note: You can substitute country-style ribs for the two cuts of pork listed in the ingredients. Serve this dish with *frijoles de olla* (plain boiled black beans).

Verdolagas Con Carne De Puerco

(Maravatio, Michoacán)

Mexicans gather and prepare many wild plants, just as their ancestors did millennia ago. One of these is *verdolagas* or purslane. Considered a weed by many home gardeners, it is really quite nutritious. But, because purslane is slightly mucilaginous, it should be parboiled and washed before using. It can be bought in "natural" foodstores, but why not collect it yourself?

1-½ lbs.	*verdolagas* (purslane), washed
¾ lb.	pork ribs
1 t.	dried thyme
	kosher salt, to taste
½ lb.	*guajillo* chiles, soaked, deveined, and seeded
½ lb.	tomatoes, roasted and peeled
4 T.	lard or canola oil
2	cloves garlic

In a large saucepan, bring enough water to cover the purslane to a boil. Plunge the purslane into the boiling water and blanch for about 2–3 minutes. Strain the purslane, rinse under cold water, and set aside. Place the pork in a large, heavy saucepan, cover with water, thyme, and a pinch of salt. Bring to a boil, reduce the heat, and simmer for 25 minutes. Meanwhile, heat a *comal* or skillet, place the chiles on it, and toast them lightly; then seed and devein. Soak the chiles in warm water until soft and set aside. Prepare the tomatoes by toasting and peeling and set aside. When the pork is done, remove it from the pan and reserve the broth. Heat the lard or oil in a heavy skillet. Add the pork and brown well on all sides. When ready to assemble the dish, place the chiles, tomatoes, and garlic in the bowl of a food processor or blender and purée. Place the sauce in a saucepan and heat. Place warm meat on a warm serving dish. Pour the chile sauce over it and top with the purslane. Adjust kosher salt, to taste.   *Serves 6*

Barbacoa de Pollo

(Sra. Carmen Villalva, Chilapa, Guerrero)

In Mexican cookery the term barbecue is closer to its original prototype than in the North American usage. The word is prehispanic Caribbean and refers to a cooking technique in which meat was wrapped in leaves and steamed in a pit filled with hot stones. This recipe is a way to do the same at home, in a *bain marie*. The basic ingredient, chicken, should be marinated overnight for best results, but several hours will do.

2		whole chickens, cut into 4 pieces (8 in all)
6		*ancho* chiles, toasted, soaked, deveined, and seeded
6		*guajillo* chiles, toasted, soaked, deveined, and seeded
10		whole black peppercorns
15		whole cumin seeds
1	t.	dried oregano
1		stick of cinnamon
3		cloves garlic
2	oz.	*mezcal* or *tequila*
		kosher salt, to taste
8		whole avocado or bay leaves
4		whole banana leaves

Cut up the chicken and set aside. Toast the chiles lightly in a heated skillet or on a *comal*. Remove the seeds and veins. Place the chiles in a bowl, cover with warm water, and soak for at least 10 minutes or until soft. Place the chiles, cloves, peppercorns, cumin, oregano, cinnamon, garlic, *mezcal* or *tequila*, and salt to taste in the bowl of a blender or food processor. Purée completely. Set the chicken in a large bowl and cover with the chile mixture. Place in the refrigerator and allow to marinate overnight. When ready to cook, place the chicken in a *bain marie* or steamer. Spread the avocado leaves over chicken, then cover with the banana leaves. Place the steamer on a heat source, bring to a medium boil, and cook the chicken for at least 45 minutes or until done, adding water to the steamer at least every 15 minutes. If making in oven with a *bain marie*, preheat the oven to 350°, set the pan in oven, and cook for about 1 hour or until the chicken is done.   *Serves 8*

Note: Serve with *salsa borracha* and avocado slices.

Churipo

(Morelia)

This is one of Mexico's classic dishes. It is likely a descendant of the Spanish *cocido*, only with some New World ingredients added to it. The *chayote*—use the porcupine-skinned variety if you can get it—should give the stew a slightly sweet undertone.

5 lbs.	stew meat, cubed
2 qts.	water
2	bay leaves
2	whole cloves
1 t.	ground cumin
2	cloves garlic, cut in half
½ lb.	*chayote* fruit, peeled and cubed
½ lb.	*guajillo* chiles, toasted, soaked, deveined, and seeded
½ lb.	carrots, medium diced
½ lb.	potatoes, peeled and quartered
½ lb.	cabbage, cut into large chunks
	kosher salt and freshly ground pepper, to taste
4	sprigs of fresh *epazote* (optional)

Place the water, meat, bay leaves, cumin, and garlic in a large pan. Bring to a boil, reduce the heat, and simmer, uncovered, for 30 minutes, or until the meat is cooked tender. Skim the froth from the top and discard. Toast the chiles on a hot *comal* or skillet. Remove the seeds and veins. Place in a bowl, cover with warm water, and soak until soft. Put the chiles in the bowl of a food processor or blender. Purée, adding enough water to make a smooth sauce. Add the vegetables and the chile mixture to the meat-broth mixture. Bring to a boil, reduce the heat, and simmer, uncovered, for 15 minutes, or until the vegetables are cooked. Season with salt and pepper, to taste. Add the *epazote* for an even better taste.   *Serves 8–10*

Manchamanteles

(Chilapa, Guerrero)

Although Dudley collected this dish from the dry hill region of Guerrero, it really comes from the coast. Another *mole*, this one has tropical products and a hint of medieval Spain in its almonds and raisins.

2	whole chickens, cut into 8–12 pieces
1 lb.	(about 2 C.) *mirepoix* (equal amounts of chopped onion, carrots, and celery)
5	*ancho* chiles, toasted, soaked, deveined, and seeded

10	*guajillo* chiles, toasted, soaked, deveined, and seeded
1 C.	lard or canola oil, plus 2 T.
⅓ C.	almonds
⅓ C.	raisins
1	whole plantain, sliced
1	slice pineapple
2	whole tomatoes
½	onion
3	cloves garlic
5	whole cloves
1	stick cinnamon, ground
	kosher salt, to taste

Place the chicken and *mirepoix* in a large, deep pan and cover with water. Bring to a boil, reduce the heat, simmer, and cook for at least 45 minutes, or until the chicken is cooked through. While the chicken is cooking, toast the chiles on a hot *comal* or skillet. Devein and seed. Set the chiles in a large bowl, cover with warm water, and soak until soft. Drain and squeeze the chiles well, reserving the water. Heat the oil in a large skillet. Add the chiles, almonds, raisins, plantain, pineapple, tomatoes, onion, garlic, and cloves and sauté until the nuts are lightly browned. Place the mixture in the bowl of a food processor or blender and purée well. Use the water from the chiles or the chicken broth to make a smooth sauce when processing. Strain the *mole* mixture, using a fine colander. In a deep saucepan or clay *cazuela*, heat 2 tablespoons of lard or canola oil and add the *mole* mixture and cinnamon, slowly stirring continuously for 10 minutes. Add 2–3 cups of chicken broth. Bring to a boil, reduce the heat, and simmer for 45 minutes. Add the chicken 20 minutes before serving time. *Serves 8–10*

Tatemado

(Morelia, Michoacán)

Tatemado is one of a group of *mole* dishes that use beef as the meat base. It is very much like the wonderful dish we had in the Purépecha village of Taracuato. It is best eaten with *corundas*.

Preheat oven to 220°.

4-½ lbs.	beef brisket, cut into medium cubes

¼ lb.	*guajillo* chiles, toasted, soaked, deveined, and seeded
¼ lb.	*pasilla* chiles, toasted, soaked, deveined, and seeded
¼ lb.	*mulatto* chiles, toasted, soaked, deveined, and seeded
1	medium onion, chopped
6	cloves garlic, chopped
1	pimento, chopped
4	cloves
4	peppercorns
4 qts.	water
1 C.	lard or vegetable oil
	kosher salt, to taste
2 lbs.	prepared corn *masa*

Cut up the meat and set aside. Toast the chiles on a hot *comal* or heavy skillet. Devein and seed. Put the chiles in a large bowl, cover with warm water, and soak until soft, reserving the water. Place the chiles, onion, pimento, pepper, cloves, and garlic in the bowl of a food processor or blender and purée. Use some of water from the chiles to make a smooth sauce. Season with kosher salt, to taste. Heat lard or vegetable oil in *olla* or heavy metal pan until hot. Add beef and sauté until just browned. Cover meat with the chile mixture. Add water to cover, stirring to mix well. Spread the prepared corn *masa* over the top of the *olla* or pot. Set the *olla* in the preheated oven and bake for 3 hours or until the meat is done.   *Serves 8–10*

Desserts

Atole de Tamarindo

(Cherán, Michoacán)

We have already seen *atole*, the pre-Columbian drink, in its purer forms, both plain and chocolate. This one contains a "foreign" ingredient, although one that is now associated with Latin American cuisine: *tamarind*. It is an Asian plant that was brought to the New World probably in the sixteenth century. The fruit itself is a brown pod with a sweet red fruit inside. It is widely available in Hispanic markets. This recipe produces a large quantity and can be cut in half. Look at it as a "party food" and serve small glasses to the assembled crowd.

2 lbs.   *tamarind*, pitted and peeled
2 lbs.   *piloncillo* or brown sugar
2 qts.   water
1 lb.   prepared corn *masa*, dissolved in water
2 C.   hot water, to dissolve *masa*

Place the water in a large saucepan or deep clay *olla* and bring to a simmer. Add the *tamarind* pods and stir continuously until the pulp dissolves. Stir in the sugar and cook until it dissolves. Meanwhile, dissolve the *masa* in 2 cups of hot water. Slowly stir the dissolved *masa* into the *tamarind* mixture and continue to stir. Cook until it becomes quite thick. Serve hot.   *Serves 8 or more*

Chongos Samoranos

(Uruapán)

3 qts.   milk
1   rennet tablet
3-³/₄ C. sugar
3   sticks of cinnamon
1 t.   ground cinnamon

Pour the milk into a heavy, deep pan and heat to a simmer. Stir in the sugar and dissolve it, adding the 3 sticks of cinnamon while stirring continuously. Once sugar is dissolved, remove the mixture from the heat and allow it to cool. Dissolve the rennet tablet in ¹/₂ cup of warm water and stir into the milk-sugar mixture. Remove the cinnamon sticks. Allow the mixture to stand in a warm place for at least 2 hours. By then, the *chongos* should be well curdled and firm. Cut into small squares and replace the pan on the stove and heat over a very low flame. The *chongos* will become yellowish and somewhat hard. Separate the squares and serve on individual plates. Sprinkle ground cinnamon over each square.   *Serves 8*

Dulce de Camote y Piña

Like sweet potato pie? The sweet potato is a native American plant, as is the pineapple. This is a classic Mexican sweet.

3		medium sweet potatoes, washed
1/2		medium pineapple, peeled
2	C.	sugar
1/2	T.	powdered cinnamon

In a deep pan heat to a boil enough water to cover the sweet potatoes. Add the sweet potatoes and cook until tender. Once cooked, peel and purée the sweet potatoes in the bowl of a food processor or blender and set aside. Place the pineapple in bowl of food processor or blender and purée. Place the pineapple in a saucepan with a little water and heat to a simmer. Gradually add the sugar and cinnamon, cooking until the sugar is dissolved. Add the sweet potatoes. Simmer at low heat, stirring constantly until you can see the bottom of the pot. When thick, remove from heat. Can be eaten hot or cold.   *Serves 4*

Dulce de Nopales

12		*nopales* (cactus paddles), peeled and chopped
1	qt.	water
2	C.	sugar
1		stick of cinnamon
1/2	t.	ground anise seed

Place the *nopales* in enough water to cover. Soak the *nopales*, changing the water frequently, until most of the gummy substance is removed. Bring 1 quart of water to a boil in a deep pan. Add the sugar, anise, and cinnamon and bring back to a boil. Cook for about 10 minutes. Add the *nopales* and boil for another 15 minutes more, until the cactus is tender. If necessary, add more water. When the mixture is syrupy, remove from the heat. Serve warm or cold.   *Serves 4*

Flan de Elote

(Morelia, Michoacán)

What would a Mexican dinner be without *flan*? Made with fresh corn, this is a particularly interesting version.

Preheat oven to 350°.

1	C.	sugar
1/3	C.	water
6	C.	fresh corn kernels, removed from the cob
7		eggs
2	6 oz.	cans condensed milk
2	C.	milk

Combine the sugar and water in a small, heavy saucepan. Bring to a boil over medium heat, washing down the sides of the pan with a brush dipped in water, until the sugar completely dissolves. Continue to cook, without stirring, until the syrup turns an even, deep amber color. Working very carefully, divide the caramelized sugar among the custard cups, tilting the cups to coat the sides and bottom with the caramel. Set the caramelized cups on a rack in a roasting pan. Place the corn in the bowl of food processor or blender and purée coarsely. Mix the corn puree with the eggs, condensed milk, and milk. Transfer the mixture to the cups. Place the roasting pan on the center rack of the oven. Pour in enough hot water to reach halfway up the sides of the cups, and loosely cover the pan with foil. Bake just until the *flans* are set, but still slightly wobbly in the center, usually 25 to 30 minutes. Do not overbake. Remove the *flans* from the water bath. Refrigerate until they are chilled, about 2 hours. Cover with plastic wrap. To unmold the *flans*, run the tip of a knife, gently around the edge of each *flan* cup. Place a serving plate over the top of the molds and invert them, shaking until the *flan* slips out. Spoon the remaining caramel onto the *flan* and serve immediately.   *Serves 8–10*

Flan de Tres Leches

(Marcos Castenanos, Michoacán)

Preheat oven to 375°.

1	C.	granulated sugar
2	C.	sweetened condensed milk
1	C.	evaporated milk
1	C.	whole milk
2	oz.	brandy or rum
1		pinch of ground cinnamon
1	t.	vanilla extract
6		whole eggs, beaten well

Place the sugar in a saucepan and set on medium heat. Melt the sugar, stirring constantly, and continue to cook until the sugar becomes caramelized (a thick, golden-brown syrup). Pour the caramel into a custard container or 8 ramekins. Mix the rest of the ingredients in a large bowl. Pour equal amounts of the custard into the ramekins. Place the ramekins in a roasting pan. Pour enough hot water in the roasting pan to reach halfway up the sides of the ramekins. Place the pan with the ramekins into the preheated oven. (The rack should be in the center position.) Bake until the custards are set, but still quite jiggly, 35–40 minutes. Remove the custards from the water and let cool in their containers on a wire rack. *Makes 8 or one large* flan

Goridas de Trigo

(Querendaro, Michoacán)

Preheat oven to 350°.

1	lb.	lard or vegetable shortening
6		whole eggs
2	lbs.	wheat flour
1	T.	baking soda
1-2/3	lbs.	*piloncillo* or brown sugar
2	qts.	whole milk

In the bowl of a food processor or by hand, whip the lard or shortening for 5 minutes. Beat in the eggs. Sift together the flour and baking powder. Beat in the rest of the ingredients. Knead the dough into a smooth texture, adding as much extra milk as needed. Pull off pieces of the dough and form into round patties about 3 inches in diameter and 1/2 inch thick. Place the patties on a greased cookie sheet. Set the baking pan in the oven and bake *gorditas* for 15 to 20 minutes, until lightly browned. *Serves 8*

Pepitorias

(Huetamo, Michoacán)

This is an unusual recipe for candy. It is like others that are made with sesame seeds, but this one has wood ash in it. The flavor is very Mexican.

4	C.	water
4-½	lbs.	pumpkin seeds
8	oz.	wood ash
2-¼	lbs.	*piloncillo* or brown sugar

In a deep saucepan or *olla*, bring the water to a simmer. Add the pumpkin seeds and the wood ash. Return to a simmer and cook for 15–20 minutes. Strain the seeds and run cold water over them until they are thoroughly cooled, about 2 minutes. In a copper *cazo* (cooking pan) or deep saucepan, place 1 cup of water and the sugar. Bring to a gentle boil and cook until the sugar is dissolved. Continue to cook until the sugar is caramelized (a thick, golden-brown syrup). Stir in the seeds and spread the mixture onto a large, lightly greased cookie sheet. Allow the mixture to cool and cut it into squares (or any other shape you like). *Serves about 8*

Authors and illustrator (left to right: Dudley Nieto, Nicolás de Jesús, and Bruce Kraig)

Notes

Chapter 1

1. Ann Barr and Paul Levy, *The Official Foodie Handbook* (London, 1984). Levy is the inventor of the now standard term, "foodie."
2. Ronald Takaki, *A Different Mirror. A History of Multicultural America* (Boston, 1993), p. 320 (quoting from Mark Reisler's, *By the Sweat of Their Brow: Mexican Immigrant Labor in the United States. 1900–1940,* [Westport, CT, 1976].)

Chapter 2

1. Mircea Eliade, *The Sacred and the Profane* (New York, 1959), pp. 44, 61.
2. Roberta H. and Peter T. Markham, *The Flayed God: The Mesoamerican Mythological Tradition: Sacred Texts and Images from pre-Columbian Mexico and Central America* (San Francisco, 1992), pp. 189, 225.
3. Emily McClung Tapia, "The Origins of Agriculture in Mesoamerica and Central America," in C. Wesley Cowan and Patty Jo Watson (eds.) *The Origins of Agriculture: An International Perspective* (Washington, D.C., 1992), p. 162.
4. Tapia, p. 149.
5. Charles B. Heiser, Jr., *Seed to Civilization: The Story of Food* (new ed., Cambridge, MA, 1990), p. 95.
6. Heiser, pp. 103–104.
7. Michael D. Coe, *Mexico* (third ed., rev., New York, 1984), p. 64.
8. Markham and Markham, p. 179–182
9. See Linda Schele and Mary Ellen Miller, *The Blood of Kings: Dynasty and Ritual in Maya Art* (New York, 1986).
10. Sophie Coe, "Aztec Cuisine," *Petits Propos Culinaires*, 19, 20, 21 (London, 1985).
11. Gretel H. Pelto, "Social Class and Diet in Contemporary Mexico," in Marvin Harris and Eric B. Ross (eds.) *Food and Evolution: Toward a Theory of Human Food Habits* (Philadelphia, 1987), pp. 532–533.
12. See Andrew Smith, *The Tomato in America: Early History, Culture, and Cookery* (Columbia, SC, 1994) for more details on this famous berry . . . yes, it is a berry.

13. Smith, pp. 152–153.
14. Frederick J. Simoons, *Food in China: A Cultural and Historical Inquiry* (Boca Raton, FL, 1991), pp. 76–77.
15. E. N. Anderson, personal communication. See also his classic book, *The Food of China* (New Haven, CT, 1977), pp. 328–329.
16. K. T. Achaya, *Indian Food: A Historical Companion* (Dehli, 1994), pp. 227–228.
17. Susan Freeman, lecture to the Culinary Historians of Chicago, 1994, and personal communication.
18. See Mexican novelist Homero Arijdis's splendid and horrifying novel, *1492* (trans. Betty Ferber, New York, 1985) for graphic scenes of the explusion.
19. Sophie Coe, *Proceedings of the Oxford Symposium on Food and Cookery* (London, 1987).

Chapter 3

1. See Chloë Sayer, *Arts and Crafts of Mexico* (San Francisco, 1990), for a good discussion of many of the art styles and techniques mentioned in this book.
2. See Sayer, pp. 83–84, for a discussion of bark paper and art.
3. See Luis Weckmann, *The Medieval Heritage of Mexico* (trans. Frances M. López-Morillas, New York, 1992), pp. 250–252, for a discussion of the European sources for such processions and how they came to Mexico. Weckmann claims them as purely European, but surely there is much Indian ritual in the ceremonies.

Chapter 4

1. Sophie Coe, "Aztec Cuisine, Part II," *Petits Propos Culinaires* 20, p. 51.
2. M. B. Coe, pp. 142–144.
3. See Eduardo Ruiz, *Michoacán Paisajes, Tradiciones, y Leyendas* (n.p., Mexico, 1940).
4. For a discussion of masks and their meaning, see Donald Cordry, *Mexican Masks* (Austin, TX, 1980).

Ingredients and Techniques

1. For a good description of chiles, see David DeWitt and Nancy Gerlach, *The Whole Chile Pepper Book* (New York, 1990).

INDEX